The
Fluvial
System

The
Fluvial
System

STANLEY A. SCHUMM

Department of Earth Resources
Colorado State University

A WILEY-INTERSCIENCE PUBLICATION

JOHN WILEY & SONS, New York • London • Sydney • Toronto

Library of Congress Cataloging in Publication Data

Schumm, Stanley Alfred, 1927–
  The fluvial system.

  "A Wiley-Interscience publication."
  Includes bibliographies and index.
  1. Rivers. 2. Watersheds. I. Title.
GB561.S35   551.4'83   77-9333
ISBN 0-471-01901-1

Printed in the United States of America

10 9 8 7 6 5 4 3 2 1

To

Ethel

for such a number of things

Preface

The origin of this book was an invitation from Dr. Desmond Pretorius of the Economic Geology Research Unit, University of the Witwatersrand, to present a short course on fluvial geomorphology to a group of South African economic geologists. He believed that recent geomorphic research could be applied to the search for and exploitation of mineral deposits in fluvial sedimentary deposits. It was necessary to review a diverse literature to assemble the needed information, and hopefully the results can be applied not only to some aspects of economic geology, sedimentology, and stratigraphy, but also to river and erosion control and land management.

This book is an attempt to consider the fluvial system and its components in such a way that the interaction of the components and the resulting degree of inherent instability of the system can be comprehended and related to some concerns of the economic geologist, geomorphologist, stratigrapher, sedimentologist, land manager, conservationist, and civil engineer. A new way of viewing the fluvial system is presented that can aid in the explanation of the complexity of landscape evolution. In short, an attempt is made to show how geomorphic concepts and a newly emerging comprehension of the landscape and its dynamics can be of value in several areas where an understanding of fluvial processes is mandatory.

Development of an understanding of any part of a river system depends to a large extent on the appreciation of both upstream and downstream controls; therefore, the fluvial system must be considered as a whole, and that is the approach used here. The organization of the book is such that the reader moves from the drainage divide in the sediment source area through the channels and valleys of the drainage basins to depositional areas in valleys, on the piedmont, and at the coast, and upstream controls are related to downstream results and vice versa. Therefore, following discussion of the independent variables that control the fluvial system and other necessary background material (Chapters One through Three), the reader begins at the drainage divide and follows water and sediment through the drainage basin (Chapter Four) and river channel (Chapter Five) to depositional sites in valleys (Chapter

Six), on the piedmont (Chapter Seven), and at the coast (Chapter Eight). The fluvial system is considered to be composed of all the erosional and depositional components of the riverine landscape.

Except in Chapter One, where the erosional evolution of a fluvial landscape is reviewed, the geomorphic and geological reader will conclude that the treatment is concerned with events and processes of relatively short duration, whereas the engineer and sedimentologist will see that the details of sediment transport and sedimentary features are ignored and the emphasis is on events and processes of long spans of time. In fact, the emphasis is on intermediate spans of time that have been neglected to a large extent by both groups.

It is difficult to define the duration of an intermediate span of time. Much depends on the size of the landform and the rate at which erosion or deposition is occurring, but neither the details of landforms and sedimentary deposits nor the denudational history of a region is the main concern. Rather features and events of moderate scale and duration are given the most attention. Bedforms, the nature of cross-stratification in sedimentary deposits, and open-channel hydraulics are essentially ignored, but the changes in channel character and the distribution of sediment types in valleys, fans, and alluvial plains are considered. In this way some components of the fluvial system are emphasized at the expense of others, but this is done to stress the aspects of the system that are important for the objective of this work.

Therefore, the book is not a detailed review; excellent books on open-channel hydraulics, geomorphology, sedimentology, and stratigraphy are available. Rather it is an attempt to present new concepts and to demonstrate that they are valid and have application. It is a personal view that is presented, but one that may have value in application, and hopefully it will lead to additional research.

The approach is empirical rather than theoretical. This is partly the result of a lack of data on the behavior of the total fluvial system. In addition, the reader will find within the text a combination of English and metric units. In general, the material is presented in the form that it first appeared, although some conversions to metric units were made.

STANLEY A. SCHUMM

Fort Collins, Colorado
April 1977

Acknowledgments

I particularly wish to thank Donald Coates, State University of New York of Binghamton, Desmond Pretorius, Economic Geology Research Unit, University of the Witwatersrand, and John Adams, Victioria University, Wellington, for their most helpful suggestions for revision of the manuscript. Frank Ethridge and M. Paul Mosley also provided useful criticisms of the text at an earlier stage of preparation. All the reviewers raised critical questions. I am sure that not all have been resolved to their satisfaction, but the book is greatly improved by their efforts.

This book is based on the results of research carried out through the years by myself and by my graduate students, and I am grateful to David Macke, William Weaver, and R. S. Parker for permission to use their unpublished data. The agencies that made the research possible through their financial support must also be acknowledged. First my years with Water Resources Division of the Geological Survey provided ample opportunity to gain field experience and an appreciation of field problems. Financial support for field and particularly for an experimental research program at Colorado State University has been provided on a continuing basis by the Army Research Office, Colorado State Agricultural Experimental Station, and the National Science Foundation. Without this support the research would have been delayed and perhaps not attempted.

S. A. S.

Contents

Tables

Symbols

A	Drainage area (km^2 or square miles)
b	Water surface width either at mean annual discharge (Leopold and Maddock), at Q_2 (Bray), or at channel bank-full width (Schumm) (feet or m)
d	Water depth either at mean annual discharge (Leopold and Maddock), at Q_2 (Bray), or at maximum bank-full depth of channel (Schumm) (feet or m)
d_{50}	Median grain size (mm)
F	Width/depth ratio
L	Channel length (miles)
M	Silt-clay in channel perimeter (percent)
P	Sinuosity (ratio of channel length to valley length or ratio of valley slope to channel slope)
Q	Mean annual water discharge (Lane) (cfs)
Qma	Mean annual flood (cfs)
Qm	Mean annual discharge (cfs)
Q_2	Discharge for flood with 2-year recurrence interval (cfs)
Q_s	Bed material load (weight or volume)
Q_b	Bed load (percentage of total load)
R	Hydraulic radius, area of channel cross section divided by wetted perimeter (feet or m)
S	Slope of energy line (percent, tangent)
Sc	Channel gradient (percent, feet/mile, tangent)
Sv	Valley floor slope (percent, feet/mile, tangent)
V	Velocity (feet/second, m/second)
λ	Meander wavelength (km, feet, miles)
τ	Tractive force (γRS; weight per unit area)
γ	Specific weight of water (weight per unit volume)
ω	Stream power (τV; foot pounds per second per foot)

The
Fluvial
System

CHAPTER ONE

Introduction

The behavior of rivers, channel networks, and interfluves and the character of their associated sedimentary deposits are of interest to a considerable variety of engineers and scientists, as well as to the citizen who is losing his backyard, cornfield, or pasture to an aggressive river. Furthermore, the economic importance of rivers as routes of commerce is great, as is the value of petroleum, uranium, gold, and placer minerals obtained from fluvial sedimentary deposits (Craig et al., 1955; Martin, 1966; Brock and Pretorius, 1964; Haughton, 1969, pp. 69–117). In addition, the amount of money spent annually on attempts to control erosion and deposition within the fluvial system is substantial.

It is a geologic truism that sediment is derived from a source area and is transported to a place of deposition. It is equally evident that one cannot understand fluvial sedimentary deposits or the morphology and behavior of a river without a clear comprehension of upstream controls, in other words, the fluvial geomorphic system in its entirety. However, the diversity of interests and expertise devoted to the study of drainage basins and river channels is great, and, as might be expected, each expert concerns himself with his specialty with the unfortunate result that rarely is thought given to the entire fluvial system, which consists of the sediment-source area, the transportation network, and the depositional sites. A unified approach has not been common because stratigraphers and sedimentologists view the finished product at the depositional site, whereas the hydrologist, geomorphologist, and engineer study the dynamic landscape of the source area and the river network.

There can be no doubt that a stable alluvial river channel in any particular location is an integration of the upstream controls of geology, climate, and land use. Therefore, to understand any part of the fluvial system, something must be known about the quantity and type of sediment, the manner in which water is supplied from the source area, and the climatic and geologic controls on that sediment and water supply. In addition, an awareness of the upstream effects of downstream channel behavior and changes of base level is required. This approach necessitates information from studies by hydrologists, watershed scientists, civil engineers, and, of course, earth scientists. These data and conclusions must then be applied to the component of the fluvial system that is of interest.

THE FLUVIAL SYSTEM

Figure 1-1 which is divided for convenience of discussion into three parts, is a sketch of an idealized fluvial system. These are referred to as

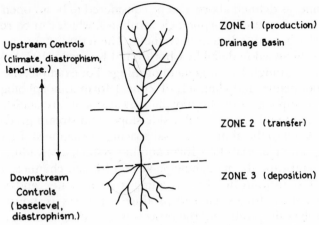

Figure 1-1 Idealized fluvial system.

Zones 1, 2, and 3 in a downstream direction. The uppermost is the drainage basin, watershed, or sediment-source area (Zone 1). This is the area from which water and sediment are derived. It is primarily the zone of sediment production, although sediment storage does occur there in important ways. Zone 2 is the transfer zone, where, for a stable channel, input of sediment can equal output. Zone 3 is the sediment sink or area of deposition.

These three subdivisions of the fluvial system may appear artificial because obviously sediments are stored, eroded, and transported in all the zones; nevertheless, within each zone one process is usually dominant, and it is convenient to think of Zone 1 as the sediment producer, and in the ideal case Zone 2 is a zone of transfer or predominant transport. Eventually the sediment is deposited in Zone 3 on an alluvial fan, alluvial plain, delta, or in deeper waters.

Zone 1 is the area of greatest interest to watershed scientists and to hydrologists, as well as to geomorphologists involved with the evolution and growth of drainage systems. Zone 2 is of major concern to the hydraulic and river-control engineer and to geomorphologists involved primarily with river-channel morphology. However, paleochannels and valley-fill deposits are preserved in the stratigraphic record, so river channels are a subject of interest to stratigraphers and sedimentologists also. Zone 3 is primarily of concern to the geologist and the coastal engineer, and the internal structure, stratigraphy, and morphology of alluvial fans, alluvial plains, deltas, and fan deltas are of critical geologic–geomorphic concern.

Each zone, as defined above, can be considered to be an open system. Each has its own set of morphologic attributes, which can be related to water discharge and sediment movement. The term system, in vogue at present, is discussed in detail by Chorley and Kennedy (1971). A system is simply a meaningful arrangement of things. For example, the divides, slopes, floodplains, and channels of Zone 1 form a morphological system. The components of the morphological system are statistically related one to the other (e.g., valley-side slopes and stream gradients are directly related to the abundance and spacing of channels). In addition, the energy and materials flow form another system, a cascading system.

In the landscape the morphologic system (slopes, channels, etc.) can be related statistically to the cascading system (water and sediment movement, shear forces, etc.) to produce a process–response system, which involves the landform, the processes operative, and the materials moved.

Chorley and Kennedy (1971) also define several types of equilibrium conditions that aid in the understanding of the process–response system. Five of these are shown and defined in Figure 1-2. Equilibrium concepts and self-regulation are discussed again later, but, without further elaboration, it should be apparent that the arrangement of landform components in Figure 1-1 forms a major process–response system with three components, Zones 1, 2, and 3.

GEOMORPHIC CONCEPTS

There is frequently a dichotomy in the thinking of geologists. On the one hand the erosional and depositional components of the fluvial system are viewed as evolving progressively through long periods of time, with major interruptions a result of climatic changes or tectonism. For example, the geomorphologist, conditioned by the erosion-cycle concept, ponders the slow progressive evolution of a landscape and its components, and the geologist visualizes the slow progressive accumulation of sediment through time. In reality, these investigators frequently concentrate on interruptions of this sequence. That is, geologist and geomorphologist rarely see a continuous record of erosion or deposition. The geomorphologist, in fact, generally concentrates his attention on the anomalous features of the landscape, for example, areas of maximum erosion and mass movement. The stratigrapher may also concentrate his studies on interruptions and changes in a depositional sequence. These changes usually appear quite abrupt in a geologic sense, and they do not conform to the idealized model of progressive

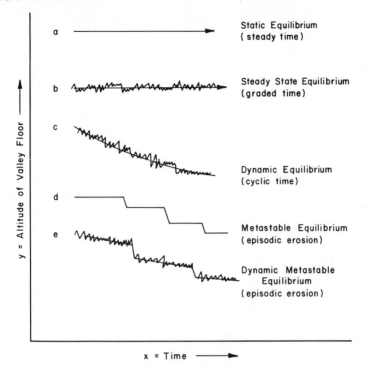

Figure 1-2 Types of equilibria based on Chorley and Kennedy (1971). Each is shown with respect to changes of valley-floor elevation with time. (a) Static equilibrium—no change with time (steady time). (b) Steady-state equilibrium—variations about a constant average condition (graded time). (c) Dynamic equilibrium—variations about a changing average condition (cyclic time). (d) Metastable equilibrium—static equilibrium separated by episodes of change as thresholds are exceeded. (e) Dynamic metastable equilibrium—dynamic equilibrium with episodic change as thresholds are exceeded.

change through time. The difference between the theoretical framework and the operating procedure appears to reflect a lack of understanding of the behavior of the complex fluvial system. Therefore, it is necessary to review a few basic geomorphic concepts.

In a widely used American textbook (Thornbury, 1969), 10 concepts are listed that are relevant to geomorphology in general and to fluvial systems in particular. However, the 10 can be collapsed into 3. The first is uniformity, which means simply that the laws of Newtonian physics and chemistry controlled the operation of past erosional and depositional processes as they do today; the second principle is that within the constraints of geology (structure) there is a determinable sequence of landscape evolution through time (stage); and the third principle, which is obviously in conflict with the second, is that both landscape history and earth history are complex. This complexity is related to the external influences of climate change and diastrophism.

An additional geomorphic concept was stated by Schumm (1973) and by Garner (1974) who concluded that geomorphic systems can be strongly influenced by thresholds. That is, abrupt changes may occur during landscape evolution, as threshold values of stress are exceeded. Before proceeding with a discussion of the fluvial system, we will further consider the concepts of uniformity, geomorphic thresholds, landscape evolution, and the complexity of geomorphic systems. These topics will appear to the reader to be most significant for the historical problems of the earth scientist, but, in fact, they are also meaningful to the engineer and land manager who are working with or against the functioning of a fluvial system.

Uniformity

Uniformity, as noted above, means the permanency of natural laws. It does not mean that catastrophic events did not or could not occur (Gretener, 1967), but it does mean that such an event is capable of a rational physical explanation. This is true of discontinuities in either depositional or erosional sequences. The stratigraphic record is replete with interruptions and breaks in the record that can be considered to be due to some change in an external variable, but, as demonstrated later, some of these events can be inherent in an erosional or depositional system as it envolves through time.

Ager (1973) takes the position that the present is too short to be the key to the past and that we rely too much on uniformitarianism in interpreting stratigraphic records. This criticism applies equally to all aspects of geology. For example, there is little question that what occurs on the surface of the earth during one lifetime is probably an inadequate basis for the discussion of the long-term erosional development of land-forms.

Ager (1973, p. 28) is concerned that one finds bedding planes, even in thick sedimentary deposits, that presumably should have accumulated uniformly through time. If sedimentation is really continuous there should be no pauses in deposition and no bedding planes. As most bedding planes are evidence of a pause in sedimentation, if not actual erosion, Ager uses this fact to conclude that the stratigraphic record is essentially "a lot of holes tied together with sediment." From a different point of view, the presence of the bedding planes and short gaps in the depositional sequence may reflect events that are taking place in the source area, or changes in the manner in which the sediment is transported to the site of deposition. In short, what may appear to be essentially minicatastrophic events in Zone 3 may be the result of normal and expectable events in Zones 1 and 2.

Ager (1973, p. 93) concludes that organic evolution, the evolution of continents and the stratigraphic column, "has been a very episodic affair, with short happenings interrupting long periods of nothing much in particular." This, as he admits, is a somewhat extreme view, but he is directing attention to apparent inconsistencies in stratigraphic and evolutionary thought. The approach taken here is that with a fuller understanding of the total fluvial system many abrupt changes in deposition, erosion, and landform evolution can be explained as a natural part of the erosional and depositional history of a fluvial system and, indeed, are uniformitarian.

Thresholds

Some discontinuities in the erosional and depositional record may be the result of the exceeding of erosional thresholds, which are the condition, level, or stage at which an effect is produced. One of the critical problems and questions in geomorphology is: Under what stress conditions will there be a dramatic change in the geomorphic system with significant modification of the landscape (e.g., Wolman and Miller, 1960)? This, of course, depends on the external stress applied and on the strength of the materials to which the stress is applied. It is in this context that thresholds are generally considered; a gradual increase in external stress eventually produces a dramatic response in the system. These are referred to as *extrinsic thresholds* (Schumm, 1973), because they depend on an external influence. A good example is the response of sediment to an increase in the velocity and depth of flow of water over it. The sediment remains immobile until movement eventually begins at a shear or velocity threshold. In addition, at higher thresholds abrupt changes in the bedforms (Figure 5-17) develop on the channel floor (Simons et al., 1965). These hydraulic thresholds show that there need not always be a progressive reaction of a system to a slowly increasing stress.

In addition, another type of threshold is inherent to the system, the *intrinsic threshold*. An example is the long-term progressive weathering of slope materials that eventually results in mass movement (Kirkby, 1973). Glacial surges that are not the result of climatic fluctuations or tectonics

(Meir and Post, 1969) reflect periodic storage and release of ice as an intrinsic threshold of glacier stability is exceeded. In semiarid regions sediment storage in a valley through time progressively increases valley slope until failure (erosion) occurs. This is a special type of intrinsic threshold, the *geomorphic threshold* (Schumm, 1973). It is the result of landform change through time to a condition of incipient instability, without a change of external influences.

A very common example of a geomorphic threshold is the progressive increase in channel sinuosity and meander amplitude until a cutoff or channel avulsion results on alluvial plains and deltas. This is due to channel lengthening and gradient reduction accompanying increases in sinuosity and delta size. Channel avulsion produces multiple delta lobes and cyclic sedimentation (Coleman and Gagliano, 1964), and when these are observed in the stratigraphic record, they may be attributed to climate change or baselevel variations rather than to the normal working of one component of fluvial systems.

Another example of a geomorphic threshold is provided by Koons (1955), who described the morphologic changes of a sandstone-capped escarpment. Beneath a vertical cliff of sandstone is a 32- to 38-degree slope of weak shale. Through time the inclined shale basal slope is eroded and reduced in height, thereby progressively forming a high vertical sandstone-capped shale cliff above the basal slope. At some critical height the cliff collapses, and the cycle begins again. The episodic retreat of this escarpment is wholly the result of changing cliff morphology under constant climatic, baselevel, and tectonic conditions.

Erosional changes, therefore, can be inherent in the development of the landform, and a change in an external variable is not required for the geomorphic threshold to be exceeded and for a significant geomorphic event and a stratigraphic result to ensue. This type of threshold has been identified and its influence has been documented for semiarid valleys and during experimental studies. Examples are discussed in greater detail in Chapters Four, Five, and Seven after the morphology and sediment yield characteristics of drainage basins is considered.

It is important to stress here that the concept of intrinsic thresholds, and especially geomorphic thresholds, means that changes in fluvial erosion and deposition need not always be attributed to external (extrinsic) influences such as climate, tectonics, and baselevel change. This conclusion is contrary to the usual geologic assumption of progressive change interrupted only by external influences, and it has significant implications for the interpretation of erosional and depositional events and the distribution of erosional and depositional features in the landscape.

Landform Evolution

A relatively simple model of landform evolution, presented by Davis in 1899 is summarized in Figure 1-3. In the Davis model a brief period of uplift and potential energy increase is followed by a long period of progressive downwearing of the uplifted terrain. The Davis model conforms to the following two of the three characteristics of a process–response system as outlined by Chorley and Kennedy (1971, p. 128):

1. Operation is controlled by the magnitude and frequency of inputs.
2. Progressive changes in the morphology and operation of the system can occur if input changes or if there is internal degradation of the system.

The speed and complexity of landform evolution are expressed by characteristic 1 and progressive landscape evolution is expressed by 2. However, there is a third characteristic of process–response systems:

3. Self-regulation or negative feedback occurs to create an equilibrium state between the variables of the morphologic and cascading components of the process–response system.

The third characteristic of process–response systems is a statement of the concept of grade.

A graded stream is defined as one that is stable; it is in equilibrium, with a balance between its transporting capacity and the amount of material supplied to it. According to Mackin (1948, p. 471) it is one

in which, over a period of years, slope is delicately adjusted to provide, with available discharge and with prevailing channel characteristics, just the velocity required for the transportation of load from the drainage basin . . . its diagnostic characteristic is that any change in any of the controlling factors will cause a displacement of the equilibrium in a direction that will tend to absorb the effect of the change.

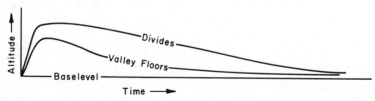

Figure 1-3   The David model of the geomorphic cycle as usually presented.

The graded stream, therefore, is a process–response system in steady-state equilibrium (Figure 1-2), and the equilibrium is maintained by self-regulation or negative feedback, which operates to counteract or reduce the effects of external change on the system so that it returns to an equilibrium condition.

The characteristics of the open process–response system, as stated above, when applied to the Davis model (Figure 1-3) are contradictory: how can the concept of grade or steady-state equilibrium fit into progressive evolution? An obvious solution to the dilemma is that, during the relatively short period when geomorphic studies are carried out, it is not possible to detect the slow progressive reduction of channel gradient and divide elevations (dynamic equilibrium), and the observer concludes that the system is at grade.

It is true that much recent geomorphic work is not concerned with the historical perspective; rather it is the workings of and relations among the components of the system that have been of major concern (Hack, 1960, 1976). Thus it is possible to view the fluvial system either as a physical system or as a historical system. In actuality the fluvial system is a physical system with a history. Hence the objective of the geomorphologist is to understand not only the physics and chemistry of the landscape, but its alteration and evolution through time. Depending on how one views the fluvial system, interpretation of events in the source area and interpretation of sedimentary deposits varies. For example, if a sample of water and sediment is taken from a river and if the quantity of sediment in that sample is used to estimate a long-term average rate of sediment production from Zone 1, the assumption is that there is a continuous uniform production and deposition of sediment (static equilibrium). However, if the samples are collected over a decade or longer, a very different picture emerges, as variations in sediment production become important (steady-rate or dynamic equilibrium).

An investigator needs to consider how to view a fluvial system for his particular needs: either as a purely physical system during a short span of time, or as a historical system that changes, because the different viewpoints strongly influence conceptions of the landscape and conclusions relating to cause and effect. For example, Schumm and Lichty (1965) suggest that landform evolution can be considered during three time spans of different duration: cyclic, graded, and steady (Figure 1-4). The cyclic time span encompasses a major period of geologic time, perhaps involving an erosion cycle. Over the long span of cyclic time a removal of material (potential energy) occurs, and the characteristics of the system progressively change (Figure 1-4a). When viewed from this

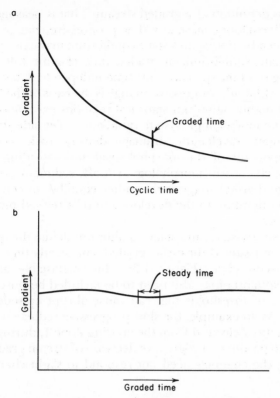

Figure 1-4   Diagram showing the concepts of cyclic, graded, and steady time as reflected in changes of stream gradient through time. (a) Progressive reduction of channel gradient during cyclic time. During graded time, a small fraction of cyclic time, the gradient remains relatively constant. (b) Fluctuations of gradient above and below a mean during graded time. Gradient is constant during the brief span of steady time. (From Schumm and Lichty, 1965.)

perspective a fluvial system is undergoing continual change (dynamic equilibrium).

The graded time span refers to a short period of cyclic time. When the system is viewed from this perspective, there is an unceasing adjustment among its components. There may be slight progressive change of the landforms, but this is masked by the fluctuations about the average values (Figure 1-4b). In other words, the progressive change during cyclic time is seen during a shorter span of time as a series of fluctuations about or approaches to an equilibrium (steady-state equilibrium). This time division is analogous to the "period of years" used by Mackin (1948,

p. 470) in his definition of a graded stream. That is, seasonal and other short-term fluctuations mask any slow progressive change.

During a steady–time span a static equilibrium may exist, in contrast to the steady-state equilibrium of graded time (Figure 1-4b). The landforms during this time span are truly time-independent, because they do not change. Although progressive change is the basis of the Davis model, the fact that highly significant statistical relations exist among the components of the morphologic system (gradient, valley side slope, channel width, meander wavelength, drainage density, rock type, etc.) and among components of the morphological and cascading system (hydraulic geometry, basin morphology, runoff, sediment yields, climate, and drainage density) suggests that other equilibrium concepts should be given consideration in the development of a revised model of landform evolution.

Dynamic, steady-state, and static equilibrium define the types of landform behavior assumed for cyclic, graded, and steady time spans in the Davisian erosion cycle (Figure 1-5a), but metastable and dynamic metastable equilibria may also need to be included because they reflect the influence of thresholds that can cause abrupt episodes of system adjustment. As an example, the slow progressive reduction of sediment size and quantity delivered from the eroding Zone 1, during cyclic time, is expected to produce a progressive decrease of stream gradient in Zone 2. However, the channels need not respond to slight changes of sedi-

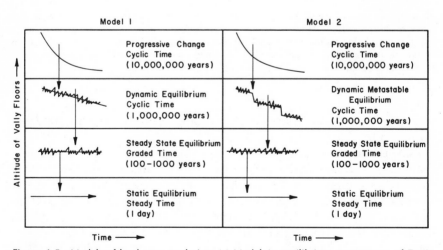

Figure 1-5   Models of landscape evolution. (a) Model 1: equilibrium components of Davis model of progressive denudation (Figure 1-2). (b) Model 2: equilibrium components of model based on episodic erosion.

ment load, but, in fact, a delay or lag of the response could occur until a threshold is exceeded. In this case the channel would respond abruptly to the slow cumulative effects of the progressive sedimentologic change.

If thresholds are a significant factor during landform evolution it is then possible to utilize the concept of dynamic metastable equilibrium to propose a modification of the classic model of progressive erosion (Schumm, 1976). This is a model that stresses periodic or episodic erosion (Figure 1-5b) resulting from the exceeding of threshold conditions. This conception has the advantage of accomodating progressive erosion, grade and periods of instability, and landscape adjustment in a single model of landscape evolution.

Complexity

The following statement by D. A. Pretorius (1973), although written for the economic geologist, is equally applicable to all aspects of geology and is an admirable statement of the problems facing the earth scientist.

> It is the nature of the history of the earth that a geologist has available to him only partial information. Occasional lines from disconnected paragraphs in obscurantist chapters are what can be read. Violence in the handling of the book through time has caused many of these chapters to be ripped and reassembled out of context. That the gist of the early chapters can be deciphered at all is a credit to perseverance and imagination not always associated with other sciences. The geologists operates at all times in an environment characterized by a high degree of uncertainty and ornamented with end-products which are the outcomes of the interactions of many complex variables. He sees only the end, and has to induce the processes and the responses that filled the time since the beginning."

Not only is the fluvial system complex, but its record is usually incomplete. This, of course, has long been recognized, and multicyclic and compound landscapes have been described that are the result of a geomorphic process operating at different rates or of two different processes (e.g., rivers and glaciers) operating on the landscape at different times.

There is, however, another type of complexity that may be of great importance. Consider the probable response of a drainage basin to rejuvenation. When baselevel is lowered, erosion and channel adjustment occur near the mouth of the basin and, in fact, the main channel probably will be adjusted to the change long before the information reaches the upstream tributaries. However, when the tributaries are in turn rejuvenated, the increased sediment production is fed into a channel that has already adjusted to the baselevel change but not to increased sediment loads from upstream. It appears that the original incision is not the only adjustment the main channel makes. In fact, a complex sequence of responses can be envisioned. The result should be reworking of sediments and terrace formation in Zones 1 and 2, and marked variations in the quantity of sediment transported to Zone 3. Hence, as with geomorphic thresholds, a complex response can also be inherent in the erosional evolution of a fluvial system (Schumm, 1973).

The complex response of a fluvial system to change is a type of complexity that is inherent in the fluvial system, and it is an addition to the classic concepts of geomorphic complexity that always refer to a response to changes that are external to the fluvial system. The validity of this concept is demonstrated in Chapter Four, but it is introduced here to alert the reader to another complication in the workings of a fluvial system that may be of major significance for the interpretation of landform and sedimentologic discontinuities.

DISCUSSION

The idealized fluvial system as defined here (Figure 1-1) is composed of three geomorphic and dynamic components: the sediment and water producer (Zone 1, drainage basin), the transfer component (Zone 2, main river channels), and the depositional area (Zone 3, alluvial fan, delta, etc.). Inherent in this idealized model is the assumption that one cannot divorce the events in the drainage basin (Zone 1) from the events in the channels downstream (Zone 2) and at the depositional sites (Zone 3). It is a true process–response system.

Two new ideas have been introduced, geomorphic thresholds and complex response. These are additions to the accepted concepts of thresholds and complexity of erosional evolution, which in turn lead to a hypothetical model of landscape evolution by episodic erosion (Figure 1-5b). The advantage of such a model, if it can be demonstrated, is that it will relieve the geologist of the need to appeal always to external controls for an explanation of erosional and depositional changes, and it will provide the land manager, conservationist, and civil engineer with an approach to preventive conservation. For example, if incipiently unstable landforms can be identified prior to their reaching a threshold, then remedial action can be taken to prevent failure, and preventive conservation will have become a reality. In addition, the influence of these types of geomorphic events on downstream deposition goes far to explain the episodic deposition favored by Ager.

REFERENCES

Ager, D. V., 1973, The nature of the stratigraphical record: Macmillan, London, 114 pp.

Brock, B. B. and Pretorius, D. A., 1964, Rand basin sedimentation and tectonics, in S. H. Haughton (editor), Some Ore Deposits of Southern Africa, vol. 1: Geological Society of South Africa, Cape Town, pp. 25–62.

Chorley, R. J. and Kennedy, B. A., 1971, Physical geography, A systems approach: Prentice-Hall, London, 370 pp.

Coleman, J. M. and Gagliano, S. M., 1964, Cyclic sedimentation on the Mississippi River deltaic plain: Gulf Coast Assoc. Geol. Soc., Trans., v. 14, pp. 67–80.

Craig, L. C. et al., 1955, Stratigraphy of the Morrison and related formations: Colorado Plateau Region: U. S. Geol. Surv. Bull. 1009-E, pp. 125–166.

Davis, W. M., 1899, The geographical cycle: Geogr. J., v. 14, pp. 481–504.

Garner, H. F., 1974, The origin of landscapes: Oxford University Press, New York, 734 pp.

Gretener, P. E., 1967, Significance of the rare event in geology: Am. Assoc. Pet. Geol., Bull. v. 51, pp. 2197–2206.

Hack, J. T., 1960, Interpretation of erosional topography in humid temperate regions: Am. J. Sci., v. 258-A, pp. 80–97.

Hack, J. T., 1976, Dynamic equilibrium and landscape evolution, in W. N. Melhorn and R. C. Flemal (editors), Theories of landform development, Publications in Geomorphology: State University of New York, Binghamton, pp. 87–102.

Haughton, S. H., 1969, Geological history of Southern Africa: Geological Society South Africa, Cape Town, 535 pp.

Kirkby, M. J., 1973, Landslides and weathering rates: Geol. Appl. Idrageol., v. 8, pp. 171–183.

Koons, Donaldson, 1955, Cliff retreat in southwestern United States: Am. J. Sci., v. 253, pp. 44–52.

Mackin, J. H., 1948, Concept of the graded river: Geol. Soc. Am. Bull., v. 59, pp. 463–512.

Martin, Rudolph, 1966, Paleogeomorphology and its application to exploration for oil and gas: Am. Assoc. Pet. Geol., Bull., v. 50, pp. 2277–2311.

Meir, M. F. and Post, Austin, 1969, What are glacier surges?: Can. J. Earth Sci., v. 6, pp. 807–816.

Pretorius, D. A., 1973, The role of E.G.R.U. in mineral exploration in South Africa: Economic Geology Research Unit, Univ. Witwatersrand Inf. Circ. 77, 16 pp.

Schumm, S. A., 1973, Geomorphic thresholds and the complex response of drainage systems, in Marie Morisawa (editor), Fluvial geomorphology, Publications in Geomorphology: State University of New York, Binghamton, pp. 299–310.

Schumm, S. A., 1976, Episodic erosion, A modification of the Davis cycle, in W. N.

Melhorn, and R. C. Flemal (editors), Theories of landform development, Publications in Geomorphology: State University of New York, Binghamton, pp. 69–85.

Schumm, S. A. and Lichty, R. W., 1965, Time, space and causality in geomorphology: Am. J. Sci., v. 263, pp. 110–119.

Simons, D. B., Richardson, E. V. and Nordin, C. F. Jr., 1965, Sedimentary structures generated by flow in alluvial channels: Soc. Econ. Paleontol. Mineral. Spec. Publ. 12, pp. 34–52.

Thornbury, W. D., 1969, Principles of geomorphology: Wiley, New York, 594 pp.

Wolman, M. G. and Miller, J. P., 1960, Magnitude and frequency of forces in geomorphic processes: J. Geol., v. 68, pp. 54–74.

CHAPTER TWO

Variables and Change

Before we proceed to a discussion of the components of the fluvial system, the independent variables (cause) that influence the morphology and dynamics of the system (effect) must be considered briefly, because system changes are referred to later. Therefore, in this chapter the endogenic and exogenic forces that act primarily on Zone 1 landforms and hydrology, and the rates at which changes occur in response to the independent variables that control the system are reviewed briefly.

The variables acting in Zone 1 determine to a large extent the hydrologic products of Zone 1, and these in turn establish the nature of channel morphology and sedimentary deposits in Zones 2 and 3. Further discussion of these relations is presented later as appropriate.

VARIABLES

A hierarchy of variables that are significant to the morphology and mechanics of Zone 1 is shown in Table 2-1. The variables are arranged in a sequence that reflects increasing degrees of dependence, insofar as this can be done for such a complex system. Note also that only upstream controls are given.

Time, initial relief, geology, and climate (variables 1 through 4; Table 2-1) are the dominant independent variables that influence the progress of the erosional denudation of a landscape and its hydrology. Vegetational type and density (variable 5) depend on lithology (soils) and climate (variables 3 and 4). As time passes the relief of the drainage system (variable 6) or mass remaining above baselevel is determined by the factors above it in the table, and relief in turn strongly influences the runoff and sediment yield per unit area within the drainage basin (variable 7). Runoff, acting on the soil and geologic materials, produces a characteristic drainage network morphology (variable 8: drainage density, channel shape, gradient, pattern) and hillslope morphology (variable 9: angle of inclination, length, profile form) within the constraints of relief, climate, lithology and time. These morphologic variables in turn strongly influence the volumes of runoff and sediment that are eventually discharged from Zone 1 (variable 10). It is this volume of sediment and water that to a major extent determines channel morphology and the nature of fluvial deposits that form in Zones 2 and 3 (variables 11 and 12).

Some of the variables given in Table 2-1, for example, geology (lithology, structure, soils) and climate (temperature, precipitation), represent

TABLE 2-1. FLUVIAL SYSTEM VARIABLES (FROM SCHUMM AND LICHTY, 1965)

Drainage system variables
1. Time
2. Initial relief
3. Geology (lithology, structure)
4. Climate
5. Vegetation (type and density)
6. Relief or volume of system above baselevel
7. Hydrology (runoff and sediment yield per unit area within Zone 1)
8. Drainage network morphology
9. Hillslope morphology
10. Hydrology (discharge of water and sediment to Zones 2 and 3)
11. Channel and valley morphology and sediment characteristics (Zone 2)
12. Depositional system morphology and sediment characteristics (Zone 3)

a group of variables and are considered as such in the discussions that follow. Other variables can be grouped for discussion purposes, for example, variables 2, 6, 8, and 9 (morphology) and variables 7 and 10 (hydrology).

Time (Variable 1)

"Time" here refers to the passage of time since the inception of the erosional process and in itself has no effect on the landscape; rather it records the accomplishments of the system. Time is discussed in some detail in the preceding chapter, where it is stated that the fluvial system can be viewed in different ways, depending on the time span considered (Figure 1-4). In fact, during periods of steady-state equilibrium (grade) or static equilibrium, time may not be a significant variable, because the system is not changing progressively during these shorter periods. This is true also of initial relief, because, during the shorter time spans, the landscape components are considered with respect to their climatic, hydrologic, and geologic environment, and present relief (variable 6).

Depending on the time span considered, time may be either an extremely important independent variable or of relatively little significance in considerations of the fluvial system. For example, during a short period of steady time, there may be continuous sedimentation, with no variation in the type of sediment deposited. During graded time, however, there is a large variation in the quantity and type of sediment transported in response to both hydrologic and other variables. During cyclic time a progressive decrease in size and quantity of sediment is likely. Therefore, it is possible to consider all three zones of the fluvial system with regard to different spans of time (Figure 1-4). For the earth scientist, cyclic and graded time have the most significance. Steady time is of concern to the hydraulic engineer and sediment-transport specialist, but for any real considerations of fluvial systems an awareness of the significance of all three is necessary.

Morphology (Variables 2, 6, 8, and 9)

The initial movement of water and sediment in Zone 1 reflects precipitation, soil characteristics, and slope. For a fluvial landscape to form, water must move and erode. The resulting drainage network and its morphologic character then influence the amount and manner in which water and sediment are discharged to Zones 2 and 3 (variable 10). The inception and effect of runoff on slopes and beneath them through the soil, although of great importance, are not discussed here; rather only the effect of two morphologic variables, relief or slope (variables 2 and 6) and drainage density (variable 8), on the hydrology of Zone 1 (variable 10) are considered.

Relief (Variables 2 and 6).   Initial relief (variable 2), which is dependent on the magnitude of uplift (Figure 1-3), and the relief at any time during the erosional development of Zone 1 (variable 6), determines the magnitude of the component of gravitational force acting along slopes and channels and the potential energy of Zone 1. Therefore, the rate at which denudational processes operate and their effects on basin morphology are significantly influenced by relief and slope. For example, drainage density (ratio of total stream length to watershed area) increases with relief and average basin slope (Gregory and Walling, 1973, p. 81). Also, drainage density and relief determine hillslope length and inclination (Strahler, 1950).

Relief and slope strongly influence the movement of water and sediment (variables 7 and 10). For example, when sediment-yield data from small drainage basins, which are underlain by sandstone and shale, are plotted against the average slope (relief/length ratio, relief of basin divided by basin length), an exponential relationship between the two variables is apparent (Figure 2-1). Although this relationship is a straight line on semilog paper, when plotted on arithmetic paper the resulting curve shows graphically the rapid exponential increase in denudation rates with the increase in relief/length ratio (Figure 2-2). It is logical to

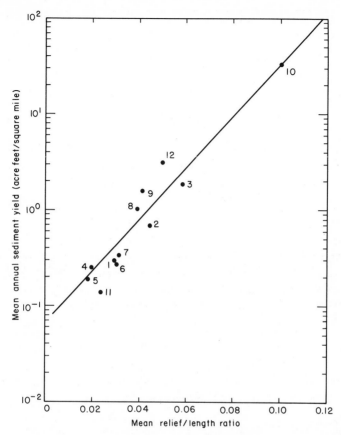

Figure 2-1 Relation of mean annual sediment yield to relief/length ratio for small drainage basins in western United States. Each point is an average value for several basins. Data from a total of 59 basins are represented. The number beside each point indicates rock type and location as follows: (1) resistant sandstone, Utah; (2) friable sandstone, Utah; (3) shale, Utah; (4) sandstone, New Mexico, Arizona; (5) conglomerate and sandstone, New Mexico, Arizona; (6) sandstone, New Mexico, Arizona; (7) sandy shale, Wyoming; (8) sandstone and shale, Wyoming; (9) shale, Wyoming; (10) shale, siltstone, Wyoming; (11) sandstone, Wyoming; (12) shale, Colorado. (From Hadley and Schumm, 1961.)

assume that the increase in denudation with an increase of slope is greater than linear simply because gravitational forces acting on a surface are proportional to the sine of the angle of inclination of that surface.

Figure 2-2 may be viewed in another manner. It can represent the change of sediment yield from one drainage basin during a cycle of erosion (high relief is analogous to the geomorphic stage of youth), and

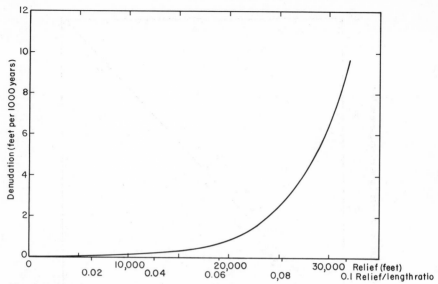

Figure 2-2   Relation of denudation rates to relief/length ratio and drainage-basin relief. Denudation rates are adjusted to drainage areas of 1500 square miles. The curve is based on the relation of Figure 2-1. (After Schumm, 1963.)

the curve then illustrates the decrease in denudation rates with time, through the erosional reduction of the landscape. As the reduction of relief takes place there is a decrease in both the quantity and size of the sediment load derived from the drainage system.

Drainage Texture (Variable 8).   The spacing of the drainage channels within Zone 1 expressed as drainage density is an index of the efficiency of Zone 1 in disposing of water and sediment. The effect of relief has already been made clear, and the effect of drainage density can be illustrated by an example from the Cornfield Wash drainage basin in northern New Mexico. Within this area of similar geology, land use, and climate, runoff and sediment-yield data were collected over a period of years for small drainage basins. Of particular interest is the fact that the channel networks in the drainage basins are not fully developed. That is, many of the valley networks do not contain a fully integrated, well-defined channel network. For example, in one basin the channel drainage density is 0.6 and in another it is 5.6. Therefore, the effect of drainage density on runoff and sediment yield can be isolated, and both mean annual runoff and sediment yield are found to be significantly greater from drainage basins with high drainage densities but similar relief/length ratios (Table 2-2).

TABLE 2-2. HYDROLOGIC AND GEOMORPHIC DATA FROM PAIRED WATERSHEDS OF SIMILAR RELIEF/LENGTH RATIOS, CORNFIELD WASH, NEW MEXICO (FROM SCHUMM, 1969)

	Drainage area (sq. miles)	Relief/ length	Drainage density	Mean annual sediment yield (acre-ft/ sq. miles)	Mean annual runoff (acre-ft/ sq. miles)
a	1.18	0.023	0.6	0.6	16.3
a'	0.87	0.026	2.1	1.7	22.1
b	0.33	0.043	3.1	3.7	44.5
b'	0.29	0.046	5.6	6.8	63.4
c	1.04	0.035	1.3	0.9	20.5
c'	0.25	0.036	3.0	2.2	36.8

Geology (Variable 3)

Geology includes the lithologic character of rocks, as well as structure, the influence of fractures (joints and faults), and other deformational features and their distribution.

Channel patterns and drainage basin shape may show pronounced structural controls (Howard, 1967). The runoff characteristics of long narrow basins differ significantly from circular drainage basins (Gregory and Walling, 1973, p. 269), but little is known concerning the effect of basin shape on sediment yield and on the eventual sedimentary deposit that results.

Rivers draining areas that differ greatly in the physical character of rocks and soils show significant morphologic differences, as the erodibility of the soils, hydrologic character of the system, and the size and quantity of sediment load moved from the basin differ (Chapter Five). On a regional basis, drainage pattern itself reflects these controls. For example, drainage density is high in a region of weak rocks and impermeable soils and low for resistant rocks and highly permeable soils (Table 2-3); photointerpreters use these differences to delineate contacts between different rock and soil types.

As important as lithology is to erosion and sediment transport, relatively little can be said other than that weak rocks erode rapidly and resistant rocks erode slowly. A difficulty is that, for most studies of sediment yield, the data have not been stratified geologically. For exam-

TABLE 2-3. LITHOLOGIC UNITS, CHEYENNE RIVER BASIN (FROM TABLE 2 AND P. 175, HADLEY AND SCHUMM, 1961)

Stratigraphic units	Mean infiltration (in/hr)	Sediment yield (acre-ft/sq. mile)	Drainage density (miles/sq. mile)
Wasatch Formation	9.2	0.13	5.4
Lance Formation	5.0	0.5	7.1
Fort Union Formation	1.3	1.3	11.4
Pierre Shale	1.0	1.4	16.1
White River group	0.18	1.8	258

ple, Figure 2-1 shows a statistically significant relation between drainage basin slope and sediment yield. However, morphology alone is not the only significant control. In Figure 2-1 basins underlain by shales and siltstones plot high, and those underlain by sandstone and conglomerates plot low. Another variable is infiltration capacity; weak rocks that produce sandy soils with a high infiltration capacity produce less runoff and therefore little sediment (Table 2-3). Therefore, there is a major lithologic control of the relation of Figure 2-1.

A major problem is that it is yet not possible to assign a quantitative assessment of erodibility to a rock type, although crystalline rocks weather and erode relatively slowly and most sedimentary rocks do so relatively rapidly (Corbel, 1964). In fact, erosion equations have been linked to soil characteristics rather than to geology. However, it is probable that a geomorphic index such as drainage density integrates both soil and rock characteristics. For example, Carlston's (1963) study of drainage density and streamflow for a variety of rock types in the eastern United States shows that drainage density is directly related to flood runoff and inversely related to baseflow. Therefore, a drainage basin underlain by relatively impermeable materials will produce a large flood, but, in turn, little water will be contributed to groundwater, and the low flow discharge will be small. This readily understood relationship explains to some extent the high sediment yields from drainage basins underlain by shales and the lower values of sediment yield from equally erodible but permeable sandstones (Figure 2-1).

The sad state of the understanding of lithologic effects on sediment yield rates is indicated by the recent work of Jensen and Painter (1974). To quantify the effects of lithology in their sediment-yield equations, they were forced to assign relative erosional values to rocks of different ages.

For example, Paleozoic rocks were assigned the number 3, Mesozoic rocks the number 5, Cenozoic rocks the number 6, and Quaternary rocks the number 2. These numbers indicate an increasing erodibility from Paleozoic to Cenozoic rocks. The reason for assigning a value of 2 to Quaternary outcrop areas is that they are frequently of low relief.

The influence of geology on landform hydrology and sedimentary deposits is great, but, as yet, only very general statements can be made about cause and effect relations. Coates' (1971) approach, which involves an evaluation of the percentage of the stratigraphic column that is composed of permeable rocks and the frequency of joints and bedding planes, has promise, but in general little or nothing quantitative has been forthcoming (Schneider, 1963; Hely and Olmstead, 1963).

Climate (Variable 4)

Geomorphologists assume that the effects of climate and climate change are reflected in erosional and depositional processes and ultimately in the landscape. For example, morphoclimatic regions have been identified wherein the climate determines to a significant extent both the efficiency and type of erosion process and the landforms that result (Stoddart, 1969; Wilson, 1968), but there is no quantitative description of these supposed differences. However, the effects of the greatly different river flow regimes experienced throughout the world (Parde, 1964; Beckinsale, 1969) and the different types of sediments provided by tropical as compared to semiarid, arctic, and arid rock weathering are detectable. For example, comparison of the hydraulic geometry of perennial streams of humid and subhumid regions with that of ephemeral streams of semiarid regions shows that, in contrast to the case of perennial streams, depth of ephemeral streams increases less rapidly and gradient decreases less rapidly in a downstream direction. This probably is due to the high water loss in ephemeral stream channels and to the increase in suspended sediment concentration in a downstream direction (Leopold et al., 1964, Table 7-5). In addition, obvious differences in the morphology of slopes of different aspect, north versus south, for example, are directly attributable to the microclimatic character of the valley sides.

For the purpose here, an extended discussion of climate and the influence on weathering and soil formations is not necessary; rather the effects of climate on vegetation and hydrology (variables 5, 7, 10) are the most important for understanding the geomorphology and hydrology of Zone 1.

Vegetation (Variable 5)

There can be no question of the highly significant effect of vegetation on landforms and erosion rates. In the United States vegetational bulk or weight increases approximately as the cube of mean annual precipitation (Langbein and Schumm, 1958), and a significant reduction in erosion and sediment yield can be anticipated as precipitation increases or as vegetation increases in a given climatic situation. Figure 2-3 shows such a relation from an experimental area in Utah. The relationship is exponential and an extrapolation of the curve indicates a maximum of 50,000 pounds per acre of erosion with zero ground cover. However, there is no reason to believe that this value will be achieved. Although in Figure 2-3 an asymptotic approach to the *y* axis is indicated by the rapid increase of erosion and small percentages of ground cover, there must exist a maximum rate of erosion for a given soil or rock type that will be reached before ground cover is zero. The curve would plateau at that value, as the dashed line suggests. If this is true, then Figure 2-3 leads to the conclusion that with less than about 8.0 percent cover, vegetation is

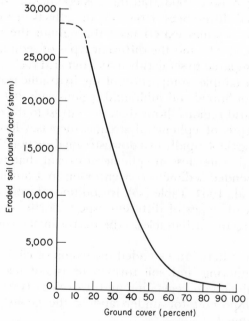

Figure 2-3   Relation of eroded soil to ground cover from an experimental watershed in Utah. Dashed extension of curve is hypothetical. (After Noble, 1965.)

probably relatively ineffective in controlling erosion. On the other hand, above about 70 percent cover, additional vegetation will not significantly reduce erosion. These limits to vegetational effectiveness for erosion control should be given consideration before expensive attempts are made to slightly improve vegetational cover in the drylands of the world. The above discussion is based on the assumption that a threshold, above which vegetational cover becomes important for erosion control, exists.

Hydrology (Variables 7 and 10)

All the previously discussed variables significantly control the runoff and sediment yield from Zone 1, which in turn, greatly influence Zones 2 and 3. In this section the products of Zone 1 are considered primarily in relation to climatic controls.

In any study of hydrologic variables only the available modern records can be utilized and many of these are of short duration. In addition, records of stream discharge are far more abundant than records of sediment loads; therefore, much more is known concerning runoff than sediment movement. Data are usually of excellent quality for humid regions but become less reliable for the drylands. Note that several important topics, such as hydrograph characteristics, subsurface flow (Freeze, 1974), and the role of subsurface flow and groundwater in chemical denudation of the landscape, are not treated here.

Runoff. Runoff is that part of precipitation that appears in surface streams (Langbein and Iseri, 1960). It is therefore water that plays the principal role in fashioning and modifying the fluvial landscape.

Langbein et al. (1949) used data from gaging stations at which the discharge was not materially affected by diversions or regulations to illustrate the general relation between climate and runoff (Figure 2-4). The position of each of the curves depends on mean annual temperature, which was adjusted to remove the effects of seasonal rainfall on runoff. For example, a given amount of precipitation yields less runoff during the warmer months of summer than during the cool winter months.

The family of curves shows that, as expected, when annual precipitation increases, annual runoff increases and that as temperature increases with constant precipitation, runoff decreases. These relations are straightforward and need no elaboration.

Sediment Yield. Sediment yield is the total amount of sediment moved from a drainage basin. It is usually calculated from measurements of the

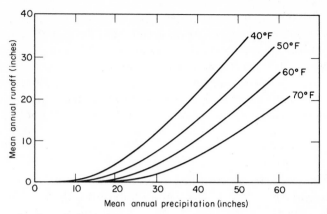

Figure 2-4 The effect of average temperature on the relation between mean annual runoff and mean annual precipitation. (After Langbein et al., 1949.)

sediment concentration in a stream of water, which does not include bed load, or from the amount of sediment deposited in a reservoir, which is a measure of total sediment load.

Langbein and Schumm (1958, Figure 2) defined the relation between annual sediment yield and annual precipitation for drainage basins averaging about 1500 square miles in the conterminous United States for an annual mean temperature of 50°F (Figure 2-5). Although precipi-

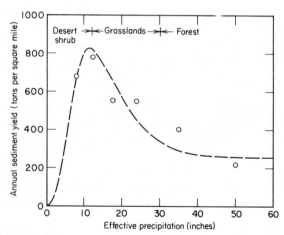

Figure 2-5 Variation of sediment yield with climate as based on data from small watersheds in the United States (From Langbein, W. B. and Schumm, S. A., 1958, Am. Geophys. Union Trans., v. 39, pp. 1076–1084.)

tation is the dominant climatic factor influencing sediment yields, the effect of temperature needs to be considered, because more precipitation is required to produce a given amount of runoff in a warm climate than in a cool climate. The curve of Figure 2-5, therefore, is the relationship between sediment yield and precipitation adjusted to an annual mean temperature of 50°F (Langbein and Schumm, 1958, p. 1076). The definition of the 50°F curve is based on known values of runoff for each drainage basin from which the sediment-yield data were obtained. These observed values of runoff were converted to an "effective precipitation," that is, the annual precipitation required to produce the known runoff at 50°F, by use of the 50°F rainfall/runoff curve of Figure 2-4. For example, if the mean annual runoff from a drainage basin is 10 inches at a mean annual temperature of 50°F, the effective precipitation required to produce this runoff is about 33 inches. To produce the same runoff at 60°F about 39 inches of precipitation is required.

The sediment yield curve reveals that at 50°F sediment yield is a maximum at about 12 inches of precipitation, and it then decreases with lesser and greater amounts of precipitation. This variation in sediment yield with precipitation can be explained by the interaction of precipitation and vegetation on runoff and erosion. As precipitation increases above zero, sediment yields increase at a rapid rate, because more runoff becomes available to move sediment. Opposing this tendency is that of the vegetation, which becomes more abundant as pecipitation increases. Above 12 inches of precipitation, sediment-yield rates decrease under the influence of the more effective grass and forest cover, but where monsoonal climates prevail, sediment-yeild rates may increase again above 50 inches of precipitation under the influence of highly seasonal climates (Fournier, 1949).

A more recent analysis by Dendy and Bolton (1976) of data from 800 drainage basins scattered throughout the United States reveals that a peak of sediment yield exists at between 1 and 3 inches of runoff. At a temperature of 50°F this corresponds to about 18 to 20 inches of precipitation. This more comprehensive set of data suggest that the peak of sediment yield occurs at slightly higher precipitation conditions.

One of the most important factors that influence sediment yield is, of course, land use. For example, Wilson (1972) shows that the sediment-yield data for areas of the humid eastern United States, where strip mining or urbanization has had an important effect on the watershed, are similar to those of arid regions. Wilson's (1973) analysis of sediment-yield data available in 1969 reveals that the Langbein-Schumm relationship tends to be valid for continental types of climates, but where there is marked seasonal variability of precipitation, sediment yields can be much greater than indicated by mean annual precipitation alone. Hence sediment yields in Mediterranean climates and monsoonal climates probably exceed those of Figure 2-5. It is possible that curves, similar to those of Figure 2-5 but higher and with a broader peak (Wilson, 1973), could be developed for seasonal climates.

An attempt by Jensen and Painter (1974) to estimate and develop empirical equations to predict sediment yield from the world's climate zones for drainage basins exceeding 5000 km shows that erosion rates are the lowest in the continental and tropical forest climates, intermediate in arid and semiarid climates, and very high in Mediterranean climates as suggested by Wilson. Extreme values in all cases occurred in areas of high altitude and relief.

RATES OF CHANGE

The preceding has demonstrated how slope and relief, geology, climate, and vegetation influence the hydrologic and erosional character of a drainage basin. However, for the longer periods of cyclic time, it is also necessary to determine the rates of endogenic (tectonics) and exogenic (denudation) processes. Of course, an understanding of the rates of geologic processes is constrained by the short period for which available data on sediment yields, runoff, and rates of deformation are available.

Orogeny

Both the erosional evolution of Zones 1 and 2 and the depositional history of Zone 3 depend to a great extent on the ratio or balance between the endogenic and exogenic forces that modify a landscape. To investigate rates of uplift, these data should be obtained by modern measures rather than be based on a study of the geologic history of an area. For example, Zeuner (1959, p. 360) presents data showing that uplift occurs at rates of a fraction of a millimeter per year when the ages of formations exposed in the Alps and Himalayas are divided by their present altitudes. These rates are obviously only minimum values for the actual rate of uplift, which probably occurred during a far shorter time.

Indeed, modern rates of uplift are far in excess of the minimum values obtained by geologic studies. Gilluly (1949) and Bandy and Marincovich (1973) list some data for areas in California that suggest that the average rate of mountain building is 25 feet or 8 per 1000 years.

Both Gutenberg (1941) and Walcott (1972) have compiled data on postglacial isostatic rebound. Maximum rebound at the head of the Gulf of Bothnia is 110 cm per 100 years or 11 m per 1000 years. Present rates of isostatic uplift in North America are 50 cm per 100 years to the north of Lake Superior, a rate of 5 m per 1000 years (Walcott, 1972).

In contrast to isostatic uplift, Lake Mead provides an example of rapid subsidence caused by the addition of 40 billion tons of water and 2 billion tons of sediment (Gould, 1960) to an area of 232 square miles (147 pounds per square inch). Subsidence is occurring there at a rate of 40 feet per 1000 years, although total subsidence is expected to be only 10 inches (Longwell, 1960).

A variety of data indicate that deformation can be rapid and that it is occurring at rates capable of influencing a fluvial system over relatively short periods of time. In fact, a map of the United States prepared by the National Geodetic Survey shows that the probable annual rates of vertical movement over broad areas of the country are remarkably rapid (Figure 2-6). Although very general in nature, the map indicates in a striking way that some problems of river stability may indeed be a result of vertical movements of the earth's surface and may therefore have a wholly endogenic cause.

While uplift may continue at these measured rates, it seems probable that the formation of mountain ranges occurs at rates comparable to the average rate measured in existing mountains; that is, at rates approaching 8 m per 1000 years.

Although a rate of uplift of 8 m per 1000 years is very slow (8 mm per year), the tilt caused by such a rate of uplift is sufficient to modify significantly the gradient of streams over several decades. It is not suggested that all problems associated with rivers and canals can be attributed to deformation, but examples can be cited where progressive tilting of the earth's surface has significantly modified the gradient of rivers. For example, Lake Victoria is drained by the Victoria Nile which flows north to Lake Kyoga (Figure 2-7). Lake Kyoga and Lake Kwania look artificial, but they are not the result of dam construction. They are, in fact, formed by uplift and eastward tilting of western Uganda. Flow in the Kafu River has been reversed, and water draining from Lake Victoria has found a new course to the north, where it flows over Murchison Falls and into Lake Albert. The geologically recent derangement of these drainage systems is the result of uplift that is apparently continuing at the present time (Holmes, 1965, p. 1057).

Another example of tectonic effects is in Iraq, where both the character of ancient irrigation systems and the Diyala River, a tributary of the Tigris near Baghdad, have been altered because of upwarping. Uplift, during the last 1000 years, caused incision of the Diyala River into its alluvial plain and abandonment of irrigation canal systems (Adams,

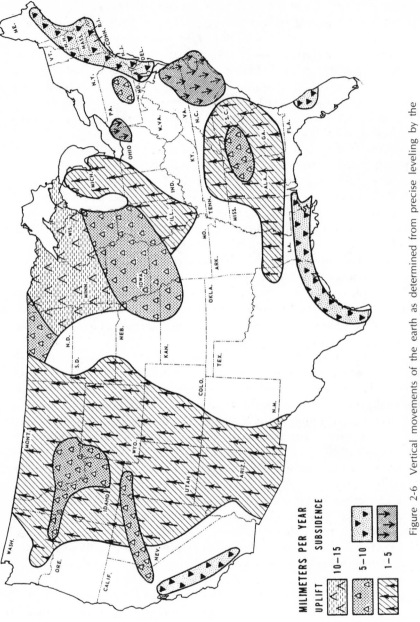

Figure 2-6 Vertical movements of the earth as determined from precise leveling by the National Geodetic Survey (U. S. Department of Commerce, 1972).

MILIMETERS PER YEAR

UPLIFT   SUBSIDENCE

10–15

5–10

1–5

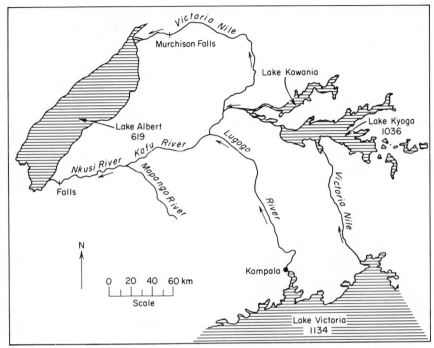

Figure 2-7   Lake Kyoga region, Uganda. Arrows show flow directions in rivers.

1965). Modern flood and river control problems in Bangladesh apparently are also partly the result of upwarping, which has displaced the Brahmaputra River to the west (Coleman, 1969).

Denudation

In contrast to sediment-yield rates, which are the weight or volume of sediment eroded from a unit area, denudation rates are generally expressed as a uniform lowering of the land surface in meters or feet per 1000 years. Obviously, no surface is lowered uniformly in this manner, but it is a convenient way to treat data. Information on rates of erosion in a variety of climatic regions under different geologic and geomorphic conditions can only be obtained from existing sediment yield data. Nevertheless, the differences between erosion and sediment production from diverse climatic regions and from areas of very different morphology at least provide clues and an order of magnitude estimate of sediment production during geologic time.

Denudation in large areas requires more time (Figure), and in early in this century Dole and Stabler (1909) concluded that the average rate of denudation for major river systems and geographical areas of the United States was 1 foot per 9120 years. The rates were calculated from data on dissolved and suspended loads of streams, and bed load was not included in the calculations (see Holeman, 1968).

Corbel (1964, p. 15) has made a worldwide compilation of erosion rates that, for the most part, includes the total sediment load of streams. His data were summarized on the basis of climate and indicate that the highest rates of erosion occur in glacial and periglacial regions (2 feet per 1000 years). Erosion also was high in the high mountain chains with Mediterranean climate (1.5 feet per 1000 years). In fact, one of the highest rates recorded in nonglacial regions was for the Durance River in southeastern France (1.7 feet per 1000 years). Corbel's data reveal that denudation rates can be considerably in excess of those reported by Dole and Stabler (1909).

Even higher denudation rates occur in small drainage areas; for example, the maximum sediment-yield rate listed by the Federal Inter-agency River Basin Committee (1953, p. 14) was measured in the Loess Hills area of Iowa. In a drainage basin of only 0.13 square mile, denudation is progressing at a rate of 42 feet per 1000 years. This high rate, however, is due to gullying in loess rather than resistant rock.

Denudation in large areas requires more time (Figure 4-8), and in general the sediment yield per unit area decreases as about the 0.15 power of drainage basin area (Brune, 1948, Figures 6 and 7; Langbein and Schumm, 1958, p. 1079). Calculations on the basis of Brune's (1948) relationship between drainage area and sediment yield indicate that the maximum denudation rate from the Loess Hills area should decrease from 24 to 10 feet per 1000 years as the size of the drainage basin is increased from 0.13 to 1500 square miles.

In addition, the denudation rate of 8.5 feet per 1000 years for the 1.06-square-mile Halls Debris Basin in California (Flaxman and High, 1955) would be about 5 feet per 1000 years for a 30-square-mile drainage basin, and about 2.8 feet per 1000 years for a 1500-square-mile basin. This rate approaches that of the Durance River mentioned by Corbel and other large drainage basins in mountainous areas.

The above modern data suggest that perhaps 3 feet or 1.0 m per 1000 years is an average maximum rate of denudation for drainage basins on the order of 1500 square miles in area. Other data suggest that this is an acceptable order of magnitude estimate of maximum denudation rates. For example, Wegman (1957, p. 6) states that the northern Alps are being lowered at a rate of about 2.0 feet per 1000 years. In addition,

Khosla (1953, p. 111) reports on the suspended sediment yield from the Kosi River above Barakshetra Bihar, India, which has a drainage basin of 23,000 square miles. Within this basin lie the highest mountain peaks in the world, Mount Everest and Mount Kanchenjunga, and the denudation rate is 3.2 feet per 1000 years.

Studies of the temperature and pressures at which certain minerals form provide information on their depths of origin. When the age of the mineral is known, a means of estimating the rate at which it approached the earth's surface through denudation is possible. It may be coincidental, but in two separate studies of this type (Clark and Jager, 1969, and Rosenfeld, 1969) denudation rates in the Alps were determined to be between 0.4 and 1.0 per year.

Several types of data indicate that 1 m per 1000 years approximates an average maximum rate of denudation which is an order of magnitude less than the average rate of orogeny. However, the denudation rates as calculated here may be high in comparison to those of the geologic past, for man's activities are known to have greatly increased erosion rates in certain areas (Meade, 1969), but Church and Ryder (1972) correctly point out that sediment production was extremely high in paraglacial situations, when fluvial activity flushed debris from glaciated drainage basins following melting of the ice. In addition, the apparent rate of sediment deposition through geologic time has increased greatly. However, the apparently great increase in production of sediment during the recent geologic past is basically due to the incompleteness of the geologic record and to the fact that much settlement is recycled through geologic time (Gilluly, 1969; Gulluly et al., 1970). For example, sediment delivered to the Pacific Ocean has been subducted and recycled into the crust of the earth. It is also possible that the continental or sediment-producing areas have progressively emerged or grown through geologic time (Hargraves, 1976). In either case the functioning of the fluvial system would not be affected.

Another aspect of sediment production that rarely receives attention is the effect of catastrophic events, such as earthquakes. A modern example from New Guinea indicates the extent to which the denudation of an area can be accelerated by the intervention of endogenic forces. Pain and Bowler (1973) report on the effects of a magnitude of earthquakes that occurred near Madang on the north coast of Papua, New Guinea. These earthquakes triggered debris avalanches that removed soil and vegetation from slopes over 60 km^2, resulting in an almost instantaneous denudation of 11.5 cm. In this region the normal denudation rate is 20 cm for 1000 years, but with earthquakes it increases to 58 cm per 1000 years, suggesting that during the early stages of the erosional development of a landscape, when tectonism is significant, mass movement triggered by earthquakes may be a very important denudational process.

DISCUSSION

It is probably not necessary to review the empirical relations presented in this chapter. For the most part they are readily comprehended, but of course more work needs to be done. For example, the relation between vegetation cover and erosion in areas of sparse vegetation needs further elaboration (Figure 2-3). If, in fact, the effect of less than 8 percent vegetative cover is negligible for soil conservation purposes, then no attempts to improve vegetation under these circumstances can be justified.

The rapid rates of uplift and subsidence reported by the National Geodetic Survey (Figure 2-6), if valid, have significant implications for river stability, especially for rivers such as the Mississippi and Ohio, which are major commercial waterways. Further detailed investigation of the possible response of modern rivers to diastrophism is certainly warranted.

The order of magnitude differences between average maximum rates of denudation and those of mountain building indicate the acceptability of Davis' assumptions concerning the beginning of the erosion cycle and have implications that are referred to later. Nevertheless, these average maximum rates as calculated do not reflect the variability of uplift and denudation rates (Yoshikawa, 1974), and locally denudation may equal maximum rates of uplift as in Taiwan (Li, 1976), where relief is great and mass movement is important.

REFERENCES

Adams, R. M., 1965, Land behind Baghdad: University of Chicago Press, Chicago, 187 pp.

Bandy, O. L. and Marincovich, Louis Jr., 1973, Rates of late Cenozoic uplift, Baldwin Hills, Los Angeles, California: Science, v. 181, pp. 653–655.

Beckinsale, R. P., 1969, River regimes: in R. J. Chorley (editor), Water, earth and man: Methuen, London, pp. 455–472.

Brune, Gunnar, 1948, Rates of sediment production in midwestern United States: Soil Conserv. Serv. Tech. Publ. 65, 40 pp.

Carlston, C. W., 1963, Drainage density and streamflow: U. S. Geol. Surv. Prof. Paper 422-C, 8 pp.

Church, Michael and Ryder, J. M., 1972, Paraglacial sedimentation: A consideration of fluvial processes conditioned by glaciation: Geol. Soc. Am. Bull., v. 83, pp. 3059–3072.

Clark, S. P. Jr. and Jager, E., 1969, Denudation rate in the Alps from geochronologic and heat flow data: Am. J. Sci., v. 267, pp. 1143–1160.

Coates, D. R., 1971, Hydrogeomorphology of Susquehanna and Delaware Basins, in M. Morisawa (editor), Quantitative geomorphology: Some aspects and applications, Publications in Geomorphology: State University of New York, Binghamton, pp. 273–306.

Coleman, J. M., 1969, Brahmaputra River: Channel processes and sedimentation: Sediment. Geol., v. 3, pp. 129–239.

Corbel, Jean, 1964, L'erosion terrestre, etude quantitative: Ann. Geogr., v. 73, pp. 385–412.

Dendy, F. E. and Bolton, G. C., 1976, Sediment-yield-runoff-drainage area relationships in the United States: J. Soil Water Conserv., v. 31, pp. 264–266.

Dole, R. B. and Stabler, H., 1909, Denudation: U. S. Geol. Surv. Water-Supply Paper 234, pp. 78–93.

Federal Inter-Agency River Basin Commission, 1953, Summary of reservoir sedimentation surveys for the United States through 1950: Subcommittee on Sedimentation, Sedimentation Bull. 5, 31 pp.

Flaxman, E. M. and High, R. D., 1955, Sedimentation in drainage basins of the Pacific Coast States: Soil Conservation Service, Portland, mimeographed.

Fournier, M. F., 1949, Les facteurs climatiques de l'erosion du sol: Bul. Assoc. Geogr. Fr. 203 (11 Juin 1949), pp. 97–103.

Freeze, Allan, 1974, Steam flow generation: Rev. Geophys. Space Phys., v. 12, pp. 627–647.

Gilluly, James, 1949, Distribution of mountain building in geologic time: Geol. Soc. Am. Bull., v. 60, pp. 561–590.

Gilluly, James, 1969, Geological perspective and the completeness of the geologic record: Geol. Soc. Am. Bull., v. 80, pp. 2303–2312.

Gilluly, James, Reed, J. C. Jr. and Cady, W. M., 1970, Sedimentary volumes and their significance: Geol. Soc. Am. Bull., v. 81, pp. 353–376.

Gould, H. R., 1960, Amount of sediment: U. S. Geol. Surv. Prof. Paper 295, pp. 195–200.

Gregory, K. J. and Walling, D. W., 1973, Drainage basin form and process: Wiley, New York, 456 pp.

Guttenberg, Beno, 1941, Changes in sealevel, postglacial uplift, and mobility of the earth's interior: Geol. Soc. Am. Bull., v. 52, pp. 721–772.

Hadley, R. F. and Schumm, S. A., 1961, Sediment sources and drainage basin characteristics in upper Cheyenne River basin: U. S. Geol. Surv. Water Supply Paper 1531-B, pp. 137–196.

Hargraves, R. B., 1976, Precambrian geologic history: Science, V. 193, pp. 363–371.

Hely, A. G. and Olmstead, F. H., 1963, Some relations between streamflow characteristics and the environment in the Delaware River Region: U. S. Geol. Surv. Prof. Paper 417-B.

Holeman, J. N., 1968, The sediment yield of major rivers of the world: Water Resour. Res., v. 4, pp. 737–747.

Holmes, A., 1965, Principles of physical geology: London, T. Nelson, 1288 pp.

Howard, A. D., 1967, Drainage analyses in geologic interpretations: A summation: Am. Assoc. Pet. Geol., Bull., v. 51, pp. 2246–2259.

Jensen, J. M. L. and Painter, R. B., 1974, Predicting sediment yield from climate and topography: J. Hydrol., v. 21, pp. 371–380.

Khosla, A. N., 1953, Silting of reservoirs: Cent. Board Irrig. Power (India) Publ. 51, 203 pp.

Langbein, W. B. et al., 1949, Annual runoff in the United States: U. S. Geol. Surv. Circ. 52, 14 pp.

Langbein, W. B. and Schumm, S. A., 1958, Yield of sediment in relation to mean annual precipitation: Am. Geophys. Union Trans., v. 39, pp. 1076–1084.

Langbein, W. B. and Iseri, K. T., 1960, General introduction and hydrologic definitions: U. S. Geol. Surv. Water-Supply Paper 1541-A, 29 pp.

Leopold, L. B., Wolman, M. G. and Miller, J. P., 1964, Fluvial processes in Geomorphology: San Francisco, Freeman, 522 pp.

Li, Y. H., 1976, Denudation of Taiwan Island since the Pleistocene epoch: Geology, v. 4, pp. 105–107.

Longwell, C. R., 1960, Interpretation of the leveling data: U. S. Geol. Surv. Prof. Paper 295, pp. 33–38.

Meade, R. H., 1969, Errors in using modern stream-load data to estimate natural rates of denudation: Geol. Soc. Am. Bull., v. 80, pp. 1265–1274.

Noble, E. L., 1965, Sediment reduction through watershed rehabilitation: U. S. Dept. Agric. Misc. Publ. 970, pp. 114–123.

Pain, C. F. and Bowler, J. M., 1973, Denudation following the November 1970 earthquake at Madang, Papua New Guinea: Z. Geomorphol. Suppl., v. 18, pp. 92–104.

Parde, M., 1964, Fleuves et rivieres: Paris, Librairie Armand Colin, 223 pp.

Rosenfeld, J. N., 1969, Stress effects around quartz inclusions in almandine and the piezo-thermometry of coexisting aluminum silicates: Am. J. Sci., v. 267, pp. 317–351.

Schneider, W. J., 1963, Areal variability of low flows in a basin of diverse geologic units: Water Resour. Res., v. 1, pp. 509–515.

Schumm, S. A., 1963, Disparity between modern rates of denudation and orogeny: U. S. Geol. Surv. Prof. Paper 454-H, 13 pp.

Schumm, S. A., 1969, A geomorphic approach to erosion control in semiarid regions: Am. Soc. Agric. Eng., Trans., v. 12, pp. 60–68.

Schumm, S. A. and Lichty, R. W., 1965, Time, space and causality in geomorphology: Am. J. Sci., v. 263, pp. 110–119.

Stoddart, D. R., 1969, Climatic geomorphology: Review and assessment: Prog. Geogr., v. 1, pp. 160–222.

Strahler, A. N., 1950, Equilibrium theory of erosional slopes approached by frequency distribution analysis: Am. J, Sci., v. 248, pp. 673–696, 800–814.

U. S. Department of Commerce, 1972, U. S. Dept. Commerce News, Friday, Sept. 22, 1972 NOAA 72-122, 3 pp.

Walcott, R. I., 1972, Late Quaternary vertical movements in eastern North America: Quantitative evidence of glacio-isostatic rebound: Rev. Geophys. Space Phys., v. 10, pp. 849–884.

Wegman, E., 1957, Tectonique vivante, denudation et phenomenes connexes: Rev. Geogr. Phys. Geol. Dynamique (2), v. 1, pp. 3–15.

Wilson, Lee, 1968, Morphogenetic classification, in R. W. Fairbridge (editor), The encyclopedia of geomorphology: Reinhold, New York, pp. 717–729.

Wilson, Lee, 1972, Seasonal sediment yield patterns of United States rivers: Water Resour. Res., v. 8, pp. 1470–1479.

Wilson, Lee, 1973, Variations in mean annual sediment yield as a function of mean annual precipitation: Am. J. Sci., v. 273, pp. 335–349.

Yoshikawa, Torao, 1974, Denudation and tectonic movement in contemporary Japan: Dept. Geogr., Univ. Tokyo Bull., No. 6, March 1974, pp. 1–14.

Zeuner, F. E., 1959, The Pleistocene period: London, Hutchinson, 446 pp.

CHAPTER THREE

Climate Change and Paleohydrology

Geologists have long been aware that the hydrologic cycle is an integral part of the cycle of denudation and reconstruction of continents and that a better understanding of the relation of sedimentary deposits and river morphology to hydrology is necessary to construct paleoenvironmental models of archaeological sites, river terraces, paleochannels, and associated terrestrial and deltaic deposits. Further, when it is possible to understand paleoclimatic and paleohydrologic variations and their effects on the fluvial system, then the same principles can be used to predict the future effects of man-induced environmental changes. Increasing weather modification efforts and the progressive regulation of river systems necessitate utilization of every method to develop a basis for prediction of the river and landscape changes that accompany alterations of hydrologic variables.

The relations among precipitation, temperature and hydrologic variables, runoff, and sediment yield are presented in Chapter Two, but those relations changed during earth history, and the influence of climate change on vegetation and in turn on runoff and erosion rates is sufficiently complex that a separate treatment of this matter is required. In fact, the complexity of these relations, especially through geologic time, necessitates a separate treatment here of paleohydrology. Only the basic relations are presented in this chapter. The effects of climate change and vegetation evolution on Zone 1 are considered in Chapter Four, and examples of how these relations can be utilized to predict river response are presented in Chapter Five.

If hydrology is the study of the waters of the earth, their distribution, composition, and movements, then paleohydrology can be defined as the science of the waters of the earth, their composition, distribution, and movement on ancient landscapes from the occurrence of the first rainfall to the beginning of historic hydrologic records. It is difficult to consider water movement on a landscape without becoming involved with the various problems of sediment transport, and therefore the inclusion of the word composition in the definition stipulates that the quantity and type of sediments moved through paleochannels must be considered a part of paleohydrology (Schumm, 1967, 1968).

It is tempting to make the uniformitarian assumption that modern hydrologic relations can be applied directly to an interpretation of sedimentologic and stratigraphic problems of the rock record. However, the very important influences of vegetation on the hydrologic cycle require consideration, and Kaiser (1931), Tricart and Cailleux (1952), and Russell (1956), among others, have warned that rates of erosion and landform evolution have been altered by the advent and progressive evolution of vegetation. Hence, to understand the functioning of fluvial systems in the past, it is mandatory that their paleohydrologic and paleoclimatic characteristics be appreciated.

The hydrologic cycle probably was operative as early as 4 billion years ago (Donn et al., 1965), although the oldest dated sediments are only 3.4 billion years old (Cloud, 1974). For there to have been a hydrologic cycle there must have been a hydrosphere; two hypotheses have been offered to explain its origin: (1) it was formed as the earth formed and is the remnant of a denser primitive atmosphere and (2) it evolved through time by the degassing of the earth.

Rubey (1951) reviews and evaluates the research, conclusions, and speculations of many investigators, and he concludes that the hydrosphere had its origin in a degassing process and that, in fact, the volume of the hydrosphere has increased through geologic time. If the process of degassing has been constant through geologic time starting about 4.5 billion years ago, then 3.4 billion years ago when the oldest sedimentary rocks formed, only 30% of the hydrosphere was present. At the beginning of the Paleozoic era about 0.5 billion years ago, 90% of the hydrosphere was present.

Although the composition of the hydrosphere probably did not change during the last 2 to 3 billion years (Cloud, 1968), other evidence indicates that the composition of the atmosphere may have been very different. Holland (1964) suggests that there was a three-stage evolution of the atmosphere. During earliest earth history, Stage 1, there was no atmosphere. During Stage 2, from about 4 to 2 billion years ago, oxygen was not abundant. Evidence for this includes the unoxidized detrital grains of uraninite—a mineral unstable in the modern atmosphere— that were identified in 2-billion-year-old and older uranium deposits in Canada and South Africa. During Stage 3, photosynthesis determined the oxidation state of the atmosphere. About 1.6 billion years ago the oxygen level reached 0.01 of the present atmosphere level and remained at about this level until all surface materials were fully oxidized by about 1.2 billion years ago (Rutten, 1970).

QUATERNARY PALEOHYDROLOGY

The simplest way to introduce the discussion of paleohydrology is to consider the existing data and to work backwards using previously developed runoff and sediment-yield relations (Figures 2-4 and 2-5). This is possible if it is assumed that during relatively recent geologic time, during the later part of the Tertiary and the entire Quaternary period, there has been no significant change of vegetation. Since this appears to be true (Kräusel, 1961, p. 230), the relations between runoff and sediment yield and between mean annual temperature and precipitation can be used to show how both sediment and runoff changed with the climatic changes of the last few million years of earth history.

To determine the effect of a climate change on sediment yields it is necessary to develop curves for temperatures other than 50°F. The rainfall–runoff curves for temperatures of 40°, 60°, and 70°F (Figure 2-4) were used to obtain the additional sediment-yield curves in Figure 3-1. These three curves were obtained by the same technique used to develop the 50°F curve of Figure 2-5.

The curves in Figure 3-1 are displaced laterally with respect to the position of the 50°F curve. They indicate that as annual temperature increases, the peak of sediment yield occurs at higher amounts of annual precipitation; that is, because of higher rates of evaporation and transpiration, less of the precipitation at higher temperatures is available to support vegetation, runoff is less, and so the peak rate of sediment yield shifts to the right. The curves of Figure 3-1 may be used to estimate changes in sediment yield as temperature or precipitation or both changed during the past. However, only the direction and magnitude of the changes are meaningful, because variations of geology and geomorphology also affect the sediment yields.

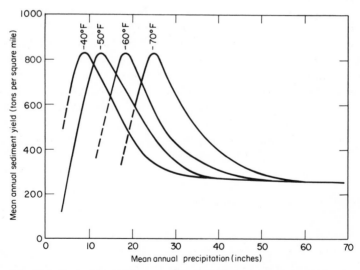

Figure 3-1   The effect of temperature on the relation between mean annual sediment yield and mean annual precipitation. (From Schumm, 1965.) Reprinted by permission of Princeton University Press.)

In addition to the amount of sediment moved, its concentration in the water by which it is moved is important, and curves have been developed to show the relation between sediment concentration and precipitation at different mean annual temperatures (Figure 3-2). To develop the curves, runoff for a given temperature was obtained from Figure 2-4 and sediment yields for a given temperature were obtained from Figure 3-1. As might be expected, for a given annual precipitation, sediment concentration increases with annual temperature, and for a given annual temperature, sediment concentration decreases with an increase in annual precipitation.

An important portion of the total load of streams, the dissolved load, was ignored in the above computations. Although the concentration of dissolved solids is greater in streams draining arid and semiarid regions, the total yield of dissolved solids is greater from humid regions (Rainwater, 1962). Changes in the amount of dissolved load would have an insignificant effect on stream activity and morphology compared to the effect of changes in the amount of either suspended load or bed load.

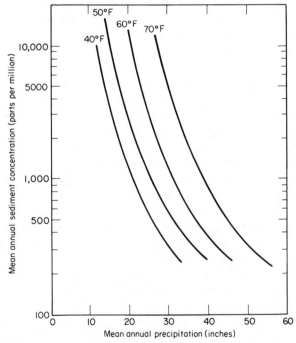

Figure 3-2   The effect of temperature on the relation between mean annual sediment concentration and mean annual precipitation. (From Schumm, 1965. Reprinted by permission of Princeton University Press.)

If Quaternary climates are known they permit the use of Figures 2-4, 3-1, and 3-2 to determine changes in the hydrology of nonglacial continental regions. For example, a change from present climatic conditions to a cooler, wetter climate causes an increase in runoff. This increase is greater for areas with initially drier climates (semiarid regions). For example, if temperature is 10°F less and precipitation is 10 inches greater, a 20-fold increase in runoff will occur in a region with a present annual precipitation of 10 inches and a present annual temperature of 50°F; however, only a two-fold increase in runoff will occur in a region of 40 inches of precipitation with an annual temperature of 50°F.

Sediment yields generally decrease with increased precipitation and decreased temperature because this type of climate change improves the vegetal cover (Figure 3-1). An exception occurs, however, when the change is from an arid (60°F and 10 inches) to a subhumid climate (50°F and 20 inches). In this case the increase in sediment yield may be explained by the assumption that the increase in runoff is more effective in promoting erosion than the improved vegetal cover is in retarding erosion.

In summary, the curves of Figures 2-4, 3-1, and 3-2, which are based on modern runoff and sediment-yield data, suggest the changes in runoff, sediment yield, and sediment concentration that can be expected with a change in climate; in the same manner it is possible to estimate Quaternary runoff, sediment yield, and sediment concentration from paleoclimatic information. One major limitation to the use of the curves is that they are applicable only to nonglacial or to pluvial regions. For these regions a decrease in temperature and an increase in precipitation cause an increase in runoff and a decrease in the sediment concentration. Sediment yield, however, can either increase or decrease depending on the temperature and precipitation before the change.

The changed relations of runoff and sediment yield during and following a climate change influence both the type and amount of sediment deposited. However, even yearly fluctuations of runoff can cause significant variations in the amount of sediment deposited. For example, Granar (1956) has established a very good correlation between varve thickness and the annual maximum discharge of the Ångerman River for the years 1920 to 1942. The relationship appears to be exponential, with varve thickness increasing greatly with an increase in the maximum discharge for any year.

In all of the preceding it has been assumed that a climate change would be gradual and the hydrologic response would be gradual. However, Knox (1972) suggests that in the northcentral United States climate change can be abrupt (Figure 3-3a), and this will trigger a response that,

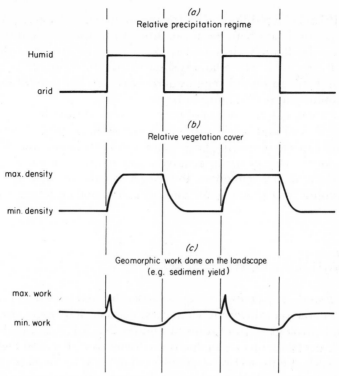

Figure 3-3 Vegetational and geomorphic response to abrupt climate change. (From Knox, 1972. Reproduced by permission from the ANNALS of the Association of American Geographers.)

although short, may be the opposite of that suggested by the sediment yield curves of Figure 3-1. He concludes that a sharp and permanent increase of precipitation, as a result of a changed circulation pattern (Knox, 1976), will cause higher slope and channel erosion until the vegetational cover can improve (Figure 3-3b). The result is a short period of very high sediment yields followed by a decrease (Figure 3-3c). It is undoubtedly true that a change of climate of any type will trigger a period of landscape instability that will produce higher erosion rates and sediment yields as the landscape and stream channels respond. However, such fluctuations may be difficult to distinguish from the effects of very large floods of rare occurrence.

Another aspect of hydrology that can be changed significantly by climate alteration is the nature of flood events. The very lack of vegetation that permits maximum erosion is also responsible for larger floods.

Knox (1972) analyzed flood data for the midwestern United States and developed a relation between mean annual precipitation and the magnitude of the flood with a 50-year recurrence interval for drainage basins of three sizes. His relations show clearly the dramatic increase in flood size between humid regions and areas with less that 20 inches of precipitation per year (Figure 3-4).

In dry areas a given amount of precipitation will run off more quickly (lag time is less) and it will produce a higher flood peak. These flash floods are capable of moving large quantities of sediment, and it is likely that a climate change from relatively wet to dry will cause channel enlargement to accommodate the larger floods, as well as channel straightening or a gradient increase to accommodate larger sediment loads.

PREQUATERNARY PALEOHYDROLOGY

Once the study of paleohydrology is carried beyond the time of modern vegetation, the very different botanical situation will strongly modify the modern hydrologic relationships of Figures 2-4, 3-1, 3-2, and 3-4. The effect of vegetation on erosion has been discussed earlier, and Figure 2-3 shows clearly the protective effect offered by a rather small percentage of vegetation cover. It is this type of relationship that must be used if an

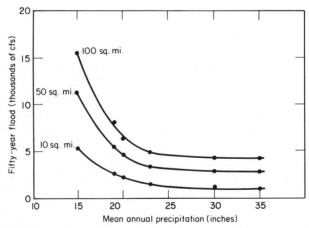

Figure 3-4   Relation between flood magnitude and mean annual precipitation for three sizes of drainage basins. (From Knox, 1972. Reproduced by permission from the ANNALS of the Association of American Geographers.)

evaluation of hydrologic conditions of the remote geologic past is to be achieved.

Fortunately, certain types of modern hydrologic data may be applicable. For example, the effect of total destruction of vegetation on the hydrologic regimen of a drainage basin may provide a glimpse into the hydrology of the distant past. An excellent example is provided by the Ducktown area of Tennessee, which was completely denuded by the poisonous effects of smelter fumes. The average annual precipitation in this general region is between 55 and 60 inches; the characteristic vegetation is oak-chestnut forest (Brater, 1939). The drainage basins from which data have been obtained are small, ranging from 6 to 89 acres, but for two basins of comparable size, the records show that peak discharges were nine times as great from the barren basin. Detailed information is not available for runoff volumes or sediment yields, but total runoff occurred in about 135 minutes for forested drainage basins but in only 35 minutes for the denuded basins, and, of course, sediment yields were increased greatly.

Another source of information is provided by drainage basins from which vegetation has been removed by burning (Anderson and Trobitz, 1949) or by small areas that have been treated to destroy the vegetation for experimental purposes. The sediment yield from these basins increased 100-fold (Storey et al., 1964).

A detailed investigation of the effect of vegetation reduction by fires on peak discharge and sediment yield for the Santa Anita Canyon and other small and moderate-size watersheds in the Los Angeles area revealed a dramatic change of hydrologic conditions (Storey et al., 1964). The basins are steep, and the response is greater than would be expected elsewhere. One year after the fire the ratio of peak discharge after the burn to peak discharge before the burn was 2.0 for large storms, with a recurrence interval between about 100 and 50 years. This ratio is 4.0 for the annual flood and increases rapidly to 10 for small storms that occur three times per year. It is largest for small runoff events that are confined within the stream channels, but the doubling of peak discharge for major storms is sufficient to cause great flood erosion, sediment transport, and downstream damage. The ratios decrease for the largest floods, because after local storage and the infiltration rate of the soil is exceeded, runoff is a very high percentage of rainfall. Hence, changing the character of the surface, in this case burning of vegetation, only doubles the peak discharge of large floods. These results indicate that, during prevegetation times, peak discharges were high and the quantity and size of sediment moved were much larger than now, when vegetation inhibits the erosional and runoff process.

For present purposes it suffices to state with confidence that the presence of vegetation will reduce total runoff from a region and that up to a limit, depending on intensity and duration of precipitation, the presence of vegetation will reduce flood peaks and increases the length of time of flooding. For example, Kittredge (1948, p. 253) states that surface runoff from areas of dense vegetation occurs only during heavy rains and is less than 3 percent of the precipitation, whereas in denuded areas runoff starts after lighter rains and may be over 60 percent of precipitation.

Caution must be exercised before the erosion rates measured in denuded areas can be applied to the erosion rates of prevegetation times. The modern rates are the result of erosion of existing soil and regolith; however, if vegetation had never been present, the rates would be slower and would be dependent on the speed of rock weathering and on the rate of erosion of weakly cemented rocks. Fairbridge (1963, p. 432, 436) suggests that the abundance of ozone during at least part of Precambrian time, and a strongly acid atmosphere in middle and late Precambrian times would have been conducive to rapid weathering and sediment production. Therefore, abundant sediment may have been available for transport even before soil development by organic processes.

Using what is known about vegetational influences on sediment yield and runoff, an attempt has been made in Figures 3-5 and 3-6 to show how the runoff and sediment-yield curves could have evolved through geologic time. As suggested by Russell (1956), four divisions of geologic time are of interest: (1) prevegetation time, (2) time during colonization of alluvial areas by primitive vegetation, (3) time during colonization of interfluves by modern types of flowering plants, and (4) time following the appearance of grasses.

It is difficult to establish the limits of these three phases of vegetational evolution. However, it is generally agreed that although vascular land plants have been identified in the Cambrian period (Andrews, 1961, p. 49), significant colonization of the land did not occur before the Devonian period (Dunbar, 1969, p. 171) about 400 million years ago.

During the vast span of time between the Devonian period and the end of the Paleozoic era, the important forms of vegetation were probably confined to nearshore and coastal-plain areas. Primitive flowering plants have been identified in sediments of the Permian and Triassic ages, but these could not have survived outside tropical rain forests (Andrews, 1961, p. 183). Conifers were abundant in the Jurassic age, and by the Middle Cretaceous period modern deciduous forests had appeared. These plants were capable of surviving seasonal changes of climate and climate fluctuations (Dunbar, 1960, pp. 304, 337). There-

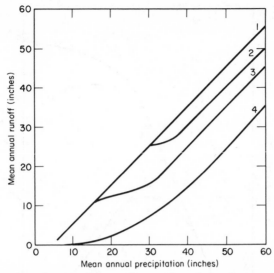

Figure 3-5 Hypothetical series of curves showing the relations between precipitation and runoff during geologic time: (1) before the appearance of land vegetation; (2) following the appearance of primitive vegetation; (3) following the appearance of flowering plants and conifers; (4) following the appearance of grasses. (From Schumm, 1968.)

fore, between the Devonian and Cretaceous periods (400 million to 135 million years ago) vegetation was progressively expanding its range as new forms evolved.

With the appearance of vegetation capable of surviving abrupt and possibly severe climatic fluctuations, the less favorable habitats were colonized, and between the Cretaceous period and the Miocene epoch (between 135 million and 25 million years ago) the interfluve or upland areas were colonized to the extent that plant cover was effective in holding weathered material on the hillslopes and lowering denudation rates. With the appearance of grasses in Miocene time (Dunbar, 1969, p. 432, 435), the effect of vegetation on the hydrologic cycle must have been as it is today.

As more paleobotanical information becomes available on the appearance and evolution of plants, it may be necessary to change the boundaries of these four periods. For example, Cloud (1974) suggests that the influence of terrestrial vegetation from as long as 1.3 billion years ago can be noticed in fluvial sediments, but, in contrast, Gregor's (1968) analysis of denudation suggests that, in fact, a major change of denudation rates took place in the Devonian period from which the first fossil land plants of any significance are found.

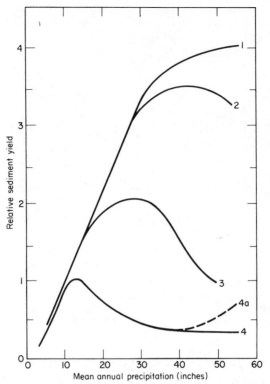

Figure 3-6   Hypothetical series of curves showing the relations between precipitation and relative sediment yield (maximum average sediment yield of today is 1) during geologic time: (1) before the appearance of land vegetation; (2) following the appearance of primitive vegetation; (3) following the appearance of flowering plants and conifers; (4) following the appearance of grasses. Curve 4a shows the increase in sediment yield rates for tropical monsoonal climates. (From Schumm, 1968.)

During Precambrian and early Paleozoic time (prior to 400 million years ago) the lack of an effective vegetation cover permitted sediment-yield rates to increase with increased precipitation to a maximum rate, dependent only on the erodibility of weathering rates of the rocks. In Figure 3-6 (curve 1) this maximum rate is arbitrarily shown to be four times as great as the average rates of sediment yield of the present. It is assumed that the severe microclimatic environment, characterized by extremes of temperatures and rapid changes of temperature at the ground surface, caused rapid mechanical weathering, and if Fairbridge is correct, chemical weathering was also rapid. The uninhibited transport of the weathered material combined with the availability of sediment to yield rapid rates of denudation. The effect of rock type itself is not shown in Figure 3-6, but the prevegetation denudation rate for weakly cemented sedimentary rocks was much greater than that shown, and it was much less for massive igneous rocks.

In Figure 3-5 curve *1* indicates that when transpiration and interception losses do not occur, runoff increases directly with precipitation after some loss due to infiltration and evaporation. This loss is assumed to have been about 5 inches, so runoff was zero from regions that received less than 5 inches of precipitation annually. At present, runoff from regions receiving less than 5 inches of annual precipitation is minimal (Langbein et al., 1949). Although curve *1* may indicate a quantity of runoff too great for even the prevegetation situation, the significant factor is that runoff increased directly with precipitation and flood peaks were much greater in the absence of vegetation.

Curve *1* indicates that runoff was about 50 percent of precipitation at 10 inches of annual precipitation, but it increased to 75 percent of precipitation at 20 inches and to 80 percent at 30 inches. Above 40 inches of precipitation, curve *4* parallels curve *1*, but it is lower and indicates a 20-inch water loss due to vegetational influences. The position of curve *1* in Figure 3-5 was established by assuming that it must be parallel to the upper portion of curve *4* and that forest vegetation can consume 20 inches of water annually in a humid region (Kittredge, 1948, Figures 19 and 20).

To summarize, during prevegetation time, runoff occurred more frequently as floods and both sediment yield and runoff increased with increased precipitation. The sediment-yield rates increased with precipitation to a plateau, depending on the erodibility of the rocks forming the drainage basin, and runoff for a given amount of precipitation was greater than at present.

As colonization of the land surface by primitive plants progressed during late Paleozoic and early Mesozoic times (between 400 million and 135 million years ago), the presence of vegetation decreased erosion in certain parts of the landscape, and the peak of the sediment-yield curve decreased somewhat (Figure 3-6, curve *2*). Also, a discontinuity appeared in the runoff–precipitation curve for those areas of greater rainfall where vegetation was present and where water was utilized by the primitive vegetation (Figure 3-5, curve *2*). Primitive vegetation probably occurred only on coastal plains and in humid valleys, and therefore, its effects initially may have been local. Sediment was shed continually from the barren hillslopes and was temporarily stored in the valleys as in prevegetation times, but, at least in the downstream areas, the vegetation would have tended to stabilize the sedimentary deposits and the stream channels.

As more modern and hardier plants evolved during the Mesozoic and early Cenozoic periods (between about 125 million and 25 million years ago), less favorable habitats were colonized and the vegetation moved up onto the interfluve areas, further decreasing sediment yields and compressing the peak of the curve (Figure 3-6, curve 3). The discontinuity in the runoff relation would have shifted into drier regions (Figure 3-5, curve 3), and, with the appearance of grasses during late Cenozoic time (about 25 million years ago), erosion and runoff conditions similar to those of the present, but without man's influence, prevailed (Figures 3-5, curve 4; 3-6, curve 4).

Gilluly (1964) concluded from an estimate of the volume of Triassic and younger sediments of the Atlantic coast of the United States that the average rate of Mesozoic and Cenozoic erosion was about equal to the present rate of erosion. However, the present erosion rate, where influenced by man's activities, may be on the average twice that of the natural rate (Douglas, 1967). For this reason curve 3 of Figure 3-6 shows Mesozoic and early Cenozoic erosion as being about double that of the present (curve 4).

The curves of Figures 3-5 and 3-6 provide some basis for paleohydrologic interpretation, and they illustrate the manner in which sediment yield and runoff vary with climate. However, the curves of Figure 3-6, although providing information on the relative volumes of sediment delivered from a system during a given climate, provide no information on the type of sediment to be expected. It is known that the material held in solution in rivers increases as the climate becomes more humid (Durum et al., 1961) and that the presence of vegetation in humid regions retards the movement of sediment from the system and promotes weathering to yield a finer-grained product (Garner, 1959). Therefore, not only will sediment yield decrease with increased precipitation, but the material will be finer for sediment-yield curves 3 and 4 of Figure 3-6; in contrast, fluvial sediments during prevegetation time (curve 1) and during colonization of the land by primitive vegetation (curve 2) were coarse-grained because extensive weathering of the material on the hillslopes was precluded by rapid erosion.

DISCUSSION

The very different hydrologic characteristics of the geologic past, as outlined above, should be reflected in the characteristics of all three zones of the fluvial system. Certainly the erosional evolution of a landscape proceeded in prevegetation times at a rate different from that of modern times, and the hydrology of the fluvial system was very different. These differences and their influences on the three zones of the fluvial systems are considered in subsequent chapters as appropriate, but perhaps a suggestion of the significance of climate change to the geologist can be given here. A climate change that increases the rate of sediment movement in Zone 1 favors the reworking of sediments and the concentration of coarse, heavy minerals to form placer deposits in Zone 1. The finer faction of both heavy minerals and normal sediments are moved downstream to Zones 2 and 3, where heavy mineral concentrations may form by additional reworking by coastal or fluvial processes. A climate change that results in increased vegetational cover and a lower erosional capability of the stream is not conducive to placer formation. Distinct periods of heavy mineral concentration in fluvial sediments can reflect significant paleohydrologic changes.

Consider also a major climate change in the Mississippi River drainage area that consists of a reversal such that the Arkansas and Missouri drainage areas are humid and the Ohio and Tennessee drainage areas are semiarid. Perhaps no significant decrease in sediment yield would result, but a striking change in the mineralogy of the deposits would appear. Hence shifting precipitation patterns can also influence the nature and quantity of sediment delivered to Zone 3.

REFERENCES

Anderson, H. W. and Trobitz, H. K., 1949, Influence of some watershed variables on a major flood: J. For., v. 47, pp. 347–356.

Andrews, H. N. Jr., 1961, Studies in paleobotany: New York, Wiley, 487 pp.

Brater, E. F., 1939, The unit hydrograph principle applied to small watersheds: Am. Soc. Civil Eng. Proc., v. 65, pp. 1191–1215.

Cloud, P. E. Jr., 1968, Atmospheric and hydrospheric evolution on the primitive Earth: Science, v. 160, pp. 729–736.

Cloud, P. E. Jr., 1974, Evolution of ecosystems: Am. Sci., v. 62, pp. 54–66.

Donn, W. L., Donn, D. B. and Valentine, W. G., 1965, On the early history of the earth: Geol. Soc. Am. Bull., v. 76, pp. 287–306.

Douglas, Ian, 1967, Man, vegetation and the sediment yields of rivers: Nature, v. 215, pp. 925–928.

Dunbar, C. O., 1969, Historical geology: New York, Wiley, 500 pp.

Durum, W. H., Heidel, S. G. and Tison, L. J., 1961, Worldwide runoff of dissolved solids: U. S. Geol. Surv. Prof. Paper 424-C, pp. 326–329.

Fairbridge, R. W., 1963, The importance of limestone and its Ca/Mg content to paleoclimatology, in Problems of climatology: Interscience, New York, 705 pp.

Garner, H. F., 1959, Stratigraphic-sedimentary significance of contemporary climate and relief in four regions of the Andes Mountains: Geol. Soc. Am. Bull., v. 70, pp. 1327–1368.

Gilluly, James, 1964, Atlantic sediments, erosion rates and the evolution of the Continental Shelf: some speculations: Geol. Soc. Am. Bull., v. 75, pp. 483–492.

Granar, Lars, 1956, Dating of recent fluvial sediments from the estuary of the Ångerman River: Geol. Foren. Stockh. Forh., v. 78, pp. 654–658.

Gregor, C. B., 1968, The rate of denudation in post-Algonkian time: Kon Neder l. Akad. Wet. Proc. B., v. 71, pp. 22–30.

Holland, H. D., 1964, On the chemical evolution of the terrestrial and cytherean atmospheres, in P. J. Brancazio and A. G. W. Cameron, (editors), The origin and evolution of atmospheres and oceans: New York, Wiley, pp. 86–100.

Kaiser, Erich, 1931, Der Grundsatz des Aktualismus in der Geologie: Z. Dtsch. Geol. Gess.: v. 83, pp. 389–407.

Kittredge, Joseph, 1948, Forest influences, McGraw-Hill, New York, 394 pp.

Knox, J. C., 1972, Valley alluviation in southwestern Wisconsin: Assoc. Am. Geogr., Ann., v. 62, pp. 401–410.

Knox, J. C., 1976, Concept of the graded stream, in W. N. Melhorn and R. C. Flemal (editors), Theories of landform development, Publications in Geomorphology: State University of New York, Binghamton, pp. 169–198.

Kräusel, R., 1961, Paleobotanical evidence of climate, in A. E. M. Nairn, (editor) Descriptive paleoclimatology: Interscience, New York, pp. 227–254.

Langbein, W. B. et al., 1949, Annual runoff in the United States: U. S. Geol. Surv. Circ. 52, 14 pp.

Rainwater, F. H., 1962, Stream composition of the conterminous United States: U. S. Geol. Surv. Hydrol. Invest. Atlas HA-61.

Rubey, W. W., 1951, Geologic history of sea water: an attempt to state the problem: Geol. Soc. Am. Bull., v. 62, pp. 1111–1148; reprinted in P. J. Brancazio and A. G. W. Cameron (editors), 1964, The origin and evolution of atmospheres and oceans: Wiley, New York, pp. 1–63.

Russell, R. J., 1956, Environomental changes through forces independent of man, in W. L. Thomas Jr., (editor), Man's role in changing the face of the earth: University of Chicago Press, Chicago, pp. 453–470.

Rutten, M. G., 1970, The history of atmospheric oxygen: Space Life Sci., v. 2, pp. 5–17.

Schumm, S. A., 1965, Quaternary paleohydrology, in H. E. Wright, Jr. and D. G. Frey, (editors), The Quaternary of the United States: Princeton University Press, Princeton, pp. 783–794.

Schumm, S. A., 1967, Paleohydrology: application of modern hydrologic data to problems of the ancient past: Int. Hydrol. Symp. Proc. Fort Collins, Colorado, v. 1, pp. 185–193.

Schumm, S. A., 1968, Speculations concerning paleohydrologic controls of terrestrial sedimentation: Geol. Soc. Am. Bull., v. 79, pp. 1573–1588.

Storey, H. C., Hobba, R. L. and Rosa, J. M., 1964, Hydrology of forest lands and range lands, Sec. 22, 52 pp., in Ven-Te Chow, (editor), Handbook of applied hydrology: McGraw-Hill, New York.

Tricart, J. and Cailleux, A., 1952, Conditions anciennes et actuelles de la genese de peneplains: Int. Geogr. Union Proc. (Washington), pp. 396–399.

CHAPTER FOUR

Drainage Basin (Zone 1)

A discussion of Zone 1 can take several forms, but in this chapter emphasis is placed on the erosional evolution of Zone 1 and the manner of drainage-basin response to change. This treatment should be of interest not only to the geomorphologist, but also to the geologist who must interpret a sedimentary deposit long after the sediment source area has been completely destroyed by erosion, and to the land manager who must work with an adjusting drainage basin and predict what can next be expected. Additional information on the morphology and hydrology of Zone 1 can be obtained from Gregory and Walling (1973).

DRAINAGE-BASIN EVOLUTION

The passage of time and the change of landform character through time determined the *stage* of development of a landform or landscape. In the Davis model a period of rapid uplift is followed by dissection and the erosional evolution of the landforms (Figure 1-3). Through time there should be a progressive removal of earth materials by erosion, and eventually a rugged landscape will be reduced to a relatively flat erosional surface, a peneplain, or pediplain (Davis, 1899). Further consideration of this erosion-cycle concept is warranted because the usual sketch of the type shown in Figure 1-3 is only the most simplistic conception of a complex process. For example, when the diagram prepared by Davis himself is inspected (Figure 4-1), it is apparent that part of his model is missing (Figure 1-3).

According to Davis (1899, pp. 254–255) the baseline extending from 0 to 5 represents the passage of time and the level to which denudation can proceed, as in Figure 1-3 the upper line (*BK*) represents divide elevation and the line *AJ* the floor of valleys. Relief at time 2 (*CD*) is increased greatly from that at time 1 (*AB*), as the streams incise and deepen their valleys. After time 2, valley floor elevation changes relatively little, but upland erosion continues. Interestingly, Davis (1899, pp. 260–261) clearly states that downwearing of the valley floor may not be a continuous process. At some stage the main river adjusts by aggradation to the increased quantities of sediment being delivered from upstream, and a valleyfill deposit is formed within the valley. Davis thus envisioned a period of aggradation during the progressive erosion of the drainage basin. This concept also was stated in an earlier paper (Davis, 1895, p. 130):

. . . streams proceed to entrench themselves in the slanting plain, and in a geologically brief period, while they are yet young, they will cut their valleys

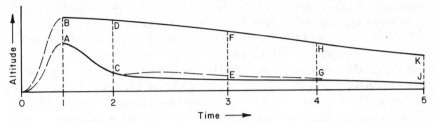

Figure 4-1 The erosion cycle of W. M. Davis (1899).

down so close to base level that they cannot for the time being cut them any deeper; that is, the streams will, of their own accord, reduce their valley lines to such a grade that their capacity to do work shall be just equal to the work they have to do. When this condition is reached, the streams may be described as having attained a "profile of equilibrium"; or, more briefly, they may be said to be *graded*. It may be noted, in passing, that inasmuch as the work that the stream has to do is constantly varying, it must as constantly seek to assume new adjustments of grade. In the normal course of river events, undisturbed by outside interference, the change in the work is so slow that the desired adjustment of capacity to work is continually maintained. It may be that during the adolescence of river life, the work to be done is on the increase, on account of the increasingly rapid delivery of land waste from the slopes of the growing valley branches; and in this case, part of the increase of waste must be laid down in the valley trough so as to steepen the grade, and thus enable the stream to gain capacity to carry the rest. Such a stream may be said to aggrade its valley . . . ; in this way certain flood plains (by no means all flood plains) may have originated. Aggrading of the valley line may often characterize the adolescence of a river's life; but later on, through maturity and old age, the work to be done decreases, and degrading is begun again, this time not to be interrupted.

The deduction by Davis that deposition may naturally follow rejuvenation of the drainage system was very astute and one that he illustrates by the dashed line (*CEG*) in Figure 4-1. This idea seems to have been ignored, but it is analogous to some aspects of the concept of complex response. The suggestion that deposition takes place naturally within the drainage system following rejuvenation is of great importance. However, before this is investigated in detail, other aspects of the long-term erosional evolution of Zone 1 are discussed.

Uplift and Denudation

In Chapter Two rates of both uplift and denudation are estimated, and they appear to support a model of rapid uplift with relatively minor erosional modification of the uplifted mass prior to cessation of uplift. This is not the only possibility, but it appears reasonable that in tectonically active areas uplift will normally exceed the rate of denudation.

There is, of course, no doubt that once uplift occurs the erosional reduction of a landscape will inevitably begin. However, some questions have been raised with regard to the cycle of erosion. For example, Gilluly's (1949) conclusion that diastrophism has not been periodic but rather almost continuous through time can be used as evidence against the uninterrupted evolution of landforms through a cycle of erosion as presented in Figures 1-3 and 4-1. This objection also can be leveled at the concept of peneplanation (Thornbury, 1969, p. 189).

Davis (1925) estimated 20 million to 200 million years were required for the planation of fault-block mountains in Utah. Recent estimates of the time involved in peneplanation involve much shorter periods; without isostatic readjustment, the continental United States could be reduced to baselevel in about 10 million years (Gilluly, 1955, p. 15). However, isostatic readjustment during erosion of such masses of rock is an extremely important factor, which may increase the time required for peneplanation by a factor of 5 or much more. For example, Holmes (1945, p. 190) believes that erosion of 4000 feet of material is required to reduce a land surface by 1000 feet; that is, there would be 3000 feet of isostatic adjustment during denudation. Therefore, Gilluly (1955), in his calculation of the time required for the planation of mountain areas, areas more than 0.2 km in elevation, allows for the erosion of 5.5 times the volume of existing mountain areas due to isostatic uplift, and he concludes that 33 million years are necessary for planation.

Isostatic adjustment to erosion occurs continuously with denudation only if the earth's crust behaves as a viscous fluid. However, the crust has considerable strength (Gunn, 1949, p. 267), and before isostatic adjustment can occur, this strength must be exceeded by the removal of rock by denudation. Indeed, even when the strength is exceeded there may be a lag before isostatic adjustment occurs, as that which allowed submergence of glaciated lands following the melting of the Pleistocene ice sheets (Charlesworth, 1957, p. 1361). Bloom (1967) concludes that a regional pressure of 10 bars (about 150 pounds per square inch) will cause isostatic adjustment.

The disparity between rates of uplift and denudation in orogenic areas (Chapter Two) suggests that isostatic adjustment to denudation is episodic (Schumm, 1963; Brown and Oliver, 1976). Orogenic uplift proceeds relatively rapidly (Figure 4-1), as demonstrated in the preceding chapter, and it may occur episodically (Hamblin, 1976). During uplift and when uplift ceases, denudation proceeds at a relatively slower rate until the strength of the crust is exceeded, when relatively rapid isostatic adjustment should occur again. This relationship is shown diagrammatically in Figure 4-2 where initial uplift is 15,000 feet (Figure 4-2b); during and following uplift, denudation rates increase to a maximum, to be followed by a decline as relief is lowered (Figure 4-2a). This sequence of events is interrupted by relatively short periods of isostatic adjustment, during and following which denudation rates again increase to a maximum. If the result is solely of isostasy, the succeeding uplifts will not reach the altitude of the initial tectonic uplift (Figure 4-2a).

Renewed tectonism can interrupt these epicycles of denudation and uplift, but if tectonism ceases after initial uplift, the sequence of erosion and isostatic adjustment may be considered analogous to a positive feedback system. Initial uplift increases denudation rates, which in turn increase the tendency for further uplift. When the removal of material per unit area is such that it exceeds the strength of the crust, isostatic adjustment occurs and the cycle begins again. These epicycles during

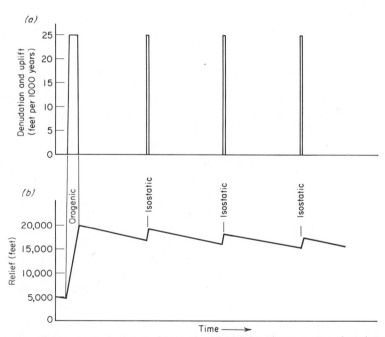

Figure 4-2 (a) Hypothetical relation of rates of uplift and denudation to time. (b) Relation of relief to time as a function of the rates of uplift and denudation shown in a. (From Schumm, 1963.)

landscape denudation occur because the components of the system, denudation and isostatic adjustment, operate at greatly different rates, and they may partly explain the occurrence of major stream terraces, multiple erosion surfaces, and some types of long-term cyclic sedimentation. From Figure 4-2 it appears that a landscape undergoing denudation is a system in dynamic metastable equilibrium (Figure 1-2).

Evidence of episodic uplift in response to denudation should appear in the stratigraphic record. For example, in sediments derived from an area subjected to cyclic uplift, gravels might recur through a great thickness of sediment. The recurrent uplift proposed by Gilluly (1949) to explain the persistence of coarse sediments in the Sespe formation may be partly the result of isostatic adjustment to denudation.

GROWTH OF DRAINAGE NETWORKS

In contrast to the geologic emphasis on events of the past, recent geomorphic research has concentrated on finding relations among climatic, hydrologic, geologic, and geomorphic variables in an effort to explain landform morphology and drainage network evolution through time (Strahler, 1964; Gregory and Walling, 1973; Smart, 1972).

Horton Analysis

The most significant development in geomorphology during the past 30 years has been the publication of a paper on drainage-basin morphology by R. E. Horton (1945). In this work he demonstrated the necessity of understanding the processes at work within a basin, and, most significantly, he demonstrated how to study a drainage network. His method of classifying the components of a stream network into channels of different order has been modified repeatedly (Scheidegger, 1970), but this dissection of Zone 1 into its components has made it possible to generate mathematical models of drainage pattern growth and quantitative descriptions of basin characteristics. Statistically the relations obtained showed that for streams of increasing order number (first-order streams are unbranched tributaries and second-order streams are formed by the junction of two first-order streams, etc.) the number, length, and drainage area of streams of each order increase. It has been argued that these relations are due simply to the expected arrangement of the components of a randomly growing network, and, in fact, such relations can be obtained from random-walk models (Smart, 1972). Nevertheless, in nature the addition of a tributary to a growing drainage network occurs where there is sufficient runoff to permit erosion of the material underlying the drainage basin (Schumm, 1956). Admittedly, much variation among tributary spacing, length, and drainage area does exist, but the pattern develops in relation to hydrologic, geomorphic, and erodibility characteristics of the basin. For example, within an area of similar earth materials there is a minimum drainage area required to support a unit length of channel. In a badland area of high drainage density this unit area was found to be about 9 square feet (Schumm, 1956). Such a relation is evidence that the drainage network develops in response to material erodibility and to the eroding force applied to the surface of the basin in a deterministic manner.

In addition, as suggested by Woldenberg (1966) and as demonstrated by Stall and Fok (1967), discharge increases with stream order number. Therefore, the Horton relations between order number and other network characteristics, in fact, link the morphologic and cascading systems of the drainage basin.

DRAINAGE-NETWORK EVOLUTION

The first detailed analysis of drainage-network growth was qualitative. Glock (1932) selected topographic maps of drainage basins in various stages of erosional development and arranged them in a sequence to show growth of the drainage patterns. The assumption is made, of course, that the drainage pattern is initiated on an essentially smooth plane due to uplift or retreat of the sea.

Glock described the phases of development as follows: *initiation*, the beginnings of the pattern and the development of a shallow skeletal drainage pattern on the undissected area; *elongation*, headward growth of the main streams; *elaboration*, the filling in of the previously undissected areas by small tributaries; *maximum extension*, the maximum development of the drainage pattern; and *abstraction*, the loss of tributaries as relief is reduced through time. The period of abstraction persists until the number of channels on the surface is reduced to a minimum. According to Glock's model, the episode starts with the rapid development of a skeletal pattern that is fleshed out as the available space is filled by tributary development. Then, through progressive reduction of relief, there is a loss of the smaller tributaries until eventually just the main skeletal drainage lines remain. This sequence, of course, takes almost as much time as is required for peneplanation. During these evolutionary changes, sediment yields from the system should follow very closely the development of the drainage system, increasing to a maximum and then decreasing after maximum extension.

The major problem with this approach is that the erosional evolution of the drainage system is not observed; rather, by selecting on maps a series of basins that are assumed to represent the drainage network in different stages of its growth and then by arranging them from youngest to oldest, space is substituted for time (ergodic hypothesis). This is an appropriate way to proceed when time is the only variable, but it must always be remembered that the sequence is only an approximation to network evolution through time.

The evolutionary development of a drainage network can also be studied experimentally, and a graphic example of drainage network development is provided by the stream networks mapped by Parker (1976). For this purpose, a 9 by 15 m container, which is referred to as the Rainfall-Erosion Facility (REF), was constructed at Colorado State University (Figure 4-3). Over this surface precipitation can be delivered at intensities ranging from 13 to about 50 mm per hour. The growth of the drainage system on this surface can be documented by mapping and photography.

Figure 4-4 shows the progressive growth of the drainage pattern by

Figure 4-3   Rainfall-erosion facility (REF) at Colorado State University. It is now housed in a building that prevents wind deflection of the precipitation.

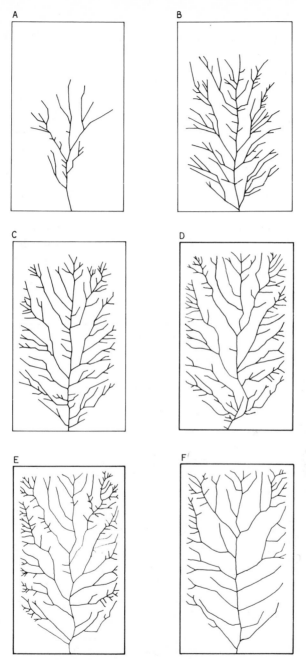

Figure 4-4   Maps of growth of drainage network in REF. Sides of rectangle are 9 by 14 m. Drainage pattern developed on a surface sloping 3.2 percent toward outlet. (From Parker, 1976.)

headward extension into the undissected drainage area (Figures 4-4*A*,*B*, *C*). When maximum extension was achieved (Figure (4-4*D*), further evolution of the system took place by abstraction, and drainage density was reduced with time. Note, however, that the reduction of drainage density and the loss of tributaries was greatest in the center of the network (Figure 4-4*E*, *F*). Drainage density near the drainage divide remained high, but it decreased in the core of the drainage basin. This was due to a reduction of slopes and stream gradients in the basin core and to the widening of the main valleys.

Drainage density, of course, increased to a maximum value as the network grew (Figure 4-5). After this, little change in the drainage density occurred for a considerable period (Figure 4-5, curve *1*), although dissection, channel lengthening and the addition of tributaries were taking place near the drainage divides. This increase in channel length of course was compensated for by abstraction near the mouth of the drainage basin.

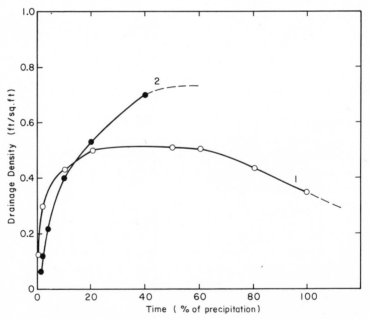

Figure 4-5   Drainage density change during two experiments in REF. Curve *1* is for pattern developed on 3.2 percent slope with stable baselevel. Curve *2* is for pattern developed on 0.75 percent slope with baselevel lowering prior to beginning of experiment. (After Parker, 1976.) Time is expressed as a percentage of the total water applied to the REF during experiment 1 (curve *1*).

Figures 4-4 and 4-5 show the evolution of a drainage network and drainage density during the erosional evolution of a small experimental drainage basin. The results indicate that there are stages of network growth that can be identified by Glock's terminology. In addition, the maps of Figure 4-4 demonstrate clearly that drainage density can vary significantly within a drainage basin, especially during the later stages of erosion (Figures 4-4E, F).

During the experiments two types of network growth were identified. Growth mode 1 occurred on a slope of 3.2 percent with no baselevel change; the evolution was similar to that described by Glock: long first-order streams quickly blocked out the drainage area, and then by elongation and elaboration the pattern was completed by the addition of tributaries (Figure 4-4). Growth mode 2 occurred on a slope of 0.75 percent with baselevel lowering. Under these conditions the drainage network grew slowly headward into the available drainage area, forming a very complete drainage pattern as it did so. Figure 4-6 shows the difference in network extension for growth modes 1 and 2, and the change of drainage density during pattern growth for each is shown in Figure 4-5.

During growth mode 1, which produced a skeleton network by elongation and then filled in the blanks by elaboration, the network formed much more rapidly, but a less complete network was developed (Figure 4-5, curve 1). Growth mode 2, which involved both elongation and elaboration equally, produced a higher drainage density with significantly shorter stream lengths (Figure 4-5, curve 2). Growth mode 2 can occur naturally, when vertical uplift or baselevel lowering rejuvenates a relatively gently sloping surface, whereas growth mode 1 controls drainage network development on more steeply sloping surfaces.

It is surprising to find that the highest drainage density developed on the gentler surface (Figure 4-5), but this is due entirely to the difference in growth modes. For example, experiments on rill formation (Mosley, 1972), which utilized the same research facility and materials as the study above, determined that when maximum rill development occurred according to growth mode 1, the drainage density of rills (D in feet per foot) increased with slope (S, percent) as follows:

$$D = 0.909 + 22.42S$$

In badlands and other areas where erosion is progressing very rapidly, it is also possible to measure landscape change, and following a short period of observation, the space for time substitution can be made with confidence because differences in stage can be identified. This type of comparison has been made for badlands in which 10 small second-order

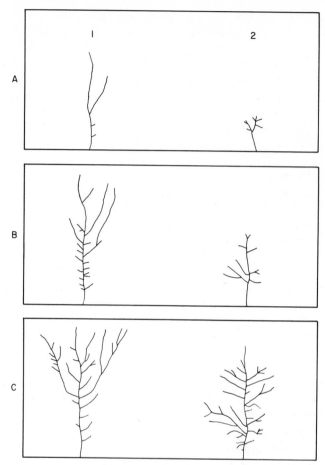

Figure 4-6   Maps of drainage pattern development by two different growth modes: (a) growth mode 1 (b) growth mode 2. (After Parker, 1976.)

drainage basins were selected in a series from mouth to head of a fifth-order drainage system (Schumm, 1956). The basin nearest the mouth of the system was older and more fully developed than those near the head. Measurements of basin characteristics permitted documentation of drainage network growth and the changes of drainage-basin morphology through time. Hypsometric curves were plotted (Figure 4-7) to show changes of basin morphology. The hypsometric curves provide a representation of the erosional development of a drainage basin through time, because the square in which the curves are plotted

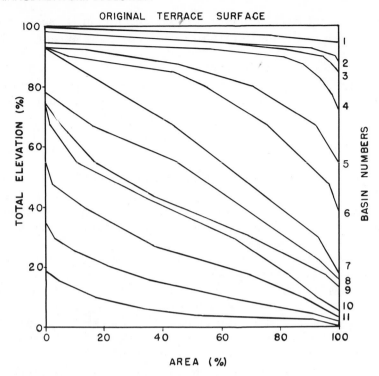

Figure 4-7 Sequence of hypsometric curves for a series of 10 second-order drainage basins. Percent of total basin area above a given datum is plotted against percentage of total relief available for erosion. The bottom two curves are hypothetical. (From Schumm, 1956.)

may be visualized as a vertical section through the mass of material to be removed as a basin evolves. Each basin occupies its relative vertical position within that square, and the curves illustrate the degradational history of the basin. That is, the 100 percent elevation line is the upper undissected surface, and the base of the diagram represents the potential erosion surface on which degradation is working. The right-hand edge of the figure is the locus of points of junction of the channels with some higher order stream. The left edge is the drainage divide. Each line therefore represents the distribution of mass within a drainage basin at a different stage of development, with the position of its mouth controlled by the degrading stream to which it is tributary.

The curves show that during erosion of a drainage basin the zone of maximum erosion migrates toward the head of the basin. That is, the vertical distance between each of the curves is greatest near the mouth of the basins (the right side of the illustration) in early stages, but it is greatest near the basin head in later stages. In addition, the shape of the curves changes with time from convex up to essentially straight and then to concave up. These changes indicate that with time the zone of maximum sediment production moves up into the basin, and stream profiles, gradients, and sediment yields should change accordingly as the area supplying the maximum amount of sediment is shifted headward.

Sediment Delivery

The evolution of the drainage network influences the hydrology of Zone 1 because, in the early stages of development, most sediment is produced near the mouth of the basin and is moved rapidly out of the basin, but as the zone of maximum erosion migrates headward (Figure 4-7), sediment is derived progressively from upstream areas. This is true for both network growth modes. Eventually, as in most drainage systems, the greatest relief and the greatest dissection (Figures 4-4D, E, F) are near the headwaters where the most sediment is produced. This situation provides an explanation for the usual decrease of sediment yield per unit area as size of a drainage basin increases (Figure 4-8).

Another explanation for this relation is based on the potential for temporary sediment storage within a drainage basin. For example, there is a very dramatic downstream increase in the area available to receive deposition within even small drainage systems. In the Cheyenne River basin of Wyoming, for example, as drainage area increases from 0.05 to 2 square miles, the percentage of the drainage area that is valley floor or

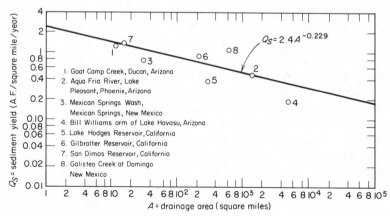

Figure 4-8   Sediment-yield decrease with increase of drainage area for drainage basins in the southwestern United States. (From Strand, 1975.)

bottomland increases from essentially 0 to approximately 60 percent (Hadley and Schumm, 1961). Thus, within any natural drainage basin there are places where sediment can be stored permanently or temporarily. This is one explanation for the inverse relationship between sediment delivery ratio (ratio of volume of sediment per unit area moved out of a basin to estimated volume of sediment per unit area produced in the basin) and drainage basin area (Figure 4-9). The estimates of sediment production from the smallest watersheds should be the most accurate; nevertheless, for basins of about 0.1 square mile the ratio ranges from 20 to 90 percent. For larger basins of about 300 square miles the ratio ranges from 3 to 20 percent. This almost order-of-magnitude range suggests that the differences are probably not all due to errors in the estimation of sediment production or in the measurement of sediment yield; rather they reflect storage of sediment within the basin (Trimble, 1975). This of course raises a question about the stability of the stored deposits and the variability of sediment yields during the evolutionary development of a drainage basin.

During one of the experimental studies the drainage basin was rejuvenated periodically to increase drainage density and the slope of the drainage system. The effect of such a rejuvenation on sediment yield is shown in Figure 4-10. The lowering of baselevel by the removal of a 10-cm-high board from the mouth of the basin at time zero increased channel erosion and sediment-yield rates dramatically. However, there was a rapid decrease in sediment yield with time, but in each case the decrease was not regular and secondary peaks of sediment production occurred (Figures 4-10 and 4-11). Note in Figure 4-11, which shows sediment yield for four drainage networks following baselevel lowering, that as the slope of the drainage basin became steeper after each baselevel lowering, sediment yield increased from run *1* to run *4*. The secondary peaks are apparent in the data for each run, and they are higher and occur earlier as relief increases.

Some of the sediment-yield variability is due to bank caving and valley side collapse following rejuvenation, but channel incision and erosion of stored alluvium produced the secondary peaks. The major sediment yield variations, therefore, can be explained by the storage and periodic flushing of alluvium from the valleys of the experimental drainage basin. This is the complex response described earlier. It appears that, as the wave of maximum erosion moves up into the drainage system following rejuvenation, major tributaries are rejuvenated in turn, and therefore the sediment delivered to the main channel increases with the result that the valley gradient, which was developed when sediment production was less, is not capable of conveying the increased sediment loads to the

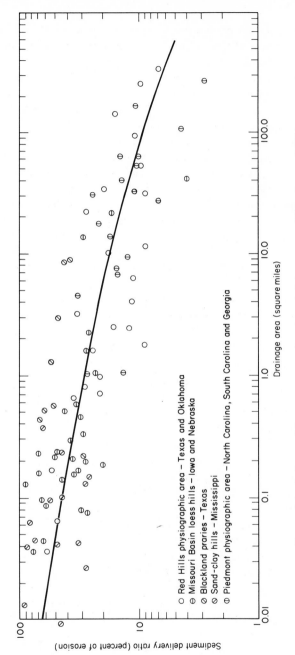

Figure 4-9 Sediment delivery ratio as a function of drainage area. (From Boyce, 1975.)

○ Red Hills physiographic area – Texas and Oklahoma
⊖ Missouri Basin loess hills – Iowa and Nebraska
⊘ Blackland praries – Texas
⊘ Sand-clay hills – Mississippi
⊕ Piedmont physiographic area – North Carolina, South Carolina and Georgia

Sediment delivery ratio (percent of erosion)

Drainage area (square miles)

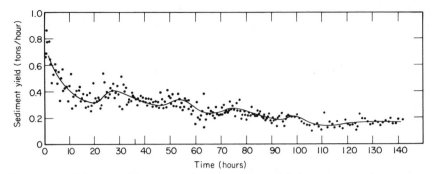

Figure 4-10 Sediment-yield variations during experimental drainage basin evolution. (From Parker, 1976.) Mean line is based on a moving mean of 3 points with an average of 10 points. Note secondary peaks at about 25, 55, 75, and 100 hours.

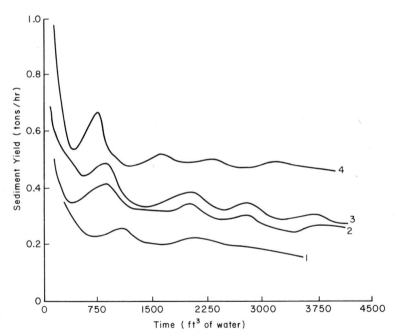

Figure 4-11 Sediment yields for four experiments with increasing relief of drainage basin. Baselevel was lowered 10 cm between experiments (Parker, 1976). Passage of time is expressed by the volume of water delivered to the surface of the REF.

mouth of the basin. As a result, deposition occurs and continues until the valley gradient is locally increased to a threshold inclination that induces renewed channel incision and flushing of the sediment down valley. Surveys of the longitudinal profile of the main channel showed that the initial incision following rejuvenation produced a relatively flat gradient, but this was then steepened by deposition as sediment loads increased (Parker, 1976).

The sequence of events is apparently related to sediment yield (Figure 4-10) as follows. Rejuvenation causes rapid channel incision at the mouth of the basin, where all the sediment produced is exported (Figure 4-10, 0 to 10 hours). As the knickpoint formed by baselevel lowering migrates up the drainage network, however, the mobilized sediment has a better chance of being stored within the valley. As the major tributaries are being rejuvenated, it is likely that sediment movement within the basin is at a maximum, but sediment yield continues to decrease (Figure 4-10, 10 to 25 hours) until some of the stored alluvium is flushed out during a period of channel incision (Figure 4-10, 25 to 30 hours). This produces the secondary peaks of high sediment yield (30, 50, and 75 hours).

If natural drainage basins, during their early erosional development or following rejuvenation, when sediment yield is large, behave as the experimental basins, then the great variability in sediment yield and sediment delivery ratios among basins and for one basin through time is understandable. In addition, the variability of sediment yield delivered from Zone 1 through time should be reflected in the behavior of the channels in Zone 2 and the nature of the sedimentary deposits of Zone 3.

COMPLEXITY OF EROSION

With the discussion of the evolution of the drainage network and the sediment production from drainage basins as background, it seems appropriate to elaborate on the two concepts of complex response and thresholds introduced in Chapter One. A full understanding of these concepts is necessary for the understanding of not only the evolution of the drainage system, but also the distribution of erosional features in the landscape and perhaps the discontinuity of the stratigraphic record in Zones 2 and 3 as well.

Complex Response

It should be clear from the preceding discussions that a simple rejuvenation of a drainage basin yields a complex erosional and sedimentological response and that the behavior of the basin itself introduces a new degree of complexity into the geomorphic processes.

Geomorphic histories are complicated, and considering the climatic changes of the past few million years of earth history, one would expect them to be so. For example, throughout the world, geologists and archaeologists have studied the details of the most recent erosional and depositional history of valleys. This consists of identifying the sequence in which alluvial deposits were emplaced and then eroded. Because of worldwide climate changes during the Quaternary period, it is logical to establish alluvial chronologies applicable to large regions. Thus a particular alluvial layer should be identifiable on a regional or even a continental basis, and correlations of these deposits over large areas can then be made.

There is no question that major climatic changes have affected erosional and depositional events, but, when Holocene alluvial chronologies are examined, it is not convincing that each depositional or erosional event occurred in response to one simultaneous external change. In fact, investigations in the southwestern United States reveal that during the last 10,000 years, the number, magnitude, and duration of erosional and depositional events in the valleys of this region not only varied from valley to valley, but also varied within the same valley (Kottlowski et al. 1965). This indicates that deposition was not in phase everywhere and that apparently at least some depositional episodes did not occur in response to a single external control.

Part of the complexity may be explained by external events (climate, baselevel change) that are not readily detectable. Climate change, uplift, or lowering of baselevel can cause incision of a channel. This incision converts the floodplain to a terrace, which is the geomorphic evidence of the erosional episode. However, a drainage system is composed of channels, hillsides, divides, floodplains, and terraces; it is complex and, in fact, little is known about the detailed morphologic response of Zone 1 to rejuvenation. That it should be complex has already been demonstrated by the sediment-yield variations obtained during the experimental study of drainage system evolution (Figures 4-10 and 4-11). However, the complexity can be illustrated further by the erosional and depositional events that take place within the drainage basin during experimentation. For example, following rejuvenation in one study, the main channel incised to form a terrace (Figure 4-12A, B). Incision occurred first at the mouth of the basin, and then progressively upstream, successively rejuvenating tributaries and scouring the alluvium previously deposited in the valley. As erosion progressed upstream, the main channel became a conveyor of upstream sediment in increasing quantities, and the inevitable result was deposition and formation of a braided stream (Figure

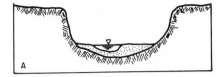

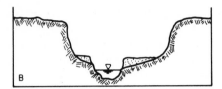

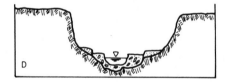

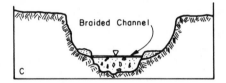

Figure 4-12   Complex response of an experimental drainage basin. (From Schumm and Parker, 1973.)

4-12*C*). However, as the tributaries eventually became adjusted to the new baselevels, sediment loads decreased, and a new phase of main-channel erosion occurred (Figure 4-12*D*). Thus initial channel incision and terrace formation were followed by deposition of an alluvial fill, channel braiding, and lateral erosion, and then, as sediment yield from upstream decreased, renewed incision formed a low alluvial terrace (Figure 4-12*D*). This low surface formed when the braided channel was converted into a better-defined channel of lower width/depth ratio, as a result of the decreased sediment loads. In nature the low surface would be either a floodplain or a low terrace.

Somewhat similar results were obtained experimentally by Lewis (1944) by rejuvenation of a very small drainage system. Initially, erosion in the headwaters was rapid and deposition occurred at the mouth of the basin, forming an alluvial plain. As the upstream gradients were decreased by erosion and the stream courses stabilized, sediment supply to the alluvial plain decreased. Because of the reduction of the sediment load, the stream cut into the alluvial plains to form a terrace. Lewis concluded that the most significant result of the experiment was that terraces were formed without any corresponding change of baselevel or discharge. The results of both experiments indicate that an event causing an erosional response within a drainage basin (tilting, changes of baselevel, climate and/or land use) creates high sediment production, which in turn causes deposition and an increase of gradient. This, then, is followed by incision of the alluvial deposits as the sediment load decreases. This sequence of events is the complex response referred to in Chapter One. However, it should be emphasized that the complexity is not simply negative feedback that restores a former condition; rather it involves the crossing of a threshold to a new equilibrium state (the metastable equilibrium of Figure 1-2).

In summary, the experimental studies demonstrate that within a complex natural system, one event can trigger a complex reaction (morphologic and/or stratigraphic) as the components of the system respond to change. This concept provides an explanation of the complexities of recent alluvial and terrace sequences and over a longer time span some stratigraphic variations. In Chapter Five field situations are described in which this process can be used to explain details of the landscape that formerly were attributed to the influence of variables external to the system, such as baselevel, climate change, and tectonics.

The magnitude of this complex response probably depends on the volumes of sediment moved, and therefore it is likely that clear evidence of complex response will only appear during early stages of an erosion cycle or during rejuvenation of high-sediment-producing areas. Nevertheless, it is these areas that produce major land management and conservation problems, and they are of considerable practical interest.

Geomorphic Thresholds

As noted above it is easy to explain a change in a fluvial system by a change in an independent variable. The apparently random distribution of erosional features in some areas and the need to explain the complex erosional history of the southwestern United States and elsewhere requires a multitude of local climatic, baselevel, or tectonic influences. Nevertheless, because the precipitation applied to the experimental drainage system discussed above was held constant, the variations in sediment yield and the adjustments of the channels cannot be attributed to changing external variables, but it is possible to explain some of these changes by use of the concept of geomorphic thresholds.

The renewal of erosion due to isostatic adjustment during progressive denudation is an example of how a threshold is crossed because of a progressive change. That is, continual erosion and removal of material from a portion of the earth's crust eventually exceeds the strength of the crust at that locality, and uplift takes place (Figure 4-2). When crossed, this threshold of crustal strength permits an isostatic response. Another example of this type of relationship is the Langbein-Schumm curve (Figure 2-6), which shows that sediment yields are directly related to annual precipitation and runoff until vegetative cover has increased sufficiently to retard erosion. At this point there is a decrease in sediment yield, with increased runoff and precipitation.

In the examples cited, an external variable changes progressively, thereby triggering abrupt changes or failure within the affected system. These *extrinsic thresholds* are discussed in Chapter One. However, as noted earlier, thresholds can also be exceeded when input is relatively constant, that is, the external variables remain constant, yet a progressive change of the system itself renders it unstable, and failure occurs. For example, in the REF, sediment storage in the valleys continued until a critical threshold slope was reached, when incision and removal of the sediment occurred. The importance of this *geomorphic threshold* in the experimental study was apparent. Obviously, when a change of slope is involved, the control is geomorphic, and the changes whereby the threshold is achieved are intrinsic to the system. For example, field studies in semiarid valleys of Wyoming, Colorado, New Mexico, and Arizona reveal that discontinuous gullies, short but troublesome gullied reaches of valley floors, can be related to the slope of the valley-floor. surface (Schumm and Hadley, 1957), and the beginning of network rejuvenation by gully erosion in these valleys tends to be localized on steeper reaches of the valley floor. Carrying this one step farther, with the concept of geomorphic thresholds in mind, it seems that for a given region of uniform geology, land-use, and climate, a critical threshold valley slope should exist above which an alluvial valley floor is unstable.

To test this hypothesis, measurements of valley-floor gradient were made in the Piceance Creek basin of western Colorado, an area with numerous discontinuous gullies but with no orderly pattern of distribution (Figure 4-13). Within this area, valleys were selected in which discontinuous gullies were present. The drainage area above each gully was measured on maps, and valley slopes were surveyed in the field. No records of runoff or flood events exist, so drainage basin area was selected as a variable, reflecting runoff and perhaps flood discharge.

Figure 4-13   Aerial photograph of valleys in Piceance Creek drainage basin, northwestern Colorado.

When valley slope is plotted against drainage area, the relationship is inverse (Figure 4-14), with gentler valley slopes being characteristic of large drainage areas. As a basis for comparison, similar measurements were made for valleys in which there were no gullies, and these data are also plotted in Figure 4-14. The lower range of slopes of the unstable valleys coincide with the higher-range slopes of the stable valleys. In other words, for a given drainage area it is possible to define a valley slope above which the valley floor is unstable (Patton and Schumm, 1975). Brice (1966) found a similar but less-well-defined relation for valleys in Nebraska.

Note that the relationship does not pertain to drainage basins smaller than about 5 square miles. In these small basins variations in vegetative cover, which is perhaps related to the aspect of the drainage basin or to

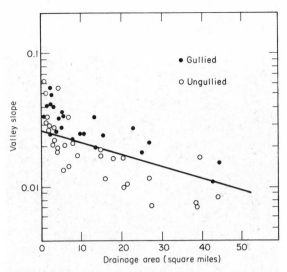

Figure 4-14   Relation between valley-floor slope and drainage area for small drainage basins, Piceance Creek area, Colorado. (From Patton and Schumm, 1975.)

variations in the properties of alluvium, prevent recognition of a critical threshold slope. Only two areas larger than 5 square miles with stable valley floors plot above the threshold line, and one may conclude that these valley floors are incipiently unstable and that a major flood may eventually cause erosion and trenching of the alluvium stored in these valleys.

Using Figure 4-14 one may define the threshold slope above which trenching or valley instability will take place in the Piceance Creek area. This has obvious implications for land management for, if the slope at which valleys are incipiently unstable can be determined, corrective measures can be taken to artificially stabilize such critical reaches as they are identified.

The concept of thresholds as applied to alluvial deposits in the western United States is shown by Figure 4-15, where the decreasing stability of an alluvial fill is represented by a line indicating increase of valley slope toward a condition of instability (line 2) with time. Of course, a similar relationship would pertain if, with constant slope, sediment loads decrease slowly with time. Superimposed on the ascending line of increasing slope are vertical lines showing the variations of valley-floor stability caused by flood events of different magnitudes. The effect of even large events is minor until the stability of the deposit has been so reduced by steepening of the valley gradient that during one major storm, erosion

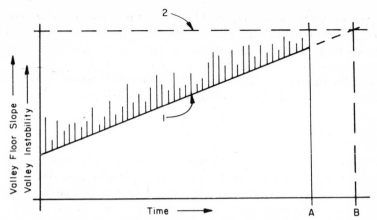

Figure 4-15 Changing valley-floor stability through time. Line *1* shows increasing instability of valley floor as it approaches failure threshold (line *2*). (From Schumm, 1968.)

begins at time A. It is important to note that the large event is only the most apparent cause of failure, as it would have occurred at time B in any case.

These studies of alluvial deposits in drylands suggest that large infrequent storms can be erosionally significant, but only when a geomorphic threshold has been exceeded are major, permanent changes the result. It is for this reason that high-magnitude, low-frequency events may at times have only minor and local effects on a landscape.

The concepts of complex response and geomorphic thresholds are supported by the response of the experimental drainage basin after rejuvenation and by the situation in the Piceance Creek area. It is not suggested that these concepts are applicable everywhere. Rather they are useful in areas of high sediment production or areas of rugged, youthful topography. Nevertheless, the natural storage, flushing, and reworking of alluvium in the valley systems of a drainage basin can be a very important aspect of the development of alluvial deposits in Zones 2 and 3.

EFFECT OF CLIMATE AND HYDROLOGY

The final topic of this chapter is a review of the response of a drainage basin, its channel network (Zone 1), and its production of sediment to climate change and to the effects of vegetation evolution and paleohydrologic controls through geologic time. Much of this material could have been presented in Chapter Three, but the preceding discussion of drainage basin morphology and evolution is basic to some aspects of this topic. Further, it seems appropriate to stress once again the effect of external variables because the concepts of complex response and geomorphic thresholds in no way invalidates conclusions reached concerning the effect of climate change on the landscape.

Climate Change

The effects of Quaternary climate changes on drainage-basin morphology were as variable as the processes operative and the materials involved. During pluvials, increased vegetal cover probably decreased slope erosion in semiarid and humid regions; however, in initially arid regions the increase in runoff probably more than compensated for the increase in vegetal cover and may have caused an increase in slope erosion. Initially arid slopes, therefore, would have been subjected to more intense erosion. Although this last statement is conjectural, the peaks of the sediment-yield curves (Figure 3-1) suggest that more sediment is exported from semiarid than from arid regions, and some of this increase must be derived from the slopes.

Moving down off the hillslopes, unchanneled extensions of the drainage networks or unchanneled alluvial deposits are encountered on valley floors of small low-order streams. To evaluate the effects of runoff changes on drainage networks, it is necessary to understand what has happened in these areas, which are not truly part of the modern drainage network.

Investigations into the relations among climate, runoff, and drainage density indicate that, within one climatic region, drainage density increases with annual runoff (Hadley and Schumm, 1961, pp. 175–176) and as the mean annual flood increases in magnitude (Carlston, 1963). Other studies suggest that in humid regions drainage density increases as the intensity of both precipitation and runoff increase (Chorley, 1957; Chorley and Morgan, 1962).

Melton (1958) has demonstrated that drainage density is related closely to channel frequency (number of channels per unit area); therefore, as the texture of topography becomes finer, not only do the existing streams lengthen but new low-order streams are added to the drainage network. In addition, Peltier (1962) found, through worldwide measurements of terrain characteristics, that for areas of comparable average slope, stream frequency is greatest in semiarid regions. Stream frequency is least in arid regions and intermediate in humid regions. The above suggests that if drainage density were to be substituted for sediment yield on the ordinate of Figure 2-5, the curve might indicate in a very general manner the variation of drainage density with climate (Schumm, 1965, p. 789).

In the clearest case, there will be zero drainage density, where precipitation is, and has been, zero. With an increase of precipitation in the arid regions, linear erosion will begin (Alimen, 1965). Therefore, drainage density should increase with precipitation in very arid regions. Other studies by Bond (1967) in southern Africa show that in areas of 50 to 60 inches of precipitation in Zambia, the headwater areas contain virtually no open channels, whereas in Botswana well-defined channels occur in areas of 15 to 22 inches of precipitation. In areas of 20–25 inches of precipitation, Bond recognizes a climatically "sensitive zone," where rivers adjust to minor climatic fluctuations. If mean annual temperature is 60°F, Bond's observations fit the curve of Figure 3-1, and they suggest that drainage density does mirror sediment yield. These conclusions are supported by more recent investigations of the influence of climate on drainage density (Abrahams, 1972; Gregory and Gardiner, 1975), which, in addition, suggest an increase of drainage density in tropical regions.

All the above indicate that both drainage density and sediment yields should be greatest in semiarid regions. The concurrence of maximum drainage densities and maximum sediment yields at the same climate suggests that the high sediment yields are a reflection of increased channel development and a more efficiently drained system. Hence, a shift to a semiarid climate from either arid or humid should allow extension of the drainage network with increased channel and hillslope erosion.

The work by Trimble (1974) in the southeastern United States has some relevance to the previous discussion. He reports that for some rivers, only about 5 percent of the eroded material has been delivered to the coast (Trimble, 1975) since agricultural activities began. Deforestation and agriculture created a serious gully problem (increase of drainage density) in the uplands and a serious aggradation problem in the valleys, where alluvium and colluvium accumulated to depths of 6 m in small to medium-sized stream valleys. This type of response would also accompany a change of climate from humid to semiarid. Subsequently, vigorous soil conservation efforts have reduced upland erosion and the alluvium stored in the valleys is being remobilized. A number of reservoirs trap this sediment, but if under natural conditions a change of climate from dry to wet were to occur the stored valley sediments would begin to move downvalley. Thus the dry period sediments might not leave the area until a more favorable runoff regime was reestablished.

This lag in the transport of sediment deposited during high-sediment-production periods is considered a normal process by Garner (1959, p. 1366).

Obviously the changed relationship of runoff and sediment yield, during and following a climate change, will influence both the type and amount of sediment deposited. For example, in arid regions, an increase in precipitation increases the sediment deposited during a unit of time. In semiarid regions an increase in precipitation decreases the amount of sediment deposited in a unit of time. In humid regions the increase in precipitation should not greatly alter the rate of sediment yield except briefly as channels adjust to increased runoff.

Vegetation and Paleohydrology

In addition to relatively short-term changes of climate and their effect on vegetation and hydrology, it is possible to use the relationships developed previously (Figures 3-5 and 3-6) to speculate about the influence of evolving vegetation and changing hydrology on landforms and sedimentary deposits through geologic time. The effects of phytological deserts on sedimentary deposits have been considered by several authors (Schwarzback, 1961, p. 68; Twenhofel, 1932, pp. 793–795; Pettijohn, 1957, p. 683). Although the mineralogy and chemical composition of sediments may be relatively unchanged throughout geologic time (for a different opinion, see Cayeux, 1941), the distribution of sediments, the form of the deposits, and the occurrence of abrupt changes of lithology may all be attributed in part to the vastly different erosion conditions and hydrology of the geologic past.

Prevegetation Period.   Before significant terrestrial vegetation appeared, the hydrologic regimen of arid regions was much as today, and even in humid regions the products of weathering were swept from hillslopes and divides into well-developed networks of stream channels. Unlike the humid regions of today, where weathering products are stored on hill-slopes, the bare hillslopes lost material rapidly as it weathered to a size that could be transported. These immature sediments accumulated in valleys and piedmont areas. Sediment production proceeded at a rapid rate in hot climates, but an arid-appearing landscape existed everywhere. Bed-load channels (see Chapter Five) were ubiquitous, and wide braided streams occupied the entire floor of alluvial valleys. Upon leaving the sediment source areas the channels were not confined, and vast alluvial-plain piedmont deposits formed. Depending on the environment of deposition, either great thicknesses of clastics accumulated or extensive sheetlike deposits formed, as floods spread across piedmont areas, reworking and sorting the sediments.

The runoff of wet years flushed vast quantities of sediment from the source areas, especially from basins where a threshold had been exceeded, whereas dry years permitted accumulation of sediment in the system, as mass wasting and local runoff continued to strip weathered material from the interfluves. Under such conditions varvelike flood deposits could have formed. Each flood event deposited a layer of sand or relatively coarse sediment, which was covered by fine sediments deposited during the waning of the flood waters. Such deposits are recognized on modern floodplains (Schumm and Lichty, 1963), and some varved Precambrian rocks, which cannot be related to glaciation (Eskola, 1932), may have formed in this manner. Of course, any isostatic or tectonic uplift in the sediment-source areas produced a pulse of sediment, which moved out of the drainage basin into the depositional areas, thereby inundating either piedmont deposits or an erosional landscape with a flood of coarse sediment (Hamblin, 1958).

Primitive Vegetation.   With the appearance of terrestrial vegetation, initially confined to the nearshore environment but eventually colonizing the alluvial valleys of sediment source areas, the delivery of sediment from interfluve areas was not inhibited and sheetlike alluvial deposits continued to form (Meckel, 1967). The presence of vegetation on coastal plains undoubtedly stabilized channels in that part of their courses, but large floods caused periodic shifts in the channel position and an influx of coarse sediment. The floods could have been responsible for some small-scale cyclic sedimentary deposits, cutouts, which occur in coal measures (Robertson, 1952; Niyogi, 1966, p. 970), as well as the ventifact reported by Mantle in an English coal swamp deposit (Schwarzback, 1961, p. 68) and the juxtaposition of meandering and straight river channels in coal measures (Thiadens and Haites, 1944, facing page 22). Hence the appearance of vegetation provided the opportunity for additional discontinuities in the stratigraphic record, and these effects were intensified as vegetation moved into the valleys of the sediment-source areas. In addition, finer channel deposits became more common.

The geomorphic threshold concept is very important in explaining the events of this time. Sediment moving off poorly vegetated hillslopes and from tributary channels could have been stored in a main valley through the stabilizing effects of vegetation. Trenching of these deposits and removal of stored sediment then took place episodically when the valley gradient was locally steepened by deposition, as described for the Piceance Creek area (Figure 4-14).

Before modern vegetation colonized interfluve areas, the situation in many ancient valleys may have resembled that of modern semiarid regions. Valley slopes and small tributaries provided an abundant supply of sediment to the main channel. During years of normal precipitation much of the sediment remained within the valley system, and these deposits then supported vegetation with its stabilizing influence. However, continued accumulation of sediment in upstream valleys caused these alluvial deposits to become less stable, as in the Piceance Creek area, and eventually a major flood triggered a phase of channel erosion and sediment movement from the source area. Perhaps, runoff was always adequate to cope with the supply of sediment in humid regions, but where erosion rates were very high and where the quantity of water percolating into coarse alluvium was large, such a sequence of events was was possible.

If one thinks in terms of a threshold flood, which, when exceeded, causes export of stored sediment from a drainage system, a climatic or hydrologic pattern can be imposed on the cycle of erosion and deposition so that floods of a certain recurrent interval or frequency trigger pulses of sediment movement from Zone 1. Thus, over a long period of years, a net accumulation of sediment occurs because of the high yield from barren interfluves and the stabilization of valley alluvium by vegetation. Steeping of the valley slope occurs during this period of sediment accumulation, and the stability of the valley or its ability to withstand erosion decreases with time (Figure 4-16). Eventually a flood of a given recurrence interval, perhaps 1000 years, will exceed the threshold of valley stability, and sediment export in excess of accumulation will occur over a short span of time, as the sediment that accumulated over a period of years is moved out of the drainage basin.

With constant climatic conditions, deposition in Zone 1 will steepen the gradient of valley floors and cause a decrease in stability of these alluvial deposits. If during 10,000 years 10 major floods (1000-year recurrence interval) occur randomly, then the coincidence of major floods and reduced valley stability will produce periods of high sediment yield, when erosion removes accumulated sediment, reduces the valley gradient, and restores the valley system to stability. According to Figure 4-16, periods of erosion will produce essentially equally spaced pulses of coarse sediment to the depositional basins. Between these periods of high and coarse sediment yield, lower rates of sediment yield will prevail and finer-grained sediments will leave the system.

During colonization of the earth by vegetation, the above process could have formed cyclic fining-upward sedimentary deposits (Allen, 1965). The stratigraphic record of this hydrologically unstable time

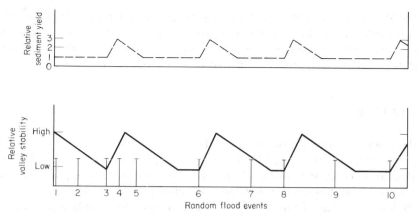

Figure 4-16   Ten randomly spaced flood events (vertical lines) of large magnitude. When they coincide with a period of low stability of valley alluvium (solid line), they cause incision and removal of accumulated sediment. High sediment yields (upper dashed line) are characteristic of short periods when the accumulated alluvium is flushed from the system. (From Schumm, 1968).

contains an abundance of interruptions and cyclic deposits (Beerbower, 1961). Other causes produce major breaks in the stratigraphic record, but hydrologic factors should not be ignored in the interpretation of ancient fluvial or nearshore sedimentary deposits.

Modern Vegetation.   As vegetation developed on interfluves and became much more effective in retarding erosion, effects of a climate change on sediment-yield rates became more pronounced. The narrowing of the peak of the sediment-yield curve, as vegetation spread over the surface of the drainage system, established a situation such that a change of climate at or below 25 inches of precipitation (Figure 3-6) would have produced considerable variation in the amount and character of sediment yield.

With the appearance of modern vegetation the rivers of humid regions became relatively stable. Rivers draining humid regions are competent to transport sediment yielded to them from vegetated valley sides. Storage of sediment as soil on interfluves provides an opportunity for additional weathering, and the resulting fluvial sediments are mature and fine grained. Under these circumstances only a major climate change, diastrophism, or man's activities can cause major changes in the type of sediment moved from the system. Further, it is probably only in subhumid and semiarid regions that pulses of sediment move out of tectonically undisturbed drainage basins at present. It is presumed that the discharge of sediment from basins in humid regions is relatively constant, except when a catastrophic hydrologic event or eustatic or tectonic changes interfere with the normal progress of landscape denudation and movement of sediment through the system.

DISCUSSION

To briefly summarize the material discussed in this chapter, one can say simply that the erosional history of a drainage basin is more complicated than previously supposed. Therefore, the sedimentary deposits resulting from the denudation of Zone 1 are also difficult to interpret. Nevertheless, the value of the concepts of geomorphic thresholds and complex response is that the investigator need not be misled by the apparent complexity of the problem. In fact, the multiple phases of erosion and deposition may clearly reflect the efforts of a drainage basin to adjust to the effects of change or to the exceeding of geomorphic thresholds, and the interpretation is actually simplified.

With the information provided in this chapter it is possible to reconsider the relatively simple erosional and depositional evolution of a landscape, as envisioned by Davis (Figure 4-1). Figure 4-2 shows that the model is complicated by isostatic adjustment to denudation. In addition, the storage and flushing of sediment from Zone 1 add another complication, and the complex response of the drainage system to external variables or to the crossing of a geomorphic threshold further increases the complexity of erosional and depositional histories. An attempt has been made in Figure 4-17 to show how the Davis model is influenced by these factors and how, during different spans of time, the erosion cycle may appear relatively simple or very complex.

During cyclic time (Figure 4-17a) the progressive denudation of the landscape is interrupted by isostatic adjustment. Between periods of isostatic adjustment, valley-floor lowering can proceed by periodic flushing of stored sediment from the drainage system (Figure 4-17b). This is the condition of dynamic metastable equilibrium of Figure 1-2. Figure 4-17c shows periods of stability and instability as part of the short-term progressive denudation and erosional evolution of a drainage system. Figure 4-17 is probably a more realistic representation of the erosion cycle than either Figure 1-2 or Figure 4-1, and it is a further elaboration of the model of episodic erosion (Figure 1-5). Obviously this model should be considered no more than a working hypothesis based on the concepts of geographic thresholds and complex response. Perhaps it is applicable only to high-sediment-producing areas of the drylands or the

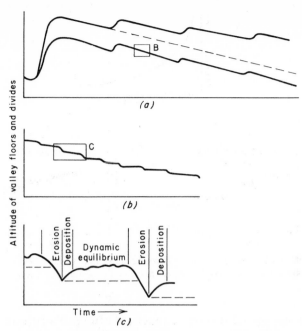

Figure 4-17 Modified concept of erosion cycle. (a) Erosion cycle following uplift as en-visioned by Davis (dashed line) and as affected by isostatic adjustment to denudation. (b) Portion of valley floor in a above showing episodic nature of decrease of valley-floor altitude. (c) Portion of valley floor in b above showing periods of dynamic equilibrium, separated by episodes of instability.

tropics, but, nevertheless, the conception is of value, as later discussions of channel, valley, piedmont and coastal landforms, and deposits em-phasize. Further, if the model of episodic erosion is valid it probably will apply only to the early stages of drainage-basin evolution and to periods following rejuvenation of Zone 1 (Figure 4-18). Dynamic equilibrium will dominate during the later stages of the erosional sequence.

The variation in channel behavior and sediment production in Zone 1 can produce some significant stratigraphic influences in Zones 2 and 3, although it is probable that such effects will be damped out when a considerable distance of transport intervenes between Zone 1 and Zone 3. However, the variability of sediment-yield data collected from mor-phologically similar drainage basins (Table 2-3) can be explained by the complex response mechanisms. For example, in Figures 4-10 and 4-11 a significant difference in sediment yield from the small experimental basin depends on when the samples were taken, either during a period

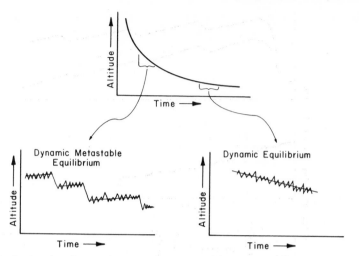

Figure 4-18   Erosional evolution of Zone 1 valley floors by both dynamic metastable equilib-rium and dynamic equilibrium, depending on stage of the geomorphic cycle.

of sediment storage or during sediment flushing. To repeat, the high degree of variability observed in modern sediment yield data may be in part related to the model of episodic erosion (Figure 4-18).

Recognition of periods when sediments are stored within Zone 1 provides an opportunity to stabilize these deposits and to reduce long-term sediment yields. Recognition of optimum periods for working with the fluvial system should provide better chances of successful land man-agement than the usual method of forcing the landscape to behave in an unnatural manner. For example, the relations between valley slope and gully distribution in the Piceance Creek area (Figure 4-14), although of local significance, suggest that similar relations could be established elsewhere, and they could be utilized by land managers as a means of identifying incipiently unstable valley floors. These areas then could be treated to prevent erosion. The preventive conservation approach has much to recommend it, and further studies of the type performed in the Piceance Creek area may be very productive in this regard.

A final point is that, although Figure 4-14 shows a critical valley slope above which gullying occurs, the figure can be used in another way to estimate valley response to altered runoff conditions. Remember that drainage area is used as a substitute for runoff. Therefore, if runoff increases, the effect would be to shift the threshold slope down for a given drainage area. Those points that plotted near but below the line would then be above it and would be susceptible to dramatic erosional alteration.

Points that fall below the new position of the line would remain stable. A careful evaluation of the morphology of Zone 1 is necessary for a reconstruction of past events and for the preparation of an environmental impact analysis. In addition, the improved comprehension of the complexity of landform evolution and response will aid in the interpretation of fluvial deposits in Zones 2 and 3.

REFERENCES

Abrahams, A. D., 1972, Drainage densities and sediment yields in eastern Australia: Aust. Geogr. Studies, v. 10, pp. 19–41.

Alimen, Henrietta, 1965, The Quaternary era in the northwest Sahara: Geol. Soc. Am. Spec. Paper 84, pp. 273–291.

Allen, J. R. L., 1965, Fining upwards cycles in alluvial successions: Geol. J. (Liverpool and Manchester), v. 4, pp. 229–246.

Beerbower, J. R., 1961, Origin of cyclothems of the Dunkard Group (Upper Pennsylvanian–Lower Permian) in Pennsylvania, West Virginia and Ohio: Geol. Soc. Am. Bull., v. 72, pp. 1029–1050.

Bloom, A. L., 1967, Pleistocene shorelines: a new test of isostasy: Geol. Soc. Am. Bull., v. 78, pp. 1433–1460.

Bond, Geoffrey, 1967, River valley morphology, stratigraphy, and paleoclimatology in southern Africa, in W. W. Bishop and J. D. Clark (editors), Background to evolution in Africa: University of Chicago Press, Chicago, pp. 303–311.

Boyce, R. C., 1975, Sediment routing with sediment delivery ratios: Agricultural Research Service, ARS-S-40, pp. 61–65.

Brice, J. C., 1966, Erosion and deposition in the loess-mantled Great Plains Medicine Creek drainage basin, Nebraska: U. S. Geol. Surv. Prof. Paper 352-H, pp. 255–339.

Brown, L. D. and Oliver, J. E., 1976, Vertical crustal movement from leveling data and their relation to geologic structure in the eastern United States: Rev. Geophys. Space Phys., v. 14, pp. 13–35.

Carlston, C. W., 1963, Drainage density and streamflow: U. S. Geol. Surv. Prof. Paper 422-C, 8 pp.

Cayeux, Lucien, 1941, Causes anciennes et causes actuelles en geologie: Paris, Masson, 79 pp.

Charlesworth, J. K., 1957, The Quaternary Era with special reference to its glaciation: Arnold, London, 2 vols., 1700 pp.

Chorley, R. J., 1957, Climate and morphology: J. Geol., v. 65, pp. 628–638.

Chorley, R. J. and Morgan, M. A., 1962, Comparison of morphometric features, Unaka Mountains, Tennessee and North Carolina, and Dartmoor, England: Geol. Soc. Am. Bull., v. 73, pp. 17–34.

Davis, W. M., 1895, The development of certain English rivers: Geogr. J., v. 5, pp. 127–146.

Davis, W. M., 1899, The geographical cycle: Geogr. J., v. 14, pp. 481–504.

Davis, W. M., 1925, The basin range problem: Natl. Acad. Sci. U. S., Proc., v. 11, pp. 387–392.

Eskola, Pentti, 1932, Conditions during the earliest geological times as indicated by the Archean rocks: Suom. Tedeakatemian Toim. Ann. Acad. Sci., Fennicae, ser. A., v. 36, 74 pp.

Garner, H. F., 1959, Stratigraphic-sedimentary significance of contemporary climate and relief in four regions of the Andes Mountains: Geol. Soc. Am. Bull., v. 70, pp. 1327–1368.

Gilluly, James, 1949, Distribution of mountain building in geologic time: Geol. Soc. Am. Bull., v. 60, pp. 561–590.

Gilluly, James, 1955, Geologic contrasts between continents and ocean basins: Geol. Soc. Am. Spec. Paper 62, pp. 7–18.

Glock, W. S., 1932, Available relief as a factor of control in the profile of a landform: J. Geol., v. 40, pp. 74–83.

Gregory, K. J. and Gardiner, V., 1975, Drainage density and climate: Z. Geomorphol., v. 19, pp. 287–298.

Gregory, K. J. and Walling, D. E., 1973, Drainage basin form and process: Wiley, New York, 456 pp.

Gunn, R., 1949, Isostasy—extended: J. Geol., v. 57, pp. 263–279.

Hadley, R. F. and Schumm, S. A., 1961, Sediment sources and drainage basin characteristics in upper Cheyenne River basin: U. S. Geol. Surv. Water-Supply Paper 1531-B, pp. 137–196.

Hamblin, W. K., 1976, Patterns of displacement along the Wasatch fault: Geology, v. 4, pp. 619–622.

Holmes, Arthur, 1945, Principles of physical geology: Ronald Press, New York, 532 pp.

Horton, R. E., 1945, Erosional development of streams and their drainage basins: Hydrophysical approach to quantitative morphology: Geol. Soc. Am. Bull., v. 50, pp. 275–370.

Kottlowski, F. E., Cooley, M. E., Ruhe, R. V., 1965, Quaternary geology of the Southwest, in H. E. Wright, Jr. and R. B. Morrison, (editors), Quaternary of the United States: Princeton University Press, Princeton, pp. 287–298.

Lewis, W. V., 1944, Stream trough experiments and terrace formation: Geol. Mag., v. 81, pp. 241–253.

Meckel, L. D., 1967, Origin of Pottsville conglomerates (Pennsylvania) in the central Appalachians: Geol. Soc. Am. Bull., v. 78, pp. 223–258.

Melton, M. A., 1958, Correlation structure of morphometric properties of drainage systems and their controlling agents: J. Geol., v. 66, pp. 442–460.

Mosley, M. P., 1972, An experimental study of rill erosion: Unpublished Thesis, Colorado State University, 118 pp.

Niyogi, Dipankar, 1966, Lower Gondwana sedimentation in Saharjuri Coalfield, Bihar, India: J. Sed. Petrol., v. 36, pp. 960–972.

Parker, R. S., 1976, Experimental study of drainage system evolution: unpublished report, Colorado State University.

Patton, P. C. and Schumm, S. A., 1975, Gully erosion, northern Colorado: a threshold phenomenon: Geology, v. 3, pp. 88–90.

Peltier, L. C., 1962, Area sampling for terrain analysis: Prof. Geogr., v. 14, pp. 24–28.

Pettijohn, F. J., 1957, Sedimentary rocks: Harper, New York, 718 pp.

Robertson, Thomas, 1952, Plant control in rhythmic sedimentation: C. R. 3rd Congr. av. etudes stratigraph. geol. Carbonifere: v. 2, pp. 515–521.

Scheidegger, A. E., 1970, Theoretical Geomorphology, 2nd ed., Springer-Verlag, Berlin, 435 pp.

Schumm, S. A., 1956, Evolution of drainage systems and slopes in badlands at Perth Amboy, New Jersey: Geol. Soc. Am. Bull., v. 67, pp. 597–646.

Schumm, S. A., 1963, The disparity between present rates of denudation and orogeny: U. S. Geol. Surv. Prof. Paper 454-H, 13 pp.

Schumm, S. A., 1965, Quaternary paleohydrology, in Quaternary of the United States: Princeton University Press, Princeton, pp. 783–794.

Schumm, S. A. and Hadley, R. F., 1957, Arroyos and the semiarid cycle of erosion: Am. J. Sci., v. 255, pp. 161–174.

Schumm, S. A. and Lichty, R. W., 1963, Channel widening and floodplain construction along Cimarron River in southwestern Kansas: U. S. Geol. Surv. Prof. Paper 352-D, pp. 71–88.

Schumm, S. A. and Parker, R. S., 1973, Implications of complex response of drainage systems for Quaternary alluvial stratigraphy: Nat. Phys. Sci., v. 243, pp. 99–100.

Schwarzback, Martin, 1961, The climatic history of Europe and North America, in A. E. M. Nairn (editor), Descriptive paleoclimatology: Interscience, New York, pp. 255–291.

Smart, J. S., 1972, Channel networks: Adv. Hydrosci., v. 8, pp. 305–346.

Stall, J. B. and Fok, Y. S., 1967, Discharge as related to stream system morphology: Int. Assoc. Sci. Hydrol. Publ. 75, pp. 224–235.

Strahler, A. N., 1964, Quantitative geomorphology of drainage basins and channel networks, in V. T. Chow (editor), Handbook of applied hydrology: McGraw-Hill, New York, Chap. 4, pp. 39–76.

Strand, R. I., 1975, Bureau of Reclamation procedures for predicting sediment yield: Agricultural Research Service, ARS-S-40, pp. 10–15.

Thiadens, A. A. and Haites, T. B., 1944, Splits and washouts in the Netherlands coal measures: Meded. Gol. Sticht. ser. C-11-1, No. 1, 51 pp.

Thornbury, W. D., 1969, Principles of geomorphology: 2nd ed., Wiley, New York, 618 pp.

Trimble, S. W., 1974, Man-induced soil erosion on the southern Piedmont 1700–1970: Soil Conservation Society of America, Ankeny, Iowa, 180 pp.

Trimble, S. W., 1975, Unsteady state denudation: Science, v. 188, p. 1207.

Twenhofel, W. H., 1932, Treatise on sedimentation: William and Wilkins, 926 pp.

Woldenberg, M. J., 1966, Horton's laws justified in terms of allometric growth and steady state in open systems: Geol. Soc. Am. Bull., v. 77, pp. 431–434.

CHAPTER FIVE

Rivers (Zone 2)

The river channel, as a conduit of the products of denudation, probably has been given more attention than any other landform. It has been studied by geomorphologists attempting to decipher the recent history of the earth's surface, by geologists seeking clues to the interpretation of fluvial deposits, and by civil engineers and others concerned with its control and management. The morphology of alluvial rivers is well known because much of the river, at least at low water, is exposed to view, and therefore, a number of quantitative relations between morphology and hydrology have been developed.

The variables that influence river morphology and the manner in which rivers respond to change are discussed in this chapter. Receiving major emphasis is the relative stability or instability of rivers. For example, when does the normal pattern shift of a channel become unstable? The local instability caused by a series of meander cutoffs that straighten and steepen part of a river's course, thereby causing increased velocity of flow, bank erosion, and channel scour above the cutoffs, may be disastrous for an engineer or landowner, but to the geomorphologist it is simply the expected result of channel-pattern evolution. A major objective of this chapter is to determine if the concepts of thresholds and complex response can be of aid in understanding the river and recognizing potentially unstable reaches of a river.

TIME AND INDEPENDENT VARIABLES

Before describing the morphology of river channels, let us inquire into the independent variables that influence both river morphology and behavior. Frequently geologists and engineers faced with this problem go their separate ways, with the geomorphologist concerned with long-term response of the river to Quaternary climate and tectonic influences, and the engineer with the effects of storm events, man-induced changes of hydrology, and the influence of modern channel morphology (width, depth, slope) on flow characteristics and sediment transport. To the geologist the passage of time or stage of landform development is important, but to the engineer it need not be. Nevertheless, it is important to realize that a river can be viewed in different ways. For example, according to Figure 1-4 and the three spans of time discussed earlier, a river can be considered unchanging or static during a steady time span, it can undergo natural and expected variations during graded time, and it can be conceived of as undergoing progressive or episodic change during a cycle time span. According to the scheme of Figure 1-2, these channels are open systems in static, steady state, or dynamic equilibrium, respectively, and the situation in each case is expectable. Of course, a channel can undergo alterations of gradient, shape, patterns, and dimensions during all three time spans if it is adjusting to major climatic, baselevel, and tectonic change.

The variables that influence channel morphology are given in order of increasing degrees of dependence in Table 5-1. This is an extension of the approach used in the earlier discussion of time (Figure 1-4) and the variables influencing Zone 1 (Table 2-1). The variables labeled as independent are not necessarily independent of each other, but for a given time span they significantly influence the dependent variables as given in Table 5-1.

A river, during a cyclic time span (millions of years), is an open system undergoing continual change (Figure 1-4), and there are no constant relations between the dependent and independent variables as they change. During this time span, only time, initial relief, geology, and paleoclimate are dependent variables (Table 5-1). Paleohydrology reflects paleoclimate, geology, and relief, but it in turn is considered to be an independent variable influencing valley dimensions because the depth, width, and especially slope of river valleys may significantly

TABLE 5-1.   THE STATUS OF RIVER VARIABLES DURING TIME SPANS OF DECREASING DURATION (AFTER SCHUMM AND LICHTY, 1963)

Variables	Status of variables during designated time spans		
	Cyclic	Graded	Steady
1. Time (stage)	Independent	Not relevant	Not relevant
2. Initial relief	Independent	Not relevant	Not relevant
3. Geology (lithology, structure)	Independent	Independent	Independent
4. Paleoclimate	Independent	Independent	Independent
5. Paleohydrology	Independent	Independent	Independent
6. Relief or volume of system above baselevel	Dependent	Independent	Independent
7. Valley dimensions (width, depth, slope)	Dependent	Independent	Independent
8. Climate (precipitation, temp., seasonality)	—	Independent	Independent
9. Vegetation (type and density)	—	Independent	Independent
10. Hydrology (mean discharge of water and sediment)	—	Independent	Independent
11. Channel morphology	—	Dependent	Independent
12. Momentary water and sediment discharge (at-a-section)	—	—	Dependent
13. Hydraulics of flow (at-a-section)	—	—	Dependent

influence the morphology of the channel that occupies the valley flow, as is demonstrated later. The remaining variables are indeterminate, for the average climatic and hydrologic conditions changed through cyclic time, as did channel morphology and, in any case, data are not available for these variables during cyclic time.

The graded time span refers to a shorter span of time (hundreds of years), during which a graded condition or steady-state equilibrium exists. When viewed from this perspective, there is a continual adjustment between elements of the system, for events occur in which negative feedback or self-regulation dominates. In other words, the progressive change of geologic time appears during graded time as a series of fluctuations about average values (Figure 1-4), and the classification of some of the variables given in Table 5-1 changes. For example, time has been eliminated as an independent variable, for, although the drainage system as a whole may be undergoing a progressive change of very small magnitude, a graded stream will show no progressive change. Initial relief also has no significance, because it is the present relief or remaining mass of the landscape that is significant. However, geology is still considered to be an independent variable because it determines to a large extent the quantity and type of sediment fed into the stream. Paleoclimate and paleohydrology may not be considered relevant to modern channel morphology, but again, if they have determined the dimensions and slope of the valley in which the river flows, then they should be retained as independent variables. Relief, climate, and vegetation, with the other variables, determine the average hydrologic regimen of a river system, and hydrology itself exerts the major influence on channel morphology, the only dependent variable during graded time.

Some of the variables that were dependent during the cyclic time span become independent during the shorter span of graded time. The hydrologic variables, runoff and sediment yield, are especially important because, during graded time, they take on a statistical significance and define the specific character of the drainage channels; however, momentary sediment and water discharge and the hydraulics of flow are still indeterminate.

During a steady time span (perhaps one month or less) a static equilibrium may exist in contrast to the steady-state equilibrium of graded time (Figure 1-5). During this brief time span, channel morphology assumes an independent status, because it has been inherited from graded time. The present or observed discharge of water and sediment and flow characteristics can be measured at a cross section at any moment during steady time, and these variables are no longer indeterminate, but are the only dependent variables. Consideration of this leads to the conclusion that helicoidal flow in meander bends (variable 13) is the result of the meander (variable 11) and not vice versa.

It is during steady time that an apparent reversal of cause and effect may occur because of feedback from the dependent to the independent variables. For example, a major flood during this brief span of time might so alter flow characteristics that a modification of channel dimensions and shape occurs. Just as water depth and velocity can be adjusted in a flume to modify sediment transport, so there is a feedback from flow velocity to sediment discharge and channel morphology. That is, as discharge momentarily increases, sediment that was previously stationary on the channel floor may be set in motion. The resulting scour, albeit minor, will influence channel depth, gradient, and shape. Thus short-term changes in velocity can cause modification of some of the variables that are described in Table 5-1 as being independent.

These modifications are usually brief and temporary, and the mean values of channel dimensions and sediment discharge are not permanently affected. Nevertheless, a temporary reversal of cause and effect can occur that, when documented quantitatively, may be a source of confusion in the interpretation of geomorphic processes. This is best demonstrated by comparing the conflicting conclusions that could result from studying fluvial processes in the hydraulic laboratory and in a natural stream. The quantity of sediment transported through a flume is dependent on the velocity and depth of the flowing water, which for a given discharge depends on flume shape and slope. An increase in sediment transport will result from an increase in the slope of the flume or an increase in discharge. In a natural stream, however, over long periods of time it is apparent that mean water and sediment discharge, and sediment size are independent variables that determine the slope of the stream and, therefore, the hydraulic characteristics at a cross section. Furthermore, over a long period of geologic (cyclic) time the independent variables of geology, relief, and climate determine the discharge of water and sediment, with all other morphologic and hydraulic variables being dependent. Confusion can only be avoided if discussion is restricted to a consideration of one time span at a time. This will prevent unprofitable arguments between engineer and earth scientist, and between classical and process-oriented geomorphologists, which is, of course, the reason that the relations of Figure 1-4 and Table 5-1 are stressed here.

During graded and steady time, channel morphology reflects the influence of a complex series of independent variables, but the discharge of water and sediment integrates most of these; and it is the nature and quantity of sediment and water moving through a channel that largely determines the morphology of stable alluvial channels.

EFFECT OF GEOLOGIC VARIABLES

Some dramatic changes of river morphology have been the result of major baselevel, tectonic, and climate changes. Before we proceed to a discussion of the influence of water and sediment discharge on stable channel morphology, it may be well to review the results of significant changes of these variables on rivers.

Baselevel and Neotectonics

Uplift or subsidence will produce channel erosion or deposition as gradient is altered, and the rapid rate at which modern uplift is occurring (Figure 2-6) is sufficient to cause modification of a river channel at present. The earth's surface, in many parts of the world, is undergoing measurable change not only by upwarping or subsidence, but also by lateral displacement. For example, many small streams are clearly offset along the San Andreas fault of California (Figure 5-1), where progressive lateral movement on the order of 2.5 cm per year has been measured.

The rates of movement along faults are highly variable, but in Chapter Two an average rate of mountain building is estimated as about 8 m per 1000 years. This rate, which initially seems insignificant in human terms, is 8 cm per decade. For many large river systems local changes of slope based on uplift of 8 cm per decade could be significant.

An example of the cumulative effect of uplift is provided by archaeological studies on the alluvial plain of the Diyala River, a major tributary to the Tigris near Baghdad (Adams, 1965). Detailed study of 6000 years of human settlement patterns shows an expansion of agricultural areas and then a progressive contraction. This is attributed to uplift, which steepened the gradient of the Diyala and caused it to incise 15 m, thereby leaving irrigation canals high and dry. Although these changes occurred over perhaps 1000 years, during one period of critical instability there was an attempt by the irrigators to armor or pave the channel of the Diyala to prevent further incison.

The production of large quantities of sediment in Zone 1 by earthquakes has been mentioned, and the increase of sediment load by such an event causes channel adjustment. In fact, Walters (1975) concluded

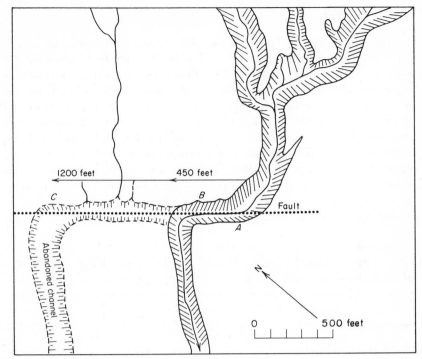

Figure 5-1   Sketch map showing offset of streams along the San Andreas Fault. (From Wallace, 1967.)

that a period of early 19th century Mississippi River instability, involving both channel widening and meander cutoffs, was due to the New Madrid earthquakes of 1811 to 1812. The Mississippi River widened, and large quantities of sediment were delivered into the river by bank caving during the earthquakes. This sediment moved downstream triggering meandor cutoffs and producing divided flow reaches by midchannel bar formation.

The geologist, of course, is not surprised to see drainage patterns that have been disrupted by warping of the earth's surface. In fact, complete reversals of drainage lines have been documented (Figure 2-7), and convexities in the longitudinal profile of both rivers and river terraces due to unwarping have been detected (Machida, 1960; Volkov et al., 1967). Further, the progressive shifting of a river toward one side of its valley has been attributed to lateral tilting (Jefferson, 1907; von Bandat, 1962, pp. 274–275; Coleman, 1969). Neotectonics certainly should not be ignored as a possible reason for modern river instability.

Climate Change

Climatic fluctuations have produced major changes of river morphology. In Table 5-2 an effort has been made to summarize the nature of river change during the Quaternary period as a result of climate change, glaciation, and climatically induced baselevel influences. For example, it is certain that, for rivers that drained from continental and valley glaciers (Table 5-2, locations 1 and 2), fluvial deposition was associated with glaciation (Zeuner, 1959, pp. 45–46). Meltwater from the glaciers transported huge loads of sediment and formed valley trains (Peltier, 1962; Kringström, 1962) and outwash plains. Following cessation of glacial erosion and the flushing of glacial debris from the valleys, the reduced sediment loads caused river incision to form terraces.

In periglacial regions (Table 5-2, location 3), Zeuner (1959, p. 49)

TABLE 5-2. SUMMARY OF CHANGES IN CHANNEL BEHAVIOR (EROSION–DEPOSITION) DURING CLIMATE CHANGE

Location or type of basin	Climate change to	River activity
1. Basin partly occupied by ice sheet	Cooler, wetter or cooler, drier	Deposition
2. Basin partly occupied by valley glacier	Cooler, wetter or cooler, drier	Deposition
3. Periglacial	Cooler, wetter or cooler, drier	Deposition
4. Coastal	Cooler	Erosion
5. Interior basin	Cooler, wetter	Deposition
6. Unglaciated continental interior, humid, perennial streams	Cooler, wetter	Erosion
7. Unglaciated continental interior, semiarid, ephemeral streams	Cooler, wetter	Erosion
8. Unglaciated continental interior, arid, ephemeral streams	Cooler, wetter	
a. Tributaries		Erosion
b. Main rivers		Deposition

concluded that as the climate became colder, and as the forests disappeared, periglacial processes of erosion, which produced much slope erosion, caused deposition of sediment in the valleys.

Near coasts (Table 5-2, location 4), late interglacial and early glacial lowering of sea level in response to climate changes caused river erosion, and conversely, the rise of sea level accompanying melting of the ice sheets caused deposition (Fisk and McFarlan, 1955). For a closed interior basin (Table 5-2, location 5) river activity was the reverse of that for the coastal situation, because during late interglaciation and early glaciation the formation of lakes due to increased runoff raised the baselevel of the streams entering the lakes.

The description of river activity in nonglaciated regions beyond the effects of changing sea level (locations 6–8) is based on the estimated hydrologic changes that accompany climate changes (Figures 2-4 and 3-1). Initial climate or the climate before the change is of critical importance here, for it determines the type of river to be considered. For example, in the humid region of location 6, the rivers were perennial, and they remained perennial following a shift to a wetter climate. The increased runoff, with a minor decrease in sediment yield (Figures 2-4 and 3-1), produced incision, or at least channel enlargement.

The situation is different for an initially semiarid region (Table 5-2, location 7), for the rivers were initially either intermittent or characterized by long periods of low flow. The smaller tributaries were ephemeral, as are many in humid regions, but many more drainage channels were present. With a shift to a wetter climate and greater runoff, the major rivers and many of the tributaries became perennial. Vegetation density increased, and, if a change of vegetation type from grass to trees occurred, many small channels and the headward portions of larger channels were obliterated. As runoff increased, sediment yield decreased, as did sediment concentration (Figure 3-2). The result was undoubtedly the enlargement and incision of the main channels. With a return to semiarid conditions, sediment yield increased, as both hillslope and channel erosion increased and runoff decreased. Deposition in the main channels probably resulted, as the tributaries again reached their maximum extent and number.

It has not always been recognized that the changes in tributary channels might not conform to changes along the larger rivers. This may not be important in humid regions, but it is of major importance in arid regions. Increased precipitation during the Pleistocene age converted ephemeral rivers to perennial ones. Increased runoff eroded the tributaries (Table 5-2, location 8a) and extended the drainage network. Sediment was flushed out of the tributary valleys into the main channels during local storms and, because the loss of water into the alluvium of the main channels was appreciable (Cornish, 1961), aggradation of the main channels probably resulted (Table 5-2, location 8b). The situation was probably similar to modern conditions along the Rio Grande, where trenching of the Rio Puerco and other tributaries during the past century has caused deposition in the Rio Grande itself (Rittenhouse, 1944).

Obviously only the simplest cases are presented in Table 5-2; for example, a major river may drain a glaciated basin, cross through a semiarid or humid region, and then enter the sea. The terrace sequence and sedimentary deposits found along this river course should be complicated and difficult to correlate. It may be concluded that the correlation of river terraces by height or number of terraces over long distances under such circumstances is unwise (Hadley, 1960).

The Nile River basin provides a good example of climatic variability within a major drainage basin. This exotic river derives its discharge from Central Africa, and any basinwide increase of precipitation will increase runoff from the headwaters, and the increased vegetal cover will decrease the sediment load of the upper Nile. However, it will also greatly increase the sediment produced by tributaries in arid Sudan and Egypt. This influx of sediment from the tributaries should cause deposition in the lower Nile valley and, in fact, Butzer and Hansen (1968) have concluded that the lower Nile aggraded during wetter periods.

The great variability of climate in large drainage basins prevents any simplistic application of the relation of Table 5-2, and this is also true for smaller drainage basins with sufficient relief to produce climatic zones within the watershed. For example, climate may range from arid or semiarid to humid or periglacial at the highest elevations, and Richmond (1962) has described the vertical shifting of such climate zones in the La Sal Mountains of Utah during the Quaternary period.

Table 5-2 suggests the manner in which channels will respond to climate change. However, remember that everything noted previously has suggested that such a change will be complex. That is, if a geomorphic threshold is exceeded, if baselevel is lowered, of if a climate change induces incision, the river probably will not respond by a straightforward downcutting to a lower level (Figure 4-12), because the channel is only one component of the adjusting fluvial systems.

EFFECT OF HYDROLOGIC VARIABLES

If the sediment and water moving through a stream channel are the primary independent variables influencing modern channel morphology, as stated earlier (Table 5-1), then it should be possible to show statistically significant relations among water discharge, the nature and quantity of sediment load, and all aspects of channel morphology, such as channel dimensions, shape, gradient, and pattern. Numerous empirical relations have been developed by geologists and engineers that relate channel morphology to water and sediment discharge, and some of these are reviewed here.

Lane (1955) summarized these relations by presenting a qualitative relation among bed-material load (Q_s), mean water discharge (Q), median sediment size (d_{50}), and gradient (S), as follows:

$$Q_s \cdot d_{50} \simeq Q \cdot S \tag{5-1}$$

He concluded that a channel will be maintained in steady-state equilibrium when changes in sediment load and sediment size are compensated for by changes in water discharge and river gradient.

Bed-material load is defined as that part of the sediment load of a stream that consists of sediment sizes that comprise a significant part of the stream bed. The emphasis on significant representation excludes the small percentage of silt and clay usually found in most bed material (Einstein, 1950, pp. 6, 7). The other component of total sediment load, as defined by Einstein, is wash load, which is part of the total load not significantly represented in the bed. It is held in suspension by the turbulence of the flowing water and it moves at the velocity of the flowing water. This distinction is necessary because, during sampling of sediment loads, bed-material load is caught in the suspended-sediment sampler, although this coarser materials may be only in temporary suspension. Einstein's definitions suggest that bed load is composed of sand-size and larger sediment, whereas suspended load is composed of sediment smaller than sand (smaller than about 0.06 to 0.07 mm). In the following text bed load is used to mean sediment larger than silt that, although often in suspension, will eventually be deposited on the bed. A sediment particle of sand size and larger normally only remains in suspension during a flood, and it is redeposited as the flood wanes. Suspended-sediment load, as used here, then refers to wash load, which is composed of silt and clay. This distinction is important because the two types of sediment have significantly different physical properties. Silt and clay have cohesion and are difficult to erode, whereas sands are moved readily, depending on size and shape (Hjulstrom, 1935; Schumm, 1960). Therefore, a river in which a large proportion of the sediment load is silt and clay should be morphologically very different from a river with a sediment load that is predominantly sand size and larger, or bed load.

Channel Dimensions and Shape

All available evidence indicates that the greater the quantity of water that moves through a channel, the larger is the cross section of that channel. Preceded by numerous studies of canal morphology and stability (Leliavsky, 1955), Leopold and Maddock (1953) demonstrated that for most rivers, the water surface width (b) and depth (d) increase with mean annual discharge (Q_m), in a downstream direction:

$$b = kQm^{0.5} \qquad\qquad\qquad (5\text{-}2)$$

$$d = kQm^{0.4} \qquad\qquad\qquad (5\text{-}3)$$

The coefficients of Equations 5-2 and 5-3 are different for each river, and when data from a number of rivers are plotted against discharge, the scatter covers an entire log cycle. That is, for a given discharge there is an order of magnitude range of width and depth. Therefore, other variables apparently influence channel dimensions.

One such hydrologic variable, which has not been given due consideration, is peak or maximum discharge. It is rare to find streams that drain geologically similar areas and yet have very different flood peaks. Two such rivers may be the Rios Guanipa and Tonoro in northeastern Venezuela (Stevens et al., 1975). Although hydrologic data were collected for only the rainy season, June through September of 1969, meteorological data indicate that the hydrologic results should be similar for longer periods. A comparison of the morphology and hydrologic character of both rivers is presented in Table 5-3. The major differences in width and sinuosity (ratio of channel to valley length) appear to be the result of the great difference in flood characteristics.

Although the records are short, they indicate that rivers with high ratios of peak to mean discharge are morphologically different from rivers with low ratios. In a general way this is substantiated by Gupta (1975) for two rivers in Jamaica. In this case the only factor that can explain the difference between the braided Yallahs River and the narrower, more sinuous Buff Bay River is the marked seasonality of precipitation in the Yallahs River drainage basin. Annual precipitation is similar in both drainage basins, but larger floods occur in the braided Yallahs channel. There have not been systematic studies of the influence of flood peaks or of the ratio of peak to mean discharge on channel morphology, but this is an area that warrants further attention.

The remaining variable that significantly controls river morphology is sediment load. Lacey (1930) concluded from an analysis of regime canal data that the wetted perimeter of a channel is directly dependent on

TABLE 5-3. CHARACTERISTICS OF RIOS TONORO AND GUANIPA (FROM STEVENS ET AL., 1975)

River	Drainage area (sq. miles)	Valley slope (ft/mile)	Channel width (ft)	Sinuosity	Median sediment size (mm)	Mean annual discharge (Q) (cfs)	Maximum annual discharge (Qp) (cfs)	Qp/Q
Tonoro	500	0.8	600	1.1	0.35	400	18,900	47
Guanipa	1100	0.7	50	2.3	0.35	600	3,700	6

discharge, but that the shape of the channel reflects the size of the sediment load. Coarse sediment produces channels of a high width/depth ratio, and fine sediment produces narrow and deep cross sections. Considerable research into the hydraulics and morphology of coarse-load Canadian rivers show that, in fact, they do differ in dimensions from the rivers studied by Leopold and Maddock (1953). For example, analysis of data from 70 reaches of gravel-fed streams in Alberta yields the following relations (Bray, 1973):

$$b = 2.38 \, Q_2^{0.527} \tag{5-4}$$

$$d = 0.266 \, Q_2^{0.333} \tag{5-5}$$

Q_2 is the discharge for a flood with a 2-year recurrence interval, and b and d are average water surface width and depth, respectively, at the 2-year discharge. Comparison with Equations 5-2 and 5-3 indicates that the gravel-bed streams at a given discharge will be wider and shallower, but according to Bray the addition of median grain size to Equations 5-4 and 5-5 did not improve them significantly.

In addition to the size of the sediment transported, the relative amounts of bed load and suspended load also significantly influence the morphology of sand-bed streams. For example, along the Smoky Hill-Kansas River system in Kansas, discharge increases in a downstream direction, but channel width decreases from about 300 feet to less than 100 feet in central Kansas. Farther east there is a marked increase in channel width. These and other changes are attributed to changes in the type of sediment load introduced by major tributary streams (Schumm, 1968). Tributaries introduce large suspended-sediment loads where the width decreases, and large bed-loads or sand loads are added where width increases.

The collection of data on channel dimensions, bed and bank sediments, and water discharge at 36 cross sections permits development of additional empirical equations for channel dimensions. All the channels are located in the semiarid to subhumid regions of the Great Plains of the United States and on the Riverine Plains of New South Wales, Australia. None of the channels contain more than about 10 percent gravel; thus bed material is sand (Schumm, 1968, pp. 40, 45). However, the channels do show a considerable range of dimensions and hydrology as follows: width 27 to 800 feet, depth 2.4 to 18 feet, width/depth ratio 4 to 75, sinuosity 1.05 to 2.5, mean annual discharge 21 to 5000 cfs.

The channels are defined as stable because there has been no progressive channel adjustment during the last 10 years of record, and they are described as alluvial channels because their bed and banks are composed of sediment that is being transported by the river. Data are not available for total sediment loads, but bed and bank samples were collected that are assumed to reflect the type of sediment transported. Although there were no systematic changes in the average size of the bed and bank materials, it was determined that the shape of the channels is closely related to the percentage of silt and clay in the sediments forming the perimeter of the channel (M). Silt–clay was measured as the sediment smaller than 0.074 mm (200 mesh sieve). The width/depth ratio (F) of these channels was found to be related to the percentage of silt–clay in the perimeter of the channel (M) according to (Figure 5-2):

$$F = 255M^{-1.08} \tag{5-6}$$

M apparently is an index of the type of sediment being transported through the channel, and it is also an indication of bank stability. For five locations, where both total sediment load data are available and where M has been calculated, it was inversely related to the percentage of the total load that is sand or bed load (Qb), at a given discharge, as follows (Schumm, 1968):

$$M = \frac{55}{Qb} \tag{5-7}$$

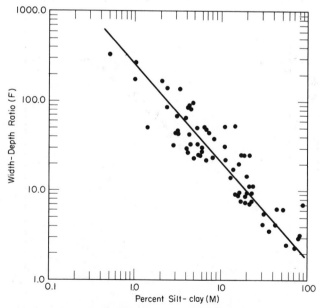

Figure 5-2   Relation between width/depth ratio and percentage of silt and clay in channel perimeter for stable alluvial streams. (After Schumm, 1960.)

Because of the great range of channel size and discharge of the channels studied, the type of sediment load is considered to be a more important control on stable channel shape than the total quantity of sediment transported through a channel. For example, in one channel a small quantity of bed load may exert the dominant control if it is the total load, whereas in another channel the same amount of bed load may exert much less influence on channel shape because it is only a small part of the total sediment load. Therefore, when suspended-sediment load and discharge are constant, an increase in the quantity of bed load will cause an increase in channel width and width/depth ratio, but this is probably related to increased gradient and velocity of flow associated with the increase of bed load (Leopold and Maddock, 1953). For example, the experimental results presented in Figure 5-3 for small channels with a constant discharge of 0.15 cfs demonstrate an increase of width/depth ratio with increased bed load (Khan, 1971). Suspended-sediment load during the experiment was not measured, but it was low and remained relatively constant; however, gradient increased with increased bed-load transport (see Figure 5-15).

In summary, for the range of channels studied, type of sediment load

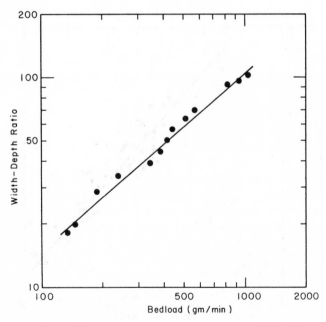

Figure 5-3   Relation between width/depth ratio and sand load in experimental channels, at constant discharge of 0.15 cfs. (From Khan, 1971).

exerts the main control on shape; therefore, for a single channel with constant discharge and amount of suspended load, a change of bed load is reflected in a change of both shape and gradient.

Further analysis of the river data produced the following relations for channel width and depth (in feet):

$$b = 37 \frac{Qm^{0.38}}{M^{0.39}} \qquad (5\text{-}8)$$

$$d = 0.6 \, M^{0.342} \, Qm^{0.29} \qquad (5\text{-}9)$$

Eighty-eight percent ($r = .93$) of the variability of width can be accounted for by mean annual discharge (Qm in cfs) and channel silt–clay or type of sediment load (M), both being about equally important. The relationship for channel depth is not as good, with about 81 percent (r = .89) of the variability of channel depth accounted for. Nevertheless, only about 40 percent of the variability of channel dimensions is accounted for by discharge alone. Note that width and depth as used here are the bank-full width and depth of the channel in contrast to water width and depth used in Equations 5-2 through 5-5.

To summarize for the alluvial rivers, no relation between size of bed sediment and channel dimensions was detected, but when an index of the type of sediment load (M) was combined with discharge, good correlations with width and depth were obtained. Hence, one may conclude that variations in channel dimensions among many rivers are probably attributable to differences of sediment type. Local changes of channel dimensions may, of course, be strongly affected by variations of resistance of bank sediments (Fisk, 1944; Simons and Albertson, 1960; Ackers, 1964).

Channel Gradient

If not influenced by uplift or variations in bedrock, the gradient of a stream will usually show a downstream decrease that is associated with an increase of discharge and a decrease in size of sediments (Shulits, 1941; Lane, 1955). In fact, Lane's relation (Equation 5-1) indicates that gradient is directly related to both bed-material load and grain size and inversely related to water discharge. Sediment size can be readily obtained at any cross section, and when samples are obtained near gaging stations, both sediment size and discharge can be related to gradient. Hack (1957) determined for streams in Virginia and Maryland that drainage area was closely related to mean annual discharge. He then used drainage area as an index of discharge and found that a ratio of median grain size (d_{50} in mm) to drainage basin area (A in square miles) was related to gradient (S_c in feet per mile) as follows:

$$S_c = 18\left(\frac{d_{50}}{A}\right)^{0.6} \tag{5-10}$$

Hack (1957) and Brush (1961) concluded that downstream decreases of stream gradient depend on the resistance of the rocks being eroded and supplied to the channels. For example, Brush found that, for a given distance downstream or length of channel (L in miles), the gradient decreased most rapidly for shale, then limestone, and least for sandstone, as shown by the following equations:

$$S_c \text{ (shale)} = 0.034L^{-0.81} \tag{5-11}$$

$$S_c \text{ (limestone)} = 0.019L^{-0.71} \tag{5-12}$$

$$S_c \text{ (sandstone)} = 0.46L^{-0.67} \tag{5-13}$$

Bray (1973) found the following expected relation among gradient, discharge (Q_2), and sediment size (d_{50}) for rivers of Alberta:

$$S_{\dot{c}} = 0.965\ Q_2^{-0.334}\ d_{50}^{0.58} \tag{5-14}$$

When data on type of sediment load (M) were used with mean annual discharge (Qm), the following multiple regression equation resulted for the Great Plains and Australian rivers:

$$S = 60M^{-0.38}Qm^{-0.32} \tag{5-15}$$

Seventy-one percent of the variability of gradient can be accounted for by Qm and M ($r = .84$, standard error is 0.07 log units). The range of grain size of the bed material was too small to permit an evaluation of the effect of grain size on the gradient of these rivers.

A plot of the slope of the alluvial valley surface on which each of the channels flowed versus gradient of the stream shows that valley slope is correlated with channel slope (Figure 5-4). This seems trivial, but if, in fact, the valley slope reflects past discharges and sediment loads (Table 5-1) then it is an independent variable influencing modern channel gradient. It is interesting that in Figure 5-4, for channels with a low silt–clay content, the gradient and valley slope are almost identical, and for others with a high silt–clay content the valley slope is three times that of the channel gradient. This suggests that, although the valley slope can exert an important influence on the gradient of a modern channel, the difference between valley and channel slope can be the result of a change of the type of sediment moved through the channel (Schumm,

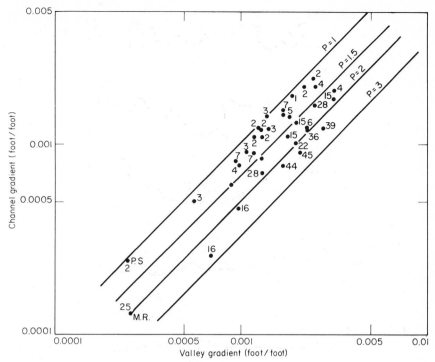

Figure 5-4   Relations between alluvial valley slope and channel gradient. Numbers beside points indicate percentage of silt–clay in channels (M). Four lines of equal sinuosity (P) are shown. M. R. identifies Murrumbidgee River and P. S. identifies paleochannel 2 (Figure 5-34). (From Schumm, 1968.)

1968, p. 51). This matter is considered again when variability of channel patterns is discussed.

In summary, the gradient of a stream is strongly influenced by the hydrology and geology of the drainage basin. The latter provides sediment of various quantities and sizes, and the former provides the transporting medium; together they determine the longitudinal profile and gradient of an alluvial river.

Channel Patterns

Rivers display a continuum of patterns from straight to highly sinuous (Figure 5-5). It should be emphasized that any division between straight and meandering channels is arbitrary, and that a meandering stream may be of low sinuosity, perhaps as low as 1.2, if the channel displays a repeating pattern of bends.

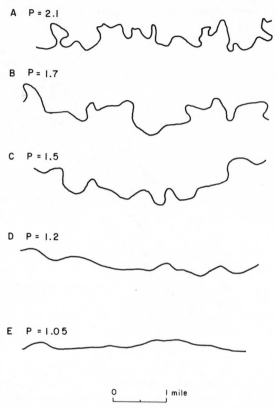

Figure 5-5   Examples of channel patterns. *P* is sinuosity (ratio of channel to valley length). (From S. A. Schumm, 1963, Sinuosity of alluvial rivers on the Great Plains: Geol. Soc. Am. Bull., v. 74, pp. 1089–1100.)

Popov (1964) makes a useful distinction between several types of straight channels based on the morphology of the channel flow as follows: straight channel with transverse dunes or bars, straight channel with alternate bars, and straight channel with midstream bars (braided). In addition, sinuous channels have been subdivided on the basis of variations in channel width and bar pattern (Figure 5-6).

The channel patterns described above and in Figures 5-5 and 5-6 are single-channel patterns, but multiple-channel patterns also exist. Although at low water, braided streams have islands of sediment or relatively permanent vegetated islands exposed in the channels, this should not obscure the fact that the islands are in a single, large channel.

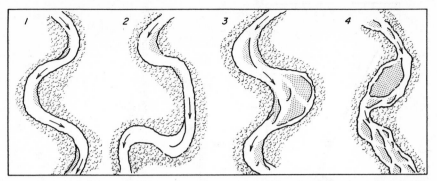

Figure 5-6 Variability of sinuous channel patterns. (*1*) Sinuous channel, uniform width, narrow point bars. (*2*) Sinuous point-bar channel, wider at bends. (*3*) Point-bar braided channel, wider at bends. (*4*) Island-braided channel, variable width. (From Culbertson et al., 1967.)

However, any type of single channel can be part of a multiple-channel distributary system (e.g., Figure 5-29).

All previous work on meandering has demonstrated that meander dimensions are related to the discharge of water through the channel (Leopold and Wolman, 1957; Dury, 1964; Speight, 1965, 1967); and, in fact, the channel need not meander to have a pool and crossing or pool and riffle spacing related to discharge (Keller, 1975). Dury (1964) found that meander wavelength (λ in feet) is related to mean annual flood (Qma in cfs) as follows (Figure 5-7):

$$\lambda = 30 \; Qma^{0.5} \tag{5-16}$$

Note that there is a 10-fold variation of meander wavelength at a given discharge (Figure 5-7). When information on type of sediment load (M) is included, the following vastly improved relation is obtained for both mean annual discharge (Qm in cfs) and mean annual flood (Qma in cfs):

$$\lambda = 1890 \; \frac{Qm^{0.34}}{M^{0.74}} \tag{5-17}$$

($r = .96$; standard error is 0.16 log units);

$$\lambda = \frac{Qma^{0.48}}{M^{0.74}} \tag{5-18}$$

($r = .93$; standard error is 0.19 log units). Additional relations among

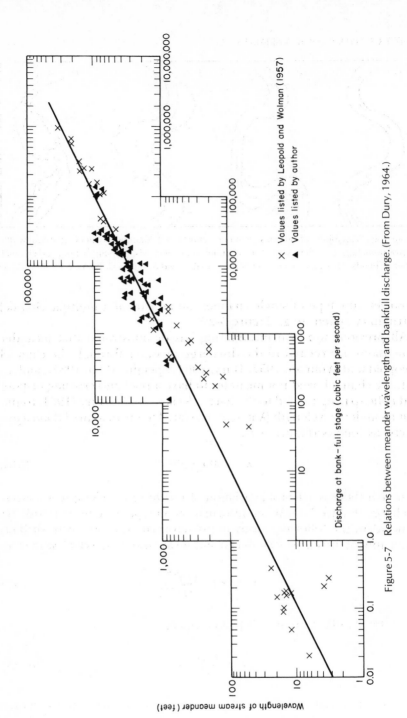

Figure 5-7   Relations between meander wavelength and bankfull discharge. (From Dury, 1964.)

channel width, discharge, and width of the meander belt have been reviewed by Leliavsky (1955, pp. 133–135).

For stable alluvial rivers of the Great Plains, the degree of meandering or the sinuosity (P, ratio of channel length to valley length) is related to M as follows ($r = .91$):

$$P = 0.94 \, M^{0.25} \tag{5-19}$$

Hence, Equations 5-6 and 5-19 show that streams transporting little bed load are relatively narrow, deep, and sinuous. However, it is true that rivers that transport small quantities of sand are not always sinuous, and some rivers that appear to be transporting only very fine sediment are straight.

Sinuosity.   A partial explanation of these sinuosity differences among rivers may reside in the relations of Figure 5-4. If tectonic factors have not modified valley slope, the gradient of the alluvial surface should be at just that inclination required for the movement of the water–sediment mixture through the valley. The fact that the surface of the alluvium is too steep requires an explanation that depends on an understanding of the changes in stream regimen during perhaps the past 15,000 years. All the rivers flow on the upper surface of alluvium that fills valleys cut into bedrock. The deep valleys and the alluvium probably are the result of changes in baselevel, climate, and hydrologic conditions during and following the Pleistocene epoch, but the alluvial fill may also be due to the type of deposition proposed by Davis (Figure 4-1) or that observed in the REF (Figure 4-12).

The alluvium filling the valleys decreases in size from gravel and coarse sand at the base of the deposit to silt, clay, or fine sand at the present valley surface, presumably reflecting changed sediment transport conditions and availability of coarse sediment. Great variability of sediment type occurs in these alluvial deposits, but all available information shows a decrease in size of the alluvium toward the surface of the fill.

Depending on the type of rocks exposed within a drainage basin, the sediment load of one of these rivers might have changed from gravel and sand to sand alone or from silt, clay, sand, and gravel to predominantly silt and clay during deposition in the valley (see Figure 6-1). For example, in a stream draining areas underlain by sandstone, the size and quantity of the sediment decreased, but the proportion of bed load to total load probably changed little. A stream draining areas of sandstone and shale underwent not only a decrease in the size of sediment load, but also a reduction in the ratio of bed load to total load. As a result a stream draining areas of mixed sediments, after deposition of the coarser sediment ceased, was flowing on alluvium with a gradient in excess of that required for transport of the finer load. A reduction of gradient by degradation could ony be partly effective, for with incision the stream would encounter the coarser sediments transported during a previous regime, and the development of an armor of coarse sediment would prevent further degradation. The formation of a sinuous course appears to have been the only alternative. Rivers draining areas of relatively coarse or sandy sediments were less affected by the change in size and type of sediment load and continued to flow on a gradient that is today essentially that of the valley itself, because they have been transporting relatively large amounts of bed load throughout their history.

An increase in sinuosity and the accompanying decrease in stream gradient reflects the need to dissipate energy, in excess of that expended in friction and sediment transport, that became available as the bed load decreased. Thus the rivers with sandy channels (low M) plot high (low sinuosity) in Figure 5-4, and the rivers with high silt–clay channels plot low.

Apparent exceptions to this conclusion occur; for example, streams draining mountain meadows may meander, yet their beds are composed of cobbles. An explanation is that the coarse sediment acts as an armor over which the stream meanders. Under the present regimen these coarse sediments are not moved; therefore, the predominant sediment load is transported in suspension. In addition, it appears probable that, although a stream is transporting fine sediments, the valley gradient may be so gentle as to inhibit meandering. Examples of this may be the Mississippi River below New Orleans (Fisk, 1944) and the Illinois River (Rubey, 1952). Both rivers flow on surfaces that slope very gently downstream, and both rivers are essentially straight, although they transport fine sediments.

It appears, then, as suggested in Table 5-1, that valley gradient can be an independent variable influencing the present pattern of an alluvial river. This is an appealing explanation for the development of a sinuous river course. It is not an original one, but it can be supported by field evidence. For example, the points labeled M. R. and P. S. in Figure 5-4 represent two channels on the Riverine Plain of New South Wales, Australia (Figure 5-34). One is a paleochannel (P.S.) that was functioning at least 10,000 years ago. It contains, and therefore must have transported, large quantities of sand (low M) across an alluvial plain at the slope of the plain (sinuosity about 1.0). Since the time that this channel was functioning, the climate has changed, the vegetational cover in the headwaters has improved, and the quantity of sand to be moved has decreased markedly (Schumm, 1968). The modern Murrumbidgee River (M.R.), which drains the same sediment source area, now meanders across the allluvial plain with a sinuosity of about 2. To reduce its gradient the paleochannel could have either incised into the plain or developed a sinuous course. Incision required the movement of tremendous quantities of sediment, and, to reduce the gradient by half, incision in the headwaters would have had to be very great. A much simpler means of reducing gradient was to develop a sinuous course, and it was in this way that gradient reduction was accomplished and the pattern of the Murrumbidgee River established.

Armoring.   Twice in the above account armoring of the channel is mentioned. It is well known that channel scour results in a concentration of the coarsest sediments on the floor of the channel. A splendid example is the reach of the Missouri River downstream from the Fort Randall dam. Release of sediment-free waters from the dam was expected to cause 10 feet of scour, but because of the development of an armor of gravel, 1 grain thick, scour ceased at about 3 feet (Livesey, 1963; Gessler, 1970).

Degradation of the Colorado River below Glen Canyon Dam is controlled by 10 gravel–cobble bars in the 24-km reach below the dam. The median grain size of the bar material is 100 mm (Pemberton, 1976). In this case the channel is stabilized not by a continuous armor, but by several armored locations. It is possible that the reduction of flood peaks below the dam permits the armor to form and persist. In nature a large flood probably could break the armor, thereby causing renewed incision and formation of another armor at a lower level. This episodic degradation continues until the armor is composed of sediment sufficiently large to protect the channel under all flow conditions.

The above observations indicate that under certain conditions an insignificant fraction of the alluvium (coarsest 1 percent) may significantly control the behavior and morphology of the channel.

EXPERIMENTAL STUDIES OF CHANNEL SHAPE AND PATTERN

Effect of Sediment Type

To test the theory that both width/depth ratio and channel sinuosity are strongly influenced by type of sediment load, a series of experiments were performed in a concrete recirculating flume that is 31 m long, 7 m wide, and about 0.9 m deep (Figure 5-8). In short, the work of Friedkin (1945). Tiffany and Nelson (1939), Quraishy (1944), Ackers (1964), and others was duplicated, and then an attempt was made to induce a channel to adopt a sinuous course by changing the type of sediment load introduced into it (Khan, 1971).

Initially, alternate bars developed and a meandering-thalweg channel was formed at a constant water discharge of 0.15 cfs (Figures 5-9a and b). This flow contained negligible suspended sediment, but bed load (sand) was fed at the entrance to prevent channel scour. With increasing bed load, channel width gradient and width/depth ratio increased (Figure 5-3) and depth decreased. After the development of a meandering thalweg,

Figure 5-8   Straight experimental channel. Water introduced into an initial bend at slope of 0.001. Channel width 1.2 ft.

but not a truly meandering channel (Figure 5-9a), kaolinite was mixed with the recirculating water until a concentration of 3 percent suspended sediment load (30,000 ppm) was obtained. Sand continued to be fed into the channel, but at a markedly reduced rate.

The major change in type and quantity of sediment load at constant water discharge, especially the reduction in bed load, should have caused channel scour and gradient reduction. In fact, the scour that occurred was confined to the thalweg and was relatively minor. In this way a truly meandering channel did develop (Figure 5-9c), although sinuosity was low.

A factor of major importance in the transformation of the channel was the stabilization of the alternate bars by deposition of the suspended load. Flow over the alternate bars was shallow, and deposition of suspended sediment on the bars decreased flow depths and prevented erosion of the alternate bars. The banks of the channel were also partly stabilized in this manner. When the thalweg was subjected to scour, a decrease of water level resulted, and the submerged alternate bars emerged to form point bars and a sinuous channel. The channel became narrower, deeper, and sinuous as a result of the introduction of suspended load and a decrease of bed load. Figure 5-10 shows the pattern and cross sections of a channel before and after adjustment to changed sediment loads. This experiment supports the field evidence concerning the effect of type of sediment load on channel shape, dimension, and pattern.

The experimental results indicate the possible effects of vegetation on channel shape. If a channel with alternate bars is invaded by vegetation during a long period of low flow and if the alternate bars are stabilized by vegetation, the thalweg will deepen during the next higher flows. If the vegetation is not destroyed the channel will become sinuous and the thalweg or low-water channel will become the main channel.

Effect of Slope and Sediment Load

According to Friedkin (1945), Leopold and Wolman (1957), and Lane (1957), when data for mean annual discharge or mean annual flood are plotted against gradient, braided rivers plot above the position of meandering rivers (Figure 5-11). In fact, for a given discharge there appears to be a threshold slope above which a braided channel pattern develops. Further, it has been suggested by Lane (1957, p. 38) and Ackers (1964), and confirmed by recent experiments performed by Ackers and Charlton (1971), that at very low slopes another threshold exists between straight and meandering-thalweg channels (Figure 5-11).

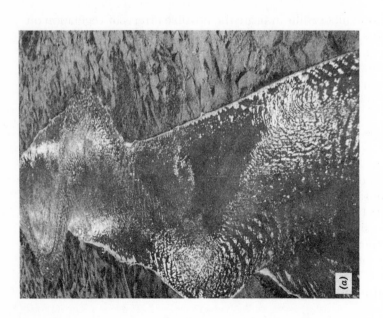

Figure 5-9 Experimental channels (a) Meandering thalweg channel formed at slope of about 0.0008. Note that alternate bars are submerged at discharge of 0.15 cfs. (b) Meandering thalweg channel at low water. Flow is toward observer. Note backwater channel between point bar and bank. (c) Meandering channel and point bars formed after introduction of suspended load. Channel width 2.2 ft. (d) Braided channel. (From Schumm and Khan, 1972.)

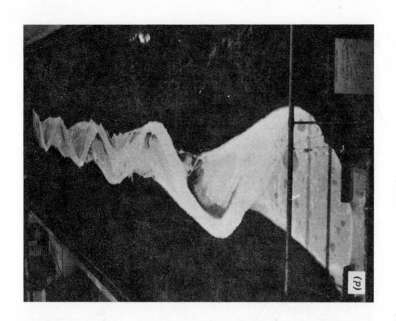

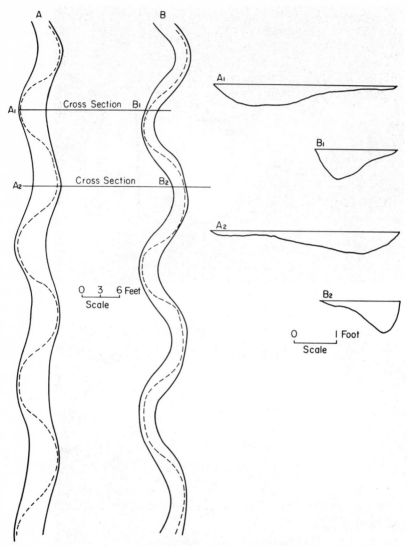

Figure 5-10 Maps showing channel (A) before and (B) after introduction of suspended-sediment load. Cross sections show changes of channel dimensions and shape. Slope was 0.0064. (From Schumm and Khan, 1972.)

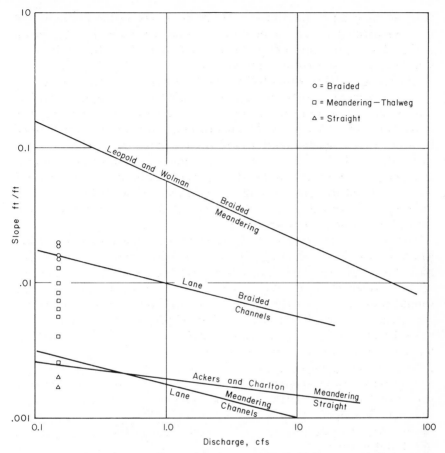

Figure 5-11 Relation between slope and discharge and threshold slopes at each discharge, as defined by Lane (1957), Leopold and Wolman (1957), and Ackers and Charlton (1971). Symbols show position of experimental channels. (From Schumm and Khan, 1973.)

Thus gradient is a variable that must be changed if a range of river patterns is to be studied experimentally. Although slope can be changed at will in the laboratory, in the field it is of course established in relation to discharge and sediment-load characteristics (Table 5-1). Nevertheless, the existence of pattern thresholds that are related to slope or sediment load were also investigated experimentally.

The studies were performed at a constant discharge of 0.15 cfs. The experiment was begun at a low slope, with water introduced at an angle to the axis of the flume. This, of course, forced the development of a bend at the head of the flume, with all its effects on the hydraulics of flow. Surprisingly, even under these conditions a channel with a meandering thalweg did not occupy the entire length of the flume until the slope was increased from 0.001 to 0.0026.

The straight channel that formed at the lowest slopes had a relatively deep and narrow cross section, and its banks were straight. Cross sections were almost uniform throughout the length of the channel. The initial bend, of course, caused bank erosion, and alternate bars formed because of the migration and deposition of bed materials. However, the size of the bends decreased sharply in the downstream direction, and the channel became straight in the lower part of the flume. Such a channel was considered straight, although a slight increase in thalweg sinuosity did occur (Figure 5-8). Within the straight channel transverse sand bars formed and migrated downstream.

The results of these experiments demonstrate that slopes exist below which a meandering thalweg will not form even though the water has moved through one bend. It had previously been assumed that this type of disturbance, especially the development of secondary flow in bends, should produce a meandering channel. However, at slopes of 0.0026 and greater, a meandering-thalweg channel formed. The channel itself was relatively straight, but a series of alternate bars developed, producing a sinuous thalweg (Figures 5-9a, b, and 5-12).

As the experiments progressed, the sinuosity of the thalweg increased with increased slope (Figure 5-12) until it reached a maximum between slopes of 0.008 and 0.013. At slopes steeper than 0.016, a braided channel developed (Figures 5-9d, and 5-13). The change from meandering-thalweg channel to braided occurred between slopes of 0.013 and 0.016.

The results of this series of experiments are summarized in Figure 5-14. With increasing flume slope at low slopes, the channel remained straight until a threshold was reached that permitted development of a meandering-thalweg (straight channel with alternate bars) channel. Thalweg sinuosity increased to a maximum of 1.25 with increased slope, and then the pattern became braided. This is, of course, only a part of the story, and other factors must be considered to explain the reaction of the channel to changed laboratory conditions. For example, it was noted earlier that, to maintain a stable channel (nonscouring, nonaggrading channel), the rate of sand feed was increased as slope increased. In Figure 5-15 the relation between slope of the model channel and sediment load is displayed. As slope was increased, the rate at which sediment moved thorugh the channel also increased. Further, the changes in rate of increase of sediment load coincide with the changes of channel

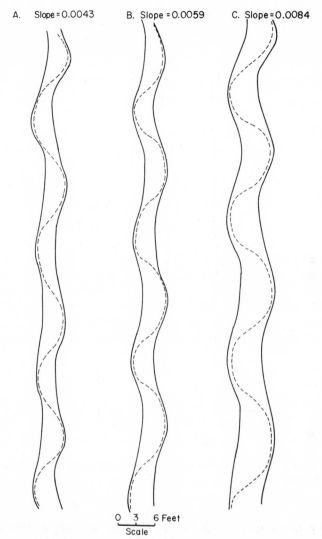

A. Slope = 0.0043   B. Slope = 0.0059   C. Slope = 0.0084

0   3   6 Feet
Scale

Figure 5-12   Meandering-thalweg channels. Solid lines show boundaries of bank-full channels. Dashed line is thalweg. Note that, in spite of thalweg sinuosity of 1.25 for channel C, a
straight line can be drawn down the center of the channel without touching either bank. (From
Schumm and Khan, 1973.)

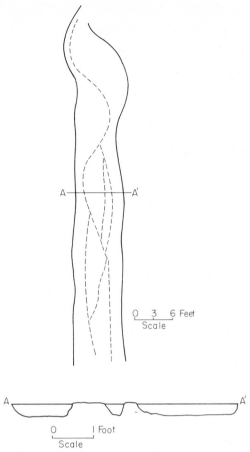

Figure 5-13   Braided channel. Dashed lines indicate positions of multiple thalwegs. (From Schumm and Khan, 1973.)

pattern. From the geologic point of view, an increase of sediment load causes an increase in slope, and this is why Figure 5-15 is plotted with slope on the ordinate. Accompanying the change of slope are major changes in channel pattern, channel cross-sectional geometry, and the hydraulics of flow in the channels.

For example, the relation between sinuosity and stream power resembles that between sinuosity and slope (Figure 5-16). Stream power, as defined by Bagnold (1966, p. 15), is the rate of work done by the fluid or the rate of energy loss per unit length of stream. It is expressed per unit width of channel as the product of tractive force (τ) and velocity (V):

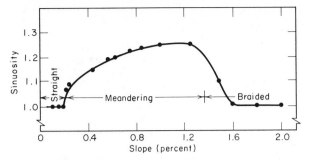

Figure 5-14   Relation between channel sinuosity and flume slope. (From Schumm and Khan, 1973.)

$$\omega = \tau V$$

Tractive force is the product of hydraulic radius and slope, and the specific weight of the fluid as follows:

$$\tau = \gamma RS$$

According to the Chezy equation, velocity is related to the depth–slope product as follows:

$$V = C \sqrt{RS}$$

Therefore, stream power is proportional to the cube of velocity. Colby (1964) has concluded that sediment transport is closely related to velocity cubed, and Yang (1972) shows that sediment transport is a function of stream power. It appears that for a given bed and bank material and discharge there is a lower threshold of stream power below which the flow is not capable of eroding the banks, and cross-channel currents are incapable of moving bed sediment to form alternate bars. There is an upper threshold of stream power, above which velocity and Froude Number are high. Bank erosion is vigorous, and a wide braided channel forms with little influence of cross-channel currents. In the zone between the upper and lower thresholds meandering occurs. The banks erode but they have sufficient resistance to preserve the sinuous pattern and cross-channel currents form alternate bars which develop into point bars.

Therefore, depending on the locations of a channel in Figure 5-16, a slight increase or decrease of stream power (velocity) can significantly alter sinuosity if the river plots near a pattern threshold. This means that

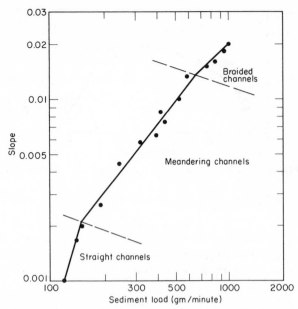

Figure 5-15   Relation between sediment load and flume slope showing increased rate of sediment transport at thresholds of pattern change. (From Schumm and Khan, 1973.)

pattern can be altered, perhaps significantly, by a change of discharge, channel roughness, or any other factor that influences velocity.

The experiments demonstrate that extrinsic threshold values of stream power, velocity or sediment load exist above which river patterns are significantly altered. Additional experiments have shown that at higher discharges, the thresholds are achieved at lower slopes (Edgar,

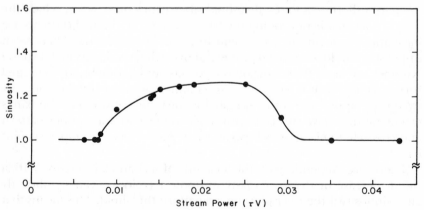

Figure 5-16   Relation between sinuosity and stream power. (Data from Khan, 1971.)

1973). As noted, threshold values of slope at a given discharge have been recognized by Lane (1957), Leopold and Wolman (1957), and Ackers and Charlton (1971), and their relations are shown on Figure 5-11. It is very difficult to attempt to extrapolate from the experimental study to natural river systems, but the curves of Lane and Ackers and Charlton fit the experimental data reasonably well, although the Leopold-Wolman relation does not, perhaps because they use bank-full rather than mean discharge. Also, slope, as used here, is slope of the initial channel or the sand surface on which the model channel developed, and it is analogous to valley slope (Sv) rather than to channel (Sc) gradient.

UNSTABLE CHANNELS

In an earlier section of this chapter the major effects of climate and tectonics on river stability are discussed. Before we proceed to a discussion of progressive changes of river morphology, which involves channel enlargement and gradient or pattern changes of significant magnitude, the topic of the relative instability of stable channels requires consideration. Again, the time span considered is important because bank erosion and river meander cutoff represent instability during a few years, but during 1000 years these processes are part of normal river behavior.

Frequently environmentalists, river engineers, and others involved in navigation and flood control consider that a river should be unchanging in shape, dimensions, and pattern. This would be very convenient. However, an alluvial river generally is continually changing its position as a consequence of hydraulic forces acting on its bed and banks, and this was always the case during the experiments just described. The changes may be slow or rapid, but it is the rule rather than the exception that banks will erode, sediments will be deposited, and floodplains, islands, chutes, and side channels will undergo modification with time. Therefore, the statistically significant empirical relations presented earlier should not lead the reader to believe that the river is static, nor, of course, should an eroding bend or local bank erosion necessarily be considered instability.

Meanders swing or shift across the valley, and the entire pattern may sweep downstream, resulting in complete reworking of floodplain alluvium. The rate at which a single bend migrates or grows depends on its shape (Hickin and Nansen, 1975) and bank stability (Daniel, 1971). Hickin (1974) shows for at least one river that meander growth at first is essentially normal to the axis of the channel, but as the amplitude of the bend increases, downstream shift of the meander becomes increasingly important.

Archaeologists have provided clear evidence that the lateral shift of channels is completely natural and to be expected. For example, the number of archaeological sites on floodplains decreases significantly with age, simply because, as floodplains are modified by river migration, the earliest sites have the greatest probability of being destroyed (Bareis, 1964; Philips et al., 1951). Lathrop (1968), working on the Rio Ucayali in the Amazon headwaters of Peru, concludes that on the average a meander loop forms and cuts off in 500 years. These loops have an amplitude of from 2 to 6 miles and an average rate of meander growth of approximately 400 feet per year.

Although the dynamic behavior of perennial streams is impressive, the modification of rivers in arid and semiarid regions and especially of ephemeral-stream channels is startling. A study of floodplain vegetation and the distribution of trees in different age groups led Everitt (1968) to conclude that about half of the Little Missouri River floodplain in western North Dakota was reworked in 69 years.

Another study shows that about one-third of the floodplain of the Missouri River, over the 170-mile reach between Glasgow and St. Charles, Missouri, was reworked by the river between 1879 and 1930 (Schmudde, 1963). On the lower Mississippi River, bend migration was on the order of 2 feet per year, whereas in the central and upper parts of the river below Cairo it was at times 1000 feet per year (Kolb, 1963). On the other hand, the meander loop pattern of the lower Ohio River has been altered very little during the past 1000 years (Alexander and Nunnally, 1972). Obviously the rate at which meanders move depends not only on the forces exerted on the banks, but also on bank resistance.

In summary, archaeological, botanical, geological, and geomorphic evidence supports the conclusion that most rivers are subject to constant changes as a normal part of their morphologic evolution. Nevertheless, these normal changes should not deter one from distinguishing between stable and unstable channels, the latter being those that are adjusting dimension, gradient pattern, and shape rapidly and progressively to changed conditions.

Bed Forms. Dramatic short-term morphologic changes also occur within the channel itself, as bed form and channel roughness change during floods. Experimental work (Figure 5-17) has shown that, as velocity of flow increases in a sand bed channel, the bed surface will successively show ripples, dunes, plane bed, antidunes, and chutes, and pools (Simons and Richardson, 1966). A large variation in resistance to flow occurs with these changes. The resistance to flow in rivers is, among other things, a function of the regime of flow and type of bed roughness generated by the interaction between the channel boundary and the

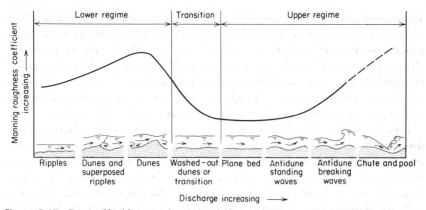

Figure 5-17   Types of bed forms and associated channel roughness. (From D. B. Simons, M. A. Stevens, and J. H. Duke, Jr., 1973, Predicting stages on sandbed rivers: J. Waterways, Harbors, Coastal Eng. Div. Am. Soc. Civil Eng., v. 99, pp. 231–243.)

water. Figure 5-17 shows the regimes of flow, the forms of bed roughness, and the resistance to flow common to sand-bed rivers. Manning's roughness coefficient (*n*) may vary from 0.01 in a sand-bed river in the lower limit of upper regime flow, to 0.04 with dunes and rough banks in the lower regime range.

Such changes in resistance to flow and, consequently, velocity are very common in alluvial channels. In fact, many rivers change from a low-flow regime condition characterized by high resistance to flow and low velocity at a low stage of discharge to an upper regime condition at high discharge, which is characterized by low resistance and higher velocity. These changes produce a more efficient channel that may actually decrease the water stage or flood peak at the highest discharge (Simons and Richardson, 1966). This effect of changing bed forms may also introduce some of the variability into the relations between discharge and channel dimensions (equations 5-2 and 5-3).

Channel Adjustment

The engineer is well aware of the type of channel response that results from his efforts to control river behavior, and engineering literature is replete with descriptions of local, but rapid, channel response to man's influence. The geologist, on the other hand, recognizes, in alluvial deposits and river terraces, evidence of long-term adjustment of entire river systems to the effects of change of climate, of mountain-building processes, and of sea-level fluctuations.

The equations developed for stable alluvial channels and reviewed above demonstrate that for most changes of hydrologic regimen, which involve both a change in discharge and type of sediment load, many aspects of channel morphology will adjust. In addition, the reaction of a channel to altered discharge and type of load may result in changes of channel dimensions contrary to those indicated by the standard regime equations. That is, it is conceivable that under certain circumstances with a decrease of discharge, depth will decrease and width will increase.

Equations 5-6, 5-8, 5-9, 5-14, 5-17, and 5-19 provide a basis for the discussion of natural and man-induced changes of river morphology, and an attempt is made here to discuss river adjustment within the framework of these equations. First, however, it should be reemphasized that they result from an analysis of stable alluvial rivers that transport only small quantities of gravel and that are, for the most part, located in subhumid and semiarid regions. Although the equations can be expected to have a wider application, the parameters are expected to change as more data from a wider range of geologic and hydrologic conditions are accumulated. Therefore, the following treatment stresses directions of change rather than magnitude.

Equations 5-2, 5-3, 5-8, 5-9, and 5-16 to 5-18 indicate that channel width (b), depth (d), and meander wavelength (λ) are directly related to discharge (Q), whereas equations 5-14 and 5-15 demonstrate that gradient (S) is inversely related to discharge. From these equations the following generalized relation is obtained:

$$Q \simeq \frac{b, d, \lambda}{S} \qquad (5\text{-}20)$$

Either mean annual discharge (Qm) or mean annual flood (Qma) could be used in this and subsequent equations. Considerable independent information is available to demonstrate that the relations expressed by equation 5-20 are valid. However, the effects of flood peaks, as discussed earlier, are not included in these relations, but they may well have the same influence as Qm and Qma.

Equations 5-8, 5-15, 5-17, and 5-18 demonstrate that channel width, meander wavelength, and gradient are inversely related to the type of sediment load (M), whereas Equations 5-9 and 5-19 indicate a direct relationship among channel depth, sinuosity (P), and type of sediment load (M). The percentage of silt–clay in the perimeter of a stable channel reflects the nature of the sediment load moving through that channel, which can be expressed as the percentage of total load that is bed load (Q_b); however, for one channel or for channels of similar average discharge, M probably will vary inversely with the quantity of bed load that moves through the channel (Equation 5-7). Therefore, $1/Q_s$ can be substituted for M in these equations if discharge is constant. From this substitution the following generalized relation is developed:

$$Q_s \simeq \frac{b, \lambda, S}{d, P} \tag{5-21}$$

Width/depth ratio, F is not included in Equation 5-21 although it is highly dependent on M or Q_s because both width and depth appear separately in the equation. Nevertheless, the relation between width/depth ratio and M (Equation 5-6) is useful for interpreting changes of channel width and depth in subsequent relations.

To discuss in more detail the effects of changing discharge and sediment load on channel morphology, a plus or minus exponent is used to indicate how, with an increase of discharge or bed load, the various aspects of channel morphology change. For the relatively straightforward cases of an increase or decrease in discharge or bed load alone, Equations 5-22 through 5-25 are obtained.

$$Q^+ \simeq b^+, d^+, \lambda^+, S^- \tag{5-22}$$

$$Q^- \simeq b^-, d^-, \lambda^-, S^+ \tag{5-23}$$

$$Q_s{}^+ \simeq b^+, d^-, \lambda^+, S^+, P^- \tag{5-24}$$

$$Q_s{}^- \simeq b^-, d^+, \lambda^-, S^-, P^+ \tag{5-25}$$

An increase or decrease in discharge alone could be caused by diversion of water into or out of a river system or climate change. An increase of Q_s can result from increased erosion in the catchment area, which can be induced by deforestation or by an increase in the area under cultivation, climate change, or uplift. A decrease of Q_s can result from improved land use, a program of soil conservation, or climate change (Figure 3-1).

An increase or decrease in discharge changes the dimensions of the channel and its gradient, but an increase or decrease in bed load at constant mean annual discharge changes not only channel dimensions, but also gradient width/depth ratio and sinuosity.

In nature, however, rarely does a change in discharge or sediment load occur alone. Generally, any change in discharge is accompanied by a change in the type of sediment load and vice versa. Under these circumstances, it should no longer be assumed that M, which can have the same value for both very large and very small streams, is related to the reciprocal of Q_s, because discharge is changing. However, changes of average discharge (Q) in a river are always considerably less than the order of magnitude differences of discharge between large and small rivers. Hence, it is probable that M can be an index of both type of sediment load (Q_b) and quantity of bed load (Q_s) in a river subject to moderate changes of average discharge.

Using the plus or minus exponents to indicate an increase or decrease in a variable, four combinations of changing discharge and sediment load can be considered. Consider for example, the case where both discharge and bed load increase, perhaps as a result of diversion of water from a bed-load channel into a suspended-load channel. Equation 5-26 suggests the nature of the resulting channel changes.

$$Q^+ Q_s^+ \simeq b^+, d^\pm, \lambda^+, S^\pm, P^-, F^+. \qquad (5\text{-}26)$$

Equation 5-19 indicates that, with an increase of both discharge and bed load, width, meander wavelength, and width/depth ratio should increase and sinuosity decrease. The influences of increasing discharge and of bed load on channel depth and gradient are in opposite directions, and it is not clear in what manner gradient and depth should change. However, by including width/depth ratio (F) in Equation 5-26 an estimate of the direction of change of depth can be obtained. Width/depth ratio is predominantly influenced by type of load (Equation 5-6) and therefore increases in Equation 5-26. This suggests that depth will remain constant or decrease, because both width and width/depth ratio increase. Channel gradient will probably increase because sinuosity decreases, thereby straightening the channel and increasing its slope.

When both Q_s and Q decrease, for example, as a result of dam construction, the reverse of Equation 5-26 pertains:

$$Q^- Q_s^- \simeq b^-, d^\pm, \lambda^-, S^\pm, P^+, F^- \qquad (5\text{-}27)$$

When, as common in nature, the changes in Q and Q_s are in opposite directions, the following relations are obtained:

$$Q^+ Q_s^- \simeq b^\pm, d^+, \lambda^\pm, S^-, P^+, F^- \qquad (5\text{-}28)$$

$$Q^- Q_s^+ \simeq b^\pm, d^-, \lambda^\pm, S^+, P^-, F^+ \qquad (5\text{-}29)$$

The situation expressed in Equation 5-28 could result from a combination of controls, for example, dam construction with impoundment of sediment and diversion of water into the channel from another source. The situation expressed by Equation 5-29 could result from increased water and land use, thereby decreasing discharge and increasing bed load; both could result from climate change (Figures 2-5 and 3-1).

Equation 5-29 shows that with an increase in discharge but a decrease in bed load, the channel depth and sinuosity will increase while gradient and width/depth ratio will decrease. With an increase in depth and a decrease in width/depth ratio, channel width will probably decrease. Meander wavelength will remain unchanged or will either increase or decrease, depending on the magnitude of the changes of discharge and load. However, as sinuosity increases, it seems likely that meander wavelength would decrease.

The above relations demonstrate qualitatively how channel metamorphosis occurs with changes of discharge and sediment load. The magnitude of the changes of channel characteristics can be estimated through the use of Equations 5-6, 5-8, 5-9, 5-15, and 5-17 to 5-19 if the magnitudes of the changes of discharge and bed load or channel silt–clay content are known.

The significantly different channel dimensions, shapes, and patterns associated with different quantities of discharge and bed load indicate that, as these independent variables change, major adjustments of channel morphology can be anticipated. When changes of channel width and depth, as well as of sinuosity and meander wavelength, are required to compensate for a hydrologic change, then a long period of channel instability can be anticipated, with considerable bank erosion and lateral shifting of the channel occurring before stability is restored. In addition, the simple scheme of erosion or deposition with climate change (Table 5-2) needs to be reconsidered with regard to the adjustment of other variables (Equations 5-20 through 5-25).

Horizontal Instability

Horizontal instability of a river may take two forms, avulsion and pattern change, avulsion being the shift of the channel from one part of the valley to another by development of a new course. Pattern change can be due to cutoffs that reduce channel sinuosity or to the growth of meanders.

Avulsion is discussed with regard to channels in Zone 3 and so only pattern change is described in this chapter.

Pattern Variability.   The same river may have patterns ranging from essentially straight to very meandering and even braided. The variations of pattern between river systems can be explained, as noted above, by differences in the geologic history of the systems and by differences in water discharge and sediment load. However, variations of sinuosity along one river that is presumably transporting constant sediment load at a constant discharge are less readily explained. If an increase of sinuosity is one means by which the gradient of a river is reduced, a serious problem arises. How can a river remain stable with essentially constant water and sediment discharge, if its gradient changes from reach to reach? Such a situation appears to invalidate the well-established regime equations that relate gradient to discharge and sediment load.

The answer appears to be that, in many cases, gradient varies only slightly, but the slope of the valley floor on which the river flows varies significantly. That is, within a valley there are reaches of valley floor that are steeper and gentler than the average gradient. To maintain a relatively constant gradient, the river lengthens its course by meandering on the steeper reaches. Thus, if other causes are eliminated, high sinuosity reaches of a channel should reflect a steeper valley slope and vice versa.

Figure 5-18 shows that the sinuosity of the Mississippi River varies with valley slope in the manner predicted from Figure 5-14. The data used to prepare Figure 5-18 were obtained from the 1911 to 1915 survey of the Mississippi River between Cairo, Illinois, and Head of Passes, Louisiana, a river distance of 1020 miles. This old survey was used because it provided information on the river before artificial cutoffs shortened the river by about 150 miles.

Although the scatter is large, the lowest sinuosity evidently occurs on the gentlest valley slopes (left side of plot), which are characteristic of the lower 200 miles of river. The low values of sinuosity at the steepest valley slopes occur where natural chute cutoffs have developed, and the flow now divides around large islands.

It should be emphasized that the length and sinuosity of meandering rivers change naturally as meander loops are enlarged and then cut off. Thus, along a given reach of a meandering river, sinuosity varies about a mean with time, hence much of the scatter in Figure 5-18. For example, the very low point (slope of 0.009, sinuosity of 1.2) represents a reach

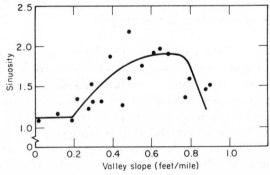

Figure 5-18   Relation between valley slope and sinuosity for the Mississippi River between Cairo, Illinois, and Head of Passes, Louisiana. Data was obtained from 1911 to 1915 surveys before modification of the channel patterns by artificial cutoffs. (From Schumm et al. 1972.)

north of Memphis, Tennessee, where several cutoffs occurred naturally
during the late 19th century.

The highest points represent a reach in which a very large bend is
prevented from cutting off by a bedrock control. Without human interference the sinuosity of very sinuous reaches will decrease because of
cutoffs; the sinuosity of the reach north of Memphis should, however,
increase, as new bends develop and enlarge.

Variations of valley slope can be caused by slight uplift, by depression
or tilting of the valley (Figure 2-7), or by a great difference in the
sediment loads carried by tributaries and the principal channel. For
example, below the junction of the Arkansas River with the Mississippi
River, the valley slope increases significantly because of the relatively
high sediment discharges from the Arkansas River during Pleistocene
time (Figure 5-19).

It is on this steep reach of the valley that the river was most sinuous.
For example, before they were cut off in 1933 and 1935, the Greenville
Bends near Greenville, Mississippi, had a sinuosity of 3.3 (Figure 5-20),
whereas the average sinuosity for the 100 miles between the junction of
the Arkansas River above Greenville and Lake Providence, Louisiana,
downstream was 2.3.

Another example of past influences on valley slope is the course of the
Jordan River between Lake Tiberias and the Dead Sea (Schattner, 1962).
Over much of this course, tributary sediments are deposited along the
flanks of the structural trough occupied by the Jordan River and do not
reach the river. Nevertheless, the influence of these tributaries on the
pattern of the modern river can be noted. Where, during the past,
alluvial fan deposits have been built into the valley, changes of the

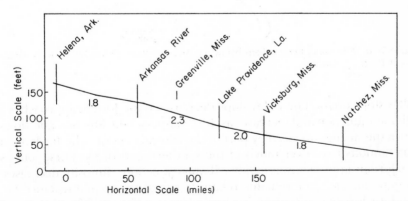

Figure 5–19 Long profile of Mississippi River valley floor, showing change of slope below the
Arkansas River confluence. Numbers below profile are sinuosity of each reach.

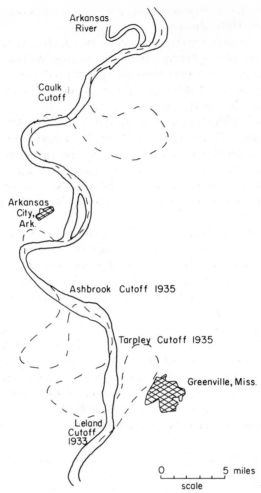

Figure 5-20 Mississippi River pattern below the Arkansas River. Dashed line shows natural precutoff river pattern.

valley slope occur. The valley slope decreases as the Jordan approaches a tributary junction and increases as the river passes the junction and flows down the steeper downvalley part of the alluvial deposit. The Jordan is a very sinuous river over much of the southern part of its course, but as the Jordan approaches a major tributary junction, sinuosity decreases. In general, the river remains relatively straight for some distance beyond the junction and sinuosity then increases. The variations in sinuosity are attributed to changes in valley slope due to tributary influence.

Pattern Instability.   In previous sections the shifting of a channel across a floodplain was considered natural, and a river behaving in such a fashion should not be considered as being unstable. However, scrutiny of maps that show river patterns over an appreciable time reveals that a reach can also change from high sinuosity to low sinuosity, and this would certainly be considered channel instability even if the change was only local.

Obviously, as a channel changes because of meander shift and the cutoff of meanders, the length of the channel changes. Figure 5-21 shows how, through time, the length of the Mississippi River has changed because of delta growth and change of position of the river within its valley, as well as the natural variations of sinuosity related to meander growth and cutoffs. The dramatic shortening of the river after 1929 is the result of artificial cutoffs.

A more detailed consideration of length variations of the Mississippi River (Figure 5-22) reveals considerable fluctuations of length through time. Major decreases of length reflect a change of the river course and the effect of cutoffs, but between these events of drastic shortening, the river length fluctuates about a mean and there appears to be a limiting

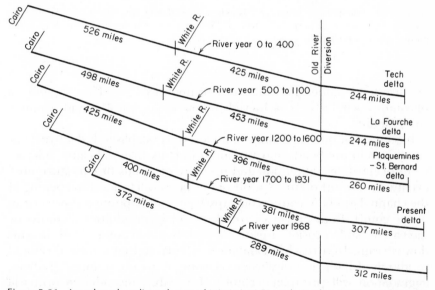

Figure 5-21   Length and gradient change of Mississippi River during last 2000 years between Cairo, Illinois, White River, Old River Diversion (Atchafalaya River), and Gulf of Mexico. Drastic shortening occurred between 1931 and 1968 due to meander cutoffs. (From B. R. Winkley, 1970, Influence of geology on the regimen of a river: Am. Soc. Civil Eng., Nat. Water Resour. Meeting (Memphis) preprint.) 1078, 35 pp.

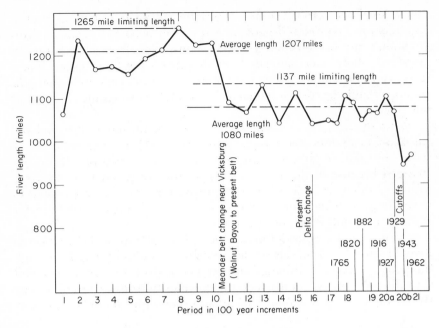

Figure 5-22   Variations in length of Mississippi River during last 2000 years. (From B. R. Winkley, 1970, Influence of geology on the regimen of a river: Am. Soc. Civil Eng., Natl. Water Resour. Meeting (Memphis) preprint 1078, 35 pp.)

or threshold value that the river cannot exceed. This suggests a maximum sinuosity is achieved followed by cutoffs and channel straightening.

It seems that once a meandering pattern is established, the hydraulic conditions in the bends and variations in bank material cause enlargement of meander amplitude and decrease of radius of curvature until eventually a cutoff occurs. Cutoff of one bend will by local steepening of the channel gradient cause scour upstream and deposition downstream of the cutoff. Both processes are likely to trigger additional cutoffs by increased bank erosion upstream and by increasing flood heights downstream. In a reach meanders may enlarge to a critical threshold condition of high sinuosity when, because of greatly reduced gradient, aggradation will precipitate cutoffs. Inevitably, meander growth will lead to a threshold of channel instability, at which point the channel will straighten out. However, this process may involve very different periods of time, depending on water discharge, sediment load, and the nature of the sediments comprising the bank material.

As Fisk (1914) and Winkley (1970) demonstrate, the Mississippi River has been subjected to considerable fluctuations of length and sinuosity through time. This natural variability (Figure 5-22) suggests that for a given river reach perhaps one way to modify the channel is to shift it toward an average sinuosity value. That is, when sinuosity is high, selective cutoffs that return the river to a moderate sinuosity may be beneficial. On the other hand, if the channel is unnaturally straight, the promotion of bend development will reduce gradient and stabilize the channel.

GEOMORPHIC APPROACH TO PATTERN INSTABILITY

A geomorphic approach to channel evaluation and management deserves further consideration. Let us consider the possible change of sinuosity of an idealized river that flows at constant discharge over a highly variable alluvial valley slope (Figure 5-23). At position 1 the channel has just sufficient velocity to move its sediment load, and any further decrease in slope by a sinuosity increase will cause aggradation; therefore, the channel of necessity remains straight. At A the threshold between straight and meandering channels is crossed at a relative slope of 2. The line AA' indicates the sinuosity at which channel gradient is 2,

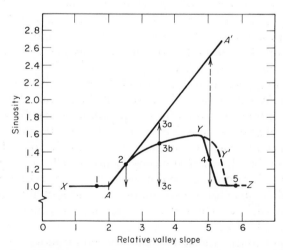

Figure 5-23   Diagram based on Figure 5-14 showing range of sinuosity with relative valley slope. The vertical lines indicate the range of sinuosity possible at a given slope. (From S. A. Schumm and R. M. Beathard, 1976, Geomorphic thresholds: an approach to river management, *in* Rivers 76, v. 1, 3rd Syposium of the Waterways: Harbors and Coastal Engineers Division of the American Society of Civil Engineers, pp. 707–724.)

as sinuosity increases with valley slope. Let us assume that at a valley slope of 2 the channel must be straight in order to transport its sediment load at a gradient of 2. Therefore, at position 2 the maximum sinuosity that can be achieved is 1.25, because at a higher sinuosity the channel gradient is less than 2. At this position sinuosity can range from 1.0 when cutoffs have occurred to 1.25, and the channel could be straightened with little channel response because the increase of gradient would be slight as sinuosity is decreased. At position 3 a maximum sinuosity of 1.7 is possible. Theoretically, it should be possible for sinuosity to achieve this value and still transport the sediment load, but practically it is not possible, as the pattern roughness of the channel increases with increased sinuosity. Therefore, the flow velocity will be decreased (Chow, 1959, p. 109), and maximum sinuosity will be less than that suggested by line AA'. The curve X, Y, Z suggests what may be an optimum sinuosity. Its shape is obviously based on the experimental results (Figure 5-14).

A considerable range of sinuosity is possible at position 3. The channel can be meandering or straight, and depending on sinuosity, the gradient of the channel will be as steep as the valley slope (3.5) when the channel is straight (3c), or gentler (2.0) when channel sinuosity is 1.75 (3a). If the average curve X, Y, Z indicates the optimum sinuosity at a given valley slope, then it is clear that the channel with a sinuosity well above this value probably is unstable, and it will revert by cutoffs toward a sinuosity of about 1.5 (3a to 3b). A straight channel at the same valley slope will develop a sinuous course in order to reduce its gradient (3c to 3b). The channel at position 3c will undoubtedly have a higher sediment load than the channels at 3a and 3b because with its steep gradient it will be eroding its channel and banks.

The river engineer should look carefully at the variations of sinuosity along a river. Where sinuosity is abnormally high, and other factors such as tributary influences and valley slope changes can be eliminated, a program of alignment by selective meander cutoffs may improve the stability of a channel as it is shifted from position 3a to 3b (Figure 5-23). On the other hand, when sinuosity is abnormally low, a shift from position 3c to 3b is beneficial and it probably can be achieved by placing dikes or other structures that induce a sinuosity into the channel. Perhaps this can be achieved by increasing roughness with artificial riffles (Keller, 1975).

At position 4 in the transition zone between meandering and braided, it may be possible to shift the threshold zone to the right ($YY'Z$) by the use of structural controls that can reduce velocity and stream power, thereby forcing a divided flow or a braided channel into the meandering mode. Hence, at position 4 a channel may shift between meandering and braided, depending on discharge and sediment-load variations. At position 5 the valley slope may be too steep and the sediment loads too great for the channel to be anything but straight, and no man-induced controls can be effective in maintaining a sinuous channel at this position in Figure 5-23.

The suggestion made here is that if one can identify the range of patterns along a river, then within that range the most appropriate channel pattern and sinuosity probably can be identified. If so, the engineer can work with the river to produce its most efficient or most stable channel. Obviously, a river can be forced into a straight configuration or it can be made more sinuous, but there is a limit to the changes that can be induced beyond which the channel cannot function without a radical morphologic adjustment as suggested by Figure 5-23. These limits probably can be determined by the use of sediment-transport equations, but in essence the approach to channel control presented here is geomorphic, and it is based on the threshold concept.

Example: Chippewa River, Wisconsin.   In most cases it is difficult to determine if a river is susceptible to the type of treatment discussed in the preceding section. Perhaps the best qualitative guide to river stability is a comparison of the morphology of numerous reaches and the determination of whether or not there has been a change in the position and morphology of the channel during the last few centuries. Another approach might be to determine the position of the river on the Leopold-Wolman (1957) or Lane (1957) gradient-discharge graphs (Figures 5-24 and 5-25). If a braided river plots among the meandering channels or vice versa, it is a likely candidate for change because it is unstable.

An example of the way that this can be done is provided by the Chippewa River of Wisconsin (Schumm and Beathard, 1976), a tributary and major sediment contributor to the upper Mississippi River (Figure 5-26). The Chippewa River rises in northern Wisconsin and flows 220 miles to the Mississippi River, entering it 75 miles below St. Paul. It is the second largest river in Wisconsin and has a drainage basin area of 9480 square miles.

From its confluence with the Mississippi to the town of Durand 16.4 miles up the valley, the Chippewa is a braided river. The main channel is characteristically broad and shallow and contains shifting sand bars. The bank-full width as measured from U. S. Geological Survey topographic maps is 1000 feet. The sinuosity of this reach is very low, being only 1.06. However, in the 42-mile reach from Durand to Eau Claire, the Chippewa River abruptly changes to a meandering configuration with a

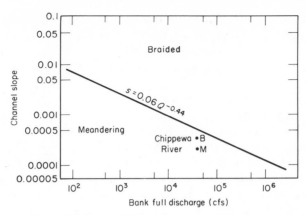

Figure 5-24 Leopold and Wolman's (1957) relation among channel patterns, channel gradient, and bank-full discharge. Letters B and M identify braided and meandering reaches of Chippewa River. (From L. B. Leopold and M. G. Wolman, 1957, River channel patterns: braided, meandering and straights: U. S. Geol. Surv. Prof. Paper 282-B.)

bank-full width of 640 feet and a sinuosity of 1.49. The valley slope and channel gradient are different for each reach of the river. The braided section has a gentler valley slope than the meandering reach upstream, 1.83 feet per mile as opposed to 2.13 feet per mile, contrary to what is expected from Figure 5-23, but the situation is reversed for channel slope; the braided reach has a channel gradient of 1.76 feet per mile, whereas the meandering reach has a gradient of 1.47 feet per mile.

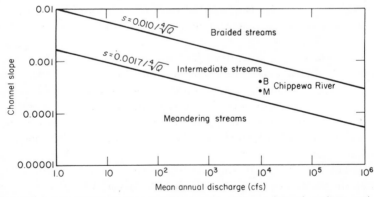

Figure 5-25 Lane's (1957) relation among channel patterns, channel gradient, and mean discharge. The regression lines were fitted to data from streams that Lane classified as highly meandering and braided. Between the two parallel lines are located streams of intermediate character ranging from meandering to braided. Letters B and M identify position of the braided and meandering reaches of the Chippewa River. (From E. W. Lane, 1957, A study of the shape of channels formed by natural streams flowing in erodible material: M. R. D. Sediment Series No. 9, U. S. Army Engineer, Division, Missouri River, Corps Engineers, Omaha, Nebraska.)

The median size of bed material upstream of Durand is coarser than 2 mm. The riverbed is bedrock controlled in several places and is composed almost entirely of coarse granules to cobble-size material. The coarse size of the bed material is attributed to armoring. Downstream of Durand, the riverbed is sand; median grain size is 0.53 mm.

There is no evidence to suggest that the Chippewa River is either progressively eroding or aggrading its channel at present. In fact, the river below Durand has remained braided during historic time. It has maintained its channel position and its pattern, but a significant narrowing as the result of the attachment of islands and the filling of chute channels has occurred near Durand, and this has resulted in a recent decrease in channel width of over 40 percent. The only other change in the lower river is a noticeable growth of its delta into the Mississippi Valley.

The relations described by Leopold and Wolman (1957) and Lane (1957) provide a means of evaluating the relative stability of the modern channel patterns of the Chippewa River. The bank-full discharge is plotted against channel slope in Figure 5-24 for both the braided and the meandering reaches of the Chippewa. The value used for the bank-full discharge is 53,082 cfs, which is the flood discharge having a return period of 2.33 years. The braided reach plots higher than the meandering reach, but both are well within the meandering zone, as defined by Leopold and Wolman. This suggests that the braided reach is anomalous; that is, according to this relation the lower Chippewa would be expected to display a meandering pattern rather than a braided one. Even when the 25-year flood of 98,416 cfs is used, the braided reach still plots within the meandering region of Figure 5-24.

When the Chippewa data are plotted on Lane's graph (Figure 5-25), the same relation exists. The Chippewa falls into the intermediate region, but within the range of scatter about the regression line for meandering streams. Again the braided reach is seen to be anomalous because it should plot much closer to or above the braided stream regression line. The position of the braided reach as plotted in both figures indicates that this reach should be meandering.

This conclusion requires an explanation that can be based on the geomorphic history of the Chippewa River. For example, we have not yet mentioned another significant morphologic feature on the Chippewa River floodplain, that is, Buffalo Slough, which occupies the southeastern edge of the floodplain (Figure 5-26). It is a sinuous remnant of the Chippewa River that was abandoned, and it is evidence of a major channel change in the Chippewa River valley.

In this survey of the upper Mississippi River, G. K. Warren (1867) included a description of the Chippewa River valley. His map and text

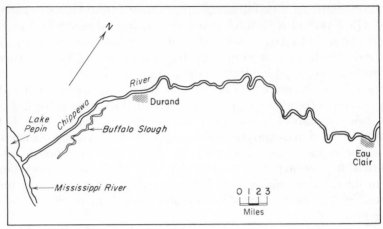

Figure 5-26   Index map of the lower Chippewa River between Eau Claire, Wisconsin, and Mississippi River.

disclose that Buffalo Slough was open and carrying flow in 1867. Flow through Buffalo Slough has decreased during historic time, and indeed flow was completely eliminated in 1876, then the upstream end of Buffalo Slough was permanently blocked. The abandonment of the former Buffalo Slough channel by the Chippewa River is the result of an avulsion, but one that took many years to complete. The channel shifted from Buffalo Slough to a straighter, steeper course along the northwestern edge of the floodplain. This more efficient route gradually captured more and more of the total discharge. The new Chippewa channel produced a divided flow or braided configuration as a result of a higher flow velocity and the resulting bank erosion. As the new channel grew, the old course deteriorated, and eventually its discharge was so reduced that the Mississippi was able to effectively dam the old channel mouth with natural levees and plug its outlet.

The sinuosity of Buffalo Slough is approximately 1.28. Although sinuosity is usually defined as the ratio of stream length to valley length, it is also the ratio of valley slope to channel slope. A sinuosity of 1.28 is therefore the ratio of the present valley slope, 1.83 feet per mile, to a channel slope of about 1.43 feet per mile. This channel slope value is very similar to the channel slope of the meandering reach upstream of Durand (1.47 feet per mile); therefore, the meandering pattern of the Buffalo Slough channel was appropriate. Although delta construction was responsible for the lower valley slope of the lower Chippewa River valley, the Buffalo Slough channel had a gradient that was not appreciably different from that in the upstream reach. Channel sinuosity decreased from 1.49 to 1.28 in a downstream direction, thereby maintaining a channel gradient of about 1.45 feet per mile.

This sinuous channel could not have transported the large amounts of sediment that the present braided channel carries to the Mississippi River, or it too would have followed a straight braided course. Therefore, the present sediment load carried by the Chippewa River is greater than that conveyed by the Buffalo Slough channel, but this is due almost entirely to the formation of the new straight, steep, braided channel, which is 400 feet wider than the old sinuous Buffalo Slough channel. It appears that the lower Chippewa has not been able to adjust as yet to its new position and steeper gradient, and the resulting bed and bank erosion has supplied large amounts of sediment to the Mississippi. The normal configuration of the lower Chippewa is sinuous, and if it could be induced to assume such a pattern the high sediment delivery from the Chippewa could be controlled. An appropriate means of channel stabilization and sediment-load reduction in this case is the development of a sinuous channel.

The suggestions made here are that if one can identify the range of patterns of a river, within that range a most appropriate channel pattern may be identified. If so, man can work with the river to produce a more efficient or a more stable channel. A river in most cases can be straightened or made more sinuous, but there is a limit beyond which the channel becomes unstable and aggradation and blockage of the channel or severe scour and bank erosion result. For example, artificial cutoffs between the Arkansas River junction and Greenville, Mississippi have now reduced the sinuosity of the Mississippi River in that reach from about 3.0 to about 1.4. This means that the river gradient has been more than doubled in this reach. The result is that the river is tending towards a braided pattern, and an extensive bank stabilization program is required to maintain the channel in this unnatural alignment. The river control engineer can be criticized for causing such a drastic change in river character. Nevertheless, the Greenville Bends (Figure 5-20) would not have persisted and, in fact, eventually they would have cut off naturally.

Vertical Instability

In addition to the pattern changes or horizontal instability discussed in the last section, the scour and fill of channels or vertical instability also produces major channel-control problems and leaves a complex record for stratigraphic and sedimentologic interpretation.

Agar (1973, p. 59) concludes that most terrestrial sedimentation is lateral rather than vertical. For example, even in stream channels the vertical deposition at a cross section may be the result of backfilling of the channel in an upstream direction. Two types of fluvial deposition result from two different controls: an upstream control related to high sediment production from the source area and a downstream control related to baselevel change. For example, progressive upvalley deposition or backfilling of a channel will occur above a dam, or whenever baselevel is raised. High sediment production will overload a channel and in this case aggradation will progressively extend downvalley (Bhamidipaty and Shen, 1971) by a process that can be referred to as downfilling.

High sediment loads can also cause local deposition or plugging of a channel with subsequent backfilling upstream, and, in fact, this seems to be the dominant process in semiarid and arid regions. The local baselevel control caused by deposition in the channel diverts the flow, gradient is reduced locally, and deposition moves progressively upstream. There can be several sites of deposition of this type in a large valley, and the local backfilling above each would eventually produce a continuous surface of deposition.

During a study of deposition of ephemeral-stream channels in the western United States it was concluded that the nature of the sediment moved through and deposited in the channel strongly influenced the processes of deposition and the nature of channel erosion (Schumm, 1961). For example, in sediments containing a large percentage of silt and clay, erosion, which was primarily by vertical incision, produced a deep, narrow trench, whereas in sandy sediments bank erosion and channel widening took place. The major difference was the change from incision to lateral erosion.

Field observations of actively aggrading channels of ephemeral streams formed the basis for the preparation of Figure 5-27. In the figure generalized cross sections of filled channels are presented. The channels shown in the figure were not observed in cross section; nevertheless, the downstream changes in channel shape and sediment character in the backfilling channels gave a good indication of the probable appearance of the channels in section. Differences in stratification appear to be related to differences in the type of sediment produced in the study areas. The following discussion of active channel aggradation, as studied in four areas in which channel deposition was typical of that sketched in Figure 5-27, explains the differences in channel-fill stratification.

In the Sage Creek, South Dakota, channel (Figure 5-27a) the percent-

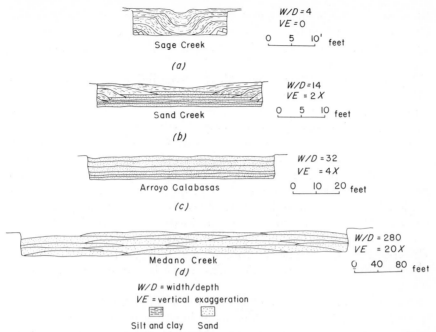

Figure 5-27   Channel-fill deposits in ephemeral-stream channels. (From Schumm, 1960.)

age of silt–clay at the stable cross sections (*M*) was about 67, as Sage Creek drained an area of siltstone and claystone. Deposition occurred initially around slump blocks that had fallen into the channel, for the highly cohesive sediment was not immediately swept away because of its resistance to disintegration. As deposition continued, it was greatest on the channel sides, causing narrowing of the channel.

In the Sand Creek, Nebraska, area (Figure 5-27*b*) the percentage of silt–clay at the stable channel sections was 20, reflecting the sandy nature of the shales exposed in the drainage area. As deposition began, the sand was deposited in essentially horizontal layers on the floor of the channel, and as this coarser material was deposited, the percentage of silt–clay increased downstream. The amount of finer sediment in the channel increased in a downstream direction and lateral deposition became important as the channel filled. The two types of deposition continued contemporaneously, fines on the banks and coarser sediments on the floor of the channel, but in the later stages of filling all the deposited material was silt–clay. Horizontally stratified sands were restricted to the lower part of the fill and progressively toward the center near the top of the fill (Figure 5-27*b*). This deposition produces a fining-upward sequence that is the result of sediment sorting in the channel. As backfilling occurs, the coarser sediments are deposited further upstream during each flood event. The result is a deposit of the type shown in Figure 5-28.

In the Arroyo Calabasas, New Mexico, channel, which drains an area of coarse Tertiary alluvium, channel silt–clay was less than 10 percent. The channel filled from bottom to top (Figure 5-27c) and stratification was relatively horizontal. The Medano Creek, Colorado, channel is 600 feet wide and it receives an abundant supply of aeolian sand from the Great Sand Dunes. Convex surfaces of deposition were noted in this wide sandy channel (Figure 5-27d). During the study the water was flowing over a width of 100 to 150 feet on a part of the channel cross section lying at an altitude several feet above the lowest part of the channel. In wide sandy channels or on floodplains where water loss into the fill is great, that part of the channel on which water is flowing may be raised by deposition. The resulting fill may appear in section as a series of overlapping convexities unless planed flat by subsequent high flood flows.

The generalized cross sections presented in Figure 5-27 are supported to some extent by observations made in other studies. For example, summarizing the literature on the subject, Shrock (1948, p. 223) states that in small shale-filled channels, the shale laminae sag slightly in the axial part and rise gently toward the sides of the channel. This type of deposit resembles that of Sage Creek channel (Figure 5-27a). Studies in estuaries of the French Coast reveal that the fine fractions of sediment are deposited on the banks of the channels, whereas the sand is deposited on the floor of the channel (Bourcart, 1947). In addition, Denson's (1956, p. 701) studies of uranium deposits led him to attribute the rise of the contact between the Shinarump member of the Chinle formation and the overlying shale of the Chinle, above the axis of a paleochannel,

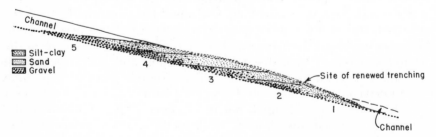

Figure 5-28 Longitudinal section through alluvial deposit formed by backfilling, showing development of graded bedding due to upstream shift of depositional units.

to a compaction of finer-grained sediments deposited along the flanks of the channel. This may be similar to deposition in the Sand Creek channel (Figure 5-27).

In summary, the type of stratification exposed in a channel-fill deposit may be dependent, to a large extent, on sediment character. Fine-grained cohesive sediments tend to adhere to the channel banks, forming concave stratification. Noncohesive sediments are deposited directly on the channel floor, causing horizontal stratification in the fill. Even convex stratification can be formed by a stream occupying only a part of a very wide sandy channel as it builds up its bed.

Actually, the channel-fill deposits are only a part of the fluvial sedimentary complex. During and after a channel has been filled, sediment-laden water spreads over the floodplain to form a variety of deposits; these are considered in the next chapter.

CLASSIFICATION

To focus attention on the most important factors that determine river morphology, and to summarize the previous material, a classification of channels may be useful. All rivers may be separated into two major groups depending on their freedom to adjust their shape and gradient. Bedrock-controlled channels are those so confined between outcrops of rock that the material forming their bed and banks determines the morphology of the channel. Alluvial channels, on the other hand, are free to adjust dimensions, shape, pattern, and gradient in response to change, and they flow through a channel with bed and banks composed of the material transported by the river under present flow conditions.

Rivers have been classified, according to their stage of development in the erosion cycle, as youthful, mature, and old (Davis, 1899), and also, according to the history of their development on a land surface, as antecedent, superposed, consequent, and subsequent (Thornbury, 1969, p. 113). However, none of these classifications considers the two independent variables, discharge and type of sediment load, on which the morphology of alluvial channels depends.

As demonstrated, discharge is an independent variable that largely determines the size of stream channels and the amplitude and wavelength of meanders. Discharge, however, is not a valid basis for a classification of stream channels unless size is considered most important, although a qualitative distinction among stream channels can be made on the basis of discharge characteristics (i.e., ephemeral and perennial streams).

The other independent variable that must be considered is sediment load. Channels are frequently referred to as muddy or sandy, or as cobble or boulder channels. This implies that size of material in and transported through the channel may be a prime consideration. It is true that in a downstream direction many river characteristics appear to change as grain size changes (Nevins, 1965), but there can be great changes in the morphology of a stream when the median grain size of bed material is essentially constant. For this reason classification is based on the nature of the sediment load or the predominant mode of sediment transport. Type of load and mode of transport are simplified here to mean the transportation of sediment as either suspended load or bed load.

Recall that the term bed load as used is synonymous with the term bed-material load, and the term suspended load as used is synonymous with the term wash load. In the channels of the Great Plains rivers, bed-material load is usually composed of sand, whereas wash load is composed of silt and clay. Although a single grain size, which would form the boundary between suspended load and bed load, cannot be selected from available sediment transport data, it is suggested that, in general, silt and clay are transported in suspension and that sand and coarser sediment are transported on or near the streambed.

On the basis of the relations discussed previously, alluvial river channels can be classified primarily according to the type of sediment load as bed-load, mixed-load, and suspended-load channels. Actually, a continuous series of channels exists, and within this classification braided, meandering, and straight channels can be recognized.

In addition to the three classes of river channels there are two major types of river systems. These may be referred to as single-channel and multiple-channel rivers (Figure 5-29). Within the single-channel category, straight channels are bed-load channels, whereas the meandering channels are mixed- or suspended-load channels. Both types have been recognized in sedimentary deposits (Moody-Stuart, 1966). Exceptions to this generalization do occur, however, because, as noted before, where valley gradient is very low, even a suspended-load channel can be straight. Braided channels are single-channel, bed-load rivers that, at low water, have islands of sediment or relatively permanent vegetated islands exposed in the channels (Doeglas, 1962). Any single channel can be part of a multiple-channel system, and, in fact, most river channels are part of a dendritic drainage pattern. However, the multiple-channel rivers considered here are those that are flowing on an alluvial surface and are distributary systems. Of the several types of multiple-channel systems, delta distributary systems have been recognized (Busch, 1959),

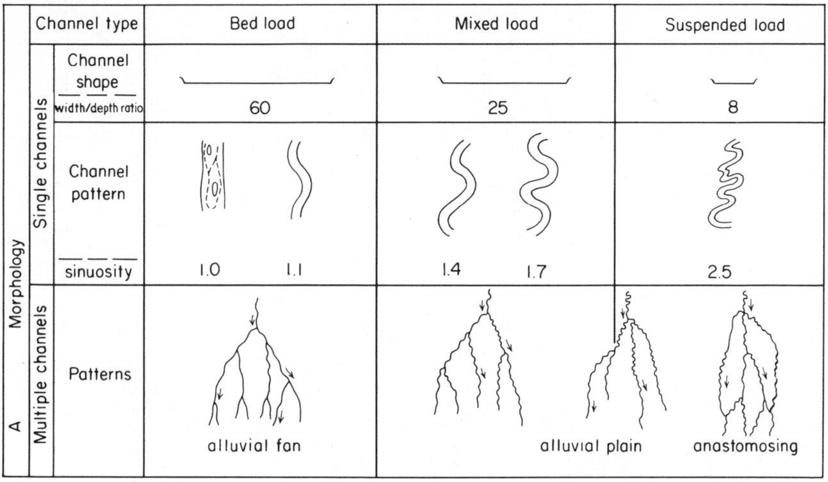

	Channel type	Bed load	Mixed load	Suspended load
Morphology / Single channels	Channel shape ⌣ / width/depth ratio	60	25	8
	Channel pattern			
	sinuosity	1.0 1.1	1.4 1.7	2.5
Multiple channels	Patterns	alluvial fan	alluvial plain	anastomosing

Figure 5-29   Types of river channels. (From Schumm, 1968.)

as have alluvial-plain and alluvial-fan systems of channels (Craig et al., 1955). Alluvial-fan distributaries will probably always be of the bed-load type, whereas alluvial-plain distributaries and delta distributaries, depending on the type of sediment moved through the channels, can be composed of any of the three channel types. The anastomosing-channel systems, however, will probably be composed primarily of suspended-load channels.

Based on the nature of unstable channel behavior during erosion and deposition as discussed earlier, a second major division of alluvial channels can be made (Table 5-4). The differences can be thought of with respect to the total sediment load delivered to the channel. An excess of total load causes deposition, a deficiency causes erosion, and between the extremes lies the stable channel. Although a given river channel often cannot be clearly identified in the field as stable, eroding, or depositing, it is possible to think of all rivers as falling into one of these three classes.

The stable channel is one that shows no progressive change in gradient, dimensions, or shape. Temporary changes occur during floods, but the stable channel, if the classification were not restricted to short segments of the river, would be identical to the graded stream as defined by Mackin (1948).

The eroding channel is one that is being progressively degraded and/or widened by bank erosion. Conversely, the depositing channel is one that is being aggraded and/or having sediment deposited on its banks. Classification of river channels on the basis of stability as eroding,

TABLE 5-4. CLASSIFICATION OF ALLUVIAL CHANNELS

Mode of sediment transport and type of channel	Channel sediment (M) (percent)	Bedload (percentage of total load)	Channel stability		
			Stable (graded stream)	Depositing (excess load)	Eroding (deficiency of load)
Suspended load	>20	<3	Stable suspended-load channel. Width/depth ratio <10; sinuosity usually >2.0; gradient, relatively gentle	Depositing suspended load channel. Major deposition on banks cause narrowing of channel; initial streambed deposition minor	Eroding suspended-load channel. Streambed erosion predominant; initial channel widening minor
Mixed load	5–20	3–11	Stable mixed-load channel. Width/depth ratio >10, <40; sinuosity usually <2.0, >1.3; gradient, moderate	Depositing mixed-load channel. Initial major deposition on banks followed by streambed deposition	Eroding mixed-load channel. Initial streambed erosion followed by channel widening
Bed load	<5	>11	Stable bed-load channel. Width/depth ratio >40; sinuosity usually <1.3; gradient, relatively steep	Depositing bed-load channel. Streambed deposition and island formation	Eroding bed-load channel. Little streambed erosion; channel widening predominant

stable, or depositing emphasizes the diversity among rivers and stream channels; each of the three classes can be considered as distinct from the others.

The classification of alluvial channels is summarized in Table 5-4. Nine subclasses of channels are shown, based on channel stability and the predominant mode of sediment transport. Although variations in the proportions of bed load and suspended load are transitional, it is possible to think in terms of a *suspended-load channel* transporting perhaps 0 to 3 percent bed load, a *bed-load channel* transporting greater than 11 percent bed load, and a *mixed-load channel* transporting from 3 to 11 percent bed load. The boundaries between these groups are based on the relation between M and the percentage of bed load (Equation 5-7) and on the known characteristics of streams having varying amounts of silt and clay in their channels. The ranges of channel shape and sinuosity are established for each subclass, but gradient is expressed qualitatively, for gradient depends to a large extent on discharge, which can vary greatly for a given value of M. Although sinuosity, as has been shown, may depend on valley slope, a characteristic sinuosity range can be established for each type of stream.

In summary, alluvial-stream channels have been classified on the basis of one of the two independent variables influencing stream morphology. Discharge is not used as a basis for the classification because it controls mainly the size of the channels. The type of material transported or the mode of its transport as bed load or suspended load appears to be a major factor determining the character of a stream channel, and the classification of channels is based on this relation. Absolute size of the sediment load may be less important than the manner in which it moves through the channel. Channel stability depends on the balance or lack of balance between sediment load and transportability, and three classes of channels result: stable, eroding, and depositing.

The classification is applicable only to segments of a river system, for the characteristics of a stream channel can change significantly within a short distance if it becomes unstable or receives sediment of a different type from a tributary. Therefore, the classification is of channels rather than of river systems, and it must be considered to be tentative until more data become available on total sediment load and the influence of sediment size on channel shape and pattern.

The classification is based on research that has been confined to sandbed streams and thus may not be applicable to gravel and cobble rivers. For a description of these channels see Galay et al. (1973), Lewis and McDonald (1973), and Kellerhals et al. (1972); However, Mollard

(1972) has, in fact, used the classification based on type of load to classify a wide range of Canadian rivers.

Bed-Load Channel Morphology

A more general but analogous classification of fluvial deposits has been developed by stratigraphers. Their fine-grained meander belt, coarse-grained meander belt, and braided stream deposits (Brown et al., 1973) are probably the result of deposition and reworking of sediments by suspended-load, mixed-load, and bed-load channels. Highly sinuous, narrow, and deep suspended-load channels, however, either are not common in the ancient rocks or have little economic significance and thus have not received the attention of stratigraphers and sedimentologists, whereas braided channels and others carrying a relatively high proportion of bed load have.

Even within one channel type the channel characteristics can vary greatly. For example, during the previously described experiments, when the bed-load channels were transporting only sand at a constant discharge, several different types of bar patterns developed as slope and sediment load were increased. The patterns are sketched in Figure 5-30 and are described as follows:

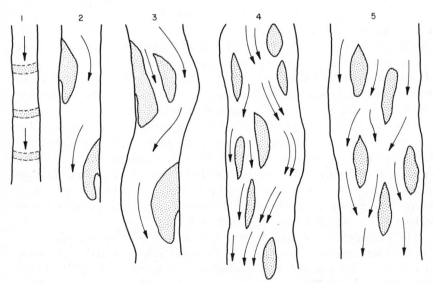

Figure 5-30   Bed-load channel bar patterns observed during experimental studies. Arrows show predominant flow directions.

1. Transverse sand waves, channel width stable, formed in the straight channel range (Figure 5-14, slope less than about 0.3).
2. Alternate bars, channel width stable, formed at lower range of meandering thalweg channels (Figure 5-14, slope between about 0.3 and 0.5).
3. Alternate bars and chutes, bank erosion, formed at upper range of meandering thalweg channels (Figure 5-14, slope between 0.5 and 1.2).
4. Point-bar braided, bank erosion significant, formed at transition between meandering thalweg and braided patterns (Figure 5-14, slope between 1.2 and 1.5).
5. Braided (Figure 5-14, slope above 1.5).

The recognition that even within one class of channel several channel floor patterns can exist may be of some aid to the stratigrapher who is attempting to classify paleochannel deposits. For example, Jacob (1973) has identified the alternate bar situation in fluvial deposits of the Paleocene Tongue River formation.

RIVER METAMORPHOSIS

The classifications presented in the preceding section indicate the range of river channel types that exist. Sedimentologic and stratigraphic studies reveal that within one sedimentary deposit fluvial sediments may change character both from the proximal to the distal part of the deposit and vertically within the deposit (Karl, 1976). This suggests drastic alterations in river morphology, as discharge and sediment load change during deposition of the fluvial sedimentary deposits.

According to the empirical relations and the classification of rivers presented earlier, a channel will undergo a complete change of morphology (river metamorphosis) if changes in discharge and sediment load are of sufficient magnitude. That is, a suspended-load channel could be converted to a mixed-load or bed-load channel. Examples of changes of this magnitude are presented in this section; first, some examples of modern or historic changes from what appear to be suspended-load or mixed-load channels to bed-load channels are cited.

Historic Examples

In the past meandering rivers have been converted to straight channels by a combination of high peak discharges and high sediment transport.

For example, the highly sinuous, relatively narrow and deep Cimarron River channel of southwestern Kansas was destroyed by the major flood of 1914. Between 1914 and 1931 the river widened from an average of 50 to 1200 feet, and the entire floodplain was destroyed. Large floods moved considerable sand and caused this transformation despite the fact that annual discharge was probably less during the drought of the 1930s. The hydrologic record is short, but an abrupt increase in annual discharge after 1940 was recorded at the Wyanoka, Oklahoma, gaging station.

Precipitation data indicate that the years 1916 to 1941 were generally a period of below-average precipitation. Thus, during years of low runoff and high floodpeaks, the Cimarron River was converted from a 50-foot wide sinuous channel characterized by low sediment transport, to a 1200-foot wide, straight bed-load river. These changes were apparently the result of climatic fluctuations, although agricultural activities within the basin may have increased the flood peaks and the sediment loads by destruction of the natural vegetation (Schumm and Lichty, 1963).

It appears that large floods override the effect of decreased mean annual discharge and that the change in Cimarron River morphology can be considered analogous to that caused by increased Q and Q_s (Equation 5-26). An increase in bed-material load must have occurred as the channel was widened and the gradient increased by straightening of the channel (decreased sinuosity), but there are no data to support this suggestion.

Smith (1940) described channel changes of several rivers in western Kansas that were of the Cimarron-type. For example, the Republican River was greatly affected by the flood of 1935. Before the flood it was a narrow stream with well-wooded banks and a perennial flow of clear water. The Republican in 1965 had a broad, shallow sandy channel with intermittent flow. The trees were mostly washed out, and the channel was filled several feet. Since then, however, regulation of flow at the Harlan County Dam has reduced both the magnitude of peak discharge and mean annual discharge, as measured at Bloomington, Nebraska. This has caused a reduction in channel capacity between 1952 and 1957 owing to the growth of willows in the channel and the formation of islands and a new floodplain (Northrup, 1965).

The Republican River example indicates that a decrease in the magnitude of peak discharges and a decrease in the movement of bed load will result in channel narrowing. After the great widening of the Cimarron River between 1914 and 1942, a period of well-above-average rainfall ensued, and although annual runoff increased, no major floods moved through the channel between 1942 and 1951. According to measurements made on aerial photographs taken in 1939 and 1954, the average width of the river decreased from 1200 to 550 feet so that, in effect, the width/depth ratio was reduced by half (Schumm and Lichty, 1963).

Equally great changes occurred along some major rivers of the western United States (Burkham, 1972). Especially impressive is the conversion of the broad North and South Platte rivers and the Arkansas River to relatively insignificant streams owing to flood-control works and diversions for irrigation. The width of these rivers as shown on topographic maps published during the latter part of the 19th century can be compared with the width shown on new maps of the same areas. For example, the North Platte River near the Wyoming–Nebraska boundary has narrowed from about 2500 to 4000 feet wide in 1890 to about 200 feet wide at present (Figure 5-31). In eastern Nebraska just upstream from the junction of the Loup River at Columbus, the river has narrowed from 4000 to 2000 feet.

The South Platte River has always been cited as a classic example of a braided stream. About 55 miles above its junction with the North Platte River, the South Platte River was about 2600 feet wide in 1897 but narrowed to about 200 feet by 1959 (Figure 5-32). The tendency of both rivers is to form one narrow well-defined channel in place of the previously wide, braided channels. In addition, the new channel is generally somewhat more sinuous than the old.

The narrowing of the North Platte can be attributed to a decrease in the mean annual flood from 13,000 cfs to 3000 cfs and to a decrease in the mean annual discharge from 2300 to 560 cfs, which resulted from river regulation and the diversion of flow for irrigation. The major decrease in annual runoff occurred about 1930. A similar change occurred on the South Platte during the drought of the 1930s. However, the annual discharge of the South Platte increased after 1940, partly as a result of transmountain diversions, whereas, because of upstream regulation, the discharge of the North Platte did not. The annual maximum discharge decreased for both rivers, and this decrease was undoubtedly the major factor determining the present channel size. Data on changes of sediment load are lacking, but it is probable that much less sand is being transported through these channels at present.

The records of relatively recent channel changes on the Great Plains of the United States reveal that, where man's activities have altered the hydrologic regimen, the wide sandy channels have changed, and, with time, they may assume the character of a mixed-load or perhaps of a suspended-load channel. It is doubtful that the adjustments will take

Figure 5-31   North Platte River at Scotts Bluff, Nebraska. View is toward Scotts Bluff from north
bank of river in (A) 1890 (U. S. Geological Survey photograph) and (B) 1960.

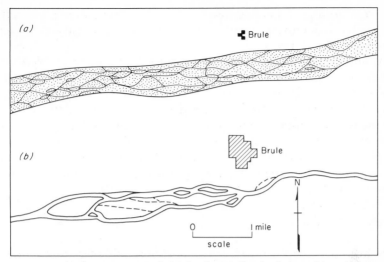

Figure 5-32   South Platte River at Brule, Nebraska. (a) Sketch of channel based on surveys made in 1897. (b) Sketch of channel based on aerial photographs taken in 1959. (From S. A. Schumm, 1969, Geomorphic: implications of climatic changes, in R. J. Charley (Editor), Water, Earth, and Man: Methuen, pp. 525–534.

place over the entire channel length because the channel changes are not in response to a climate change, which could alter the hydrologic regimen of the entire drainage basin. The tributary streams below the point of main-channel regulation still introduce their burdens of water and sediment into the main channel, and until the water and sediment yields from the tributary basins are controlled, transformation of the main channels to a suspended-load type of channel cannot be complete. Nevertheless, the tendency toward this type of change has been demonstrated locally along these rivers.

Significantly, these major changes of river character have occurred without a great change in altitude of the channel. Adjustments to altered runoff and sediment load were accomplished primarily by changes in channel shape and pattern. Of course, where a major increase in the quantity and size of sediment load occurs, aggradation will occur and may be very significant. For example, destruction of natural forest vegetation on steep slopes in the humid regions of New Zealand and replacement of this vegetation with exotic grasses have caused erosion problems of major proportions. Stable, narrow, sinuous rivers have changed to wide, straight channels as a result of an influx of coarse sediment into the channels, and aggradation and an increase in flood peaks have occurred (Grant, 1950; Campbell, 1945). A somewhat similar problem arose in California when hydraulic mining debris was fed in great quantities into the rivers draining from the gold fields of the Sierra Nevada (Gilbert, 1917).

Although data on changes of sediment load are not available for the historic examples of channel metamorphosis, it may be assumed that, as rivers are widened and steepened by destruction of their original channels, larger quantities of bed-material load are moved through the channels by the higher flood peaks. If this condition had persisted the channels would have remained wide and straight. However, with decreased flood peaks, the encroachment of vegetation into the channels formed floodplains with channel narrowing and a tendency toward development of meanders.

Geologic Examples

The historic examples of river metamorphosis, although interesting, do not provide a complete picture of river response to changes of hydrologic regimen. That is, the changes were in some cases local and temporary. However, the changes of climate and sea level during relatively recent geologic time produced examples of complete channel metamorphosis. Again, information concerning water and sediment discharge is generally indirect, but for two examples (Mississippi and Murrumbidgee Rivers) river metamorphosis can be documented in considerable detail.

One of the most intensively studied rivers of the world is the Mississippi River. The pioneering work of Fisk (1944) and his colleagues provides an unexcelled example of the effect of climate and sea-level changes on river morphology. The two factors that have determined the behavior of the Mississippi River since the maximum extent of the last glaciation are the presence of the ice sheet itself, which supplied tremendous quantities of meltwater and sediment to the Mississippi Valley, and the lowering of sea level to a maximum depth of about 130 m about 15,000 years ago (Milliman and Emery, 1968). The fall of sea level lowered the baselevel of the Mississippi River system, permitting removal of earlier deposits and scour of the floor of the valley. The details of the history as given by Fisk's (1944) report are summarized below.

During the time of maximum lowering of sea level the Mississippi River was entrenched between 400 and 450 feet (Figure 5-33a). In addition, the tributaries incised their channels to produce an irregular valley floor with an average slope of 0.83 feet per mile. The slope increased in steepness seaward, suggesting that the erosion was not complete.

When the continental ice sheet began to waste away, the introduction of water and sediment into the Mississippi Valley was greatly increased at the same time that sea level rose between 14,000 and about 4000 years ago. Deposition in the valley accompanied the rise of sea level, and the sediments presently grade upward from coarse sands and gravels through sands and silts. In effect, a wave of alluviation moved slowly upstream and into the tributary valleys so that the entire lower drainage system was affected. However, the tributary streams still transported coarse sediments, and huge alluvial fans were built into the valley.

The lack of fine sediment (silts and clays) in the lower alluvium indicates that they were transported to the sea. According to the evidence of these deposits, the Mississippi River at this time was a braided stream that shifted across the alluvial valley on a slope of about 0.75 foot per mile (Figure 5-33b).

With continued but slower rise of sea level and a decrease in the size of the sediments moving from the north and from the tributary valleys, the sediment load was eventually reduced to fine sands, silts, and clays. According to Fisk (1944, p. 22), "The braided streams, during this stage, wandered widely on the plain and built low alluvial ridges of sands and silts. . . ." The basins created between alluvial ridges received silts and clays contributed by floodwaters (Figure 5-33c). As valley alluviation continued, the gradient of the valley was reduced to about 0.60 foot per mile and the size and amount of sediment contributed to the river decreased. At this stage the river was flowing on a slope only 0.15 foot per mile less than that when it was braided. With essentially constant sea level and reduced sediment load, the river began to meander. According to Fisk (1944, p. 23) the change from a braided stream to a meandering one brought about the confinement of the Mississippi flows in a single deep channel. No longer did the river wander "freely in shallow channels across the alluvial surface as did the braided stream" (Figure 5-33d).

This outline of Mississippi River history is similar to that suggested for the rivers of the Great Plains to the extent that they too transported larger quantities of coarser sediment and apparently reduced their gradient by developing a sinuous course. The history of the Mississippi River strongly supports the idea that meandering is largely the result of a river's attempt to reduce its gradient in response to a changed hydrologic regimen.

Nevertheless, it may be questioned whether the Pleistocene rivers were truly different from those of the present, and if so, were the changes in discharge and sediment load responsible for the assumed metamorphosis? When rivers are confined to valleys, any evidence re-

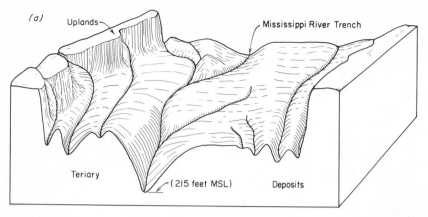

(a)

Uplands

Mississippi River Trench

Teriary

(215 feet MSL)

Deposits

(b)

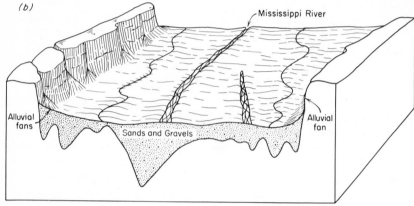

Mississippi River

Alluvial
fans

Sands and Gravels

Alluvial
fan

Valley aggradation stage I – sea level 100 feet lower than present
Valley slope ~ 0.75 feet per mile

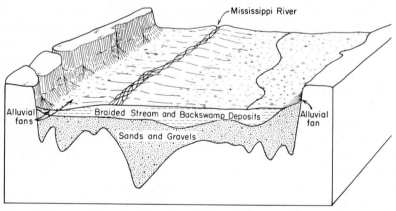

Mississippi River

Alluvial
fans

Braided Stream and Backswamp Deposits

Alluvial
fan

Sands and Gravels

Valley aggradation stage 2 – sea level 20 feet lower than present
Valley slope 0.68 feet per mile.

(c)

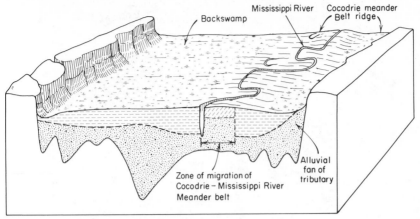

Valley aggradation stage 3 – sea level at present elevation.
Valley slope~ 0.60 feet per mile.

(d)

Figure 5-33   Mississippi River Valley Quaternary history. (From Fisk, 1944.)

lated to the dimensions of the ancient channel is destroyed by the channel adjustment. However, when the rivers flow across an alluvial plain and the position of the river shifts with time, the possibility of preservation of the paleochannel is improved. Fortunately, at least one example exists where the channels have not been destroyed by the change, and they can be studied in the field on the Riverine Plain of New South Wales, Australia (Schumm, 1968).

The sinuous Murrumbidgee River (Figure 5-34) drains from the highlands of southeastern New South Wales toward the west. It crosses the Riverine Plain, an alluvial plain that slopes at about 1.5 feet per mile, to join the Murray River at the New South Wales–Victoria border. The channel is about 200 feet wide and is confined to an irregular floodplain on which are preserved large oxbow lakes, which are evidence of a past time of high discharge (Paleochannel 1, middle arrow, Figure 5-34). The trace of an older low-sinuosity stream channel (Paleochannel 2) crosses the lower quarter of the photograph (lower arrow, Figure 5-34). In the upper half of its drainage basin the Murrumbidgee River is confined within a valley, and no evidence pertaining to its past condition exists because the old channels have been destroyed. On the alluvial plain, however, the position of the channel has shifted, and three different types of channels are visible. The morphology of these channels reflects the hydrologic regimen of the time when each channel was functioning. In Table 5-5 the dimensions and other form characteristics of these

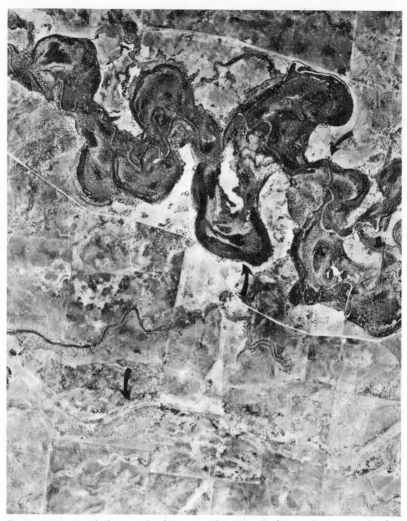

Figure 5-34. Aerial photograph of Riverine Plain near Darlington Point, New South Wales, Australia. Murrumbidgee River (upper arrow) is 200 feet wide and follows meandering course on floodplain that shows evidence of large meander scours and oxbow lake of young Paleochannel 1 (middle arrow). On surface of alluvial plain trace of old Paleochannel 2 (lower arrow) is visibel. (Photograph courtesy of New South Wales Lands Department.)

TABLE 5-5. MORPHOLOGY OF RIVERINE PLAINS CHANNELS

Location (1)	Channel width, (ft) (2)	Channel depth, (ft) (3)	Width/ depth ratio F (4)	Sinuosity S (5)	Gradient S (ft/mile) (6)	Meander wave-length λ (ft) (7)	Median grain size (mm) (8)	Channel silt–clay, M (percent) (9)	Bedload Q_s (percent) (10)	Bank-full discharge, (ft³/sec) (11)	Sand discharge at bank full (tons/day)[a] (12)
Murrumbidgee River (upper arrow, Fig. 5-34)	220	21	10	2.0	0.7	2,800	0.57	25	2.2	11,000	2,000
Paleochannel 1 (middle arrow, Fig. 5-34)	460	35	13	1.7	0.8	7,000	—	16	3.4	51,000[b]	21,000
Paleochannel 2 (lower arrow, Fig. 5-34)	600	9	67	1.1	2.0	18,000	0.55	1.6	34	23,000[b]	54,000

[a]Calculated by Colby's technique.
[b]Calculated by use of Manning equation and channel area.

169

three channels are presented together with data on sediment character-istics and hydrology. Pedologic and geomorphic evidence from the Riverine Plain indicates that the oldest of the paleochannels was functioning during a climate drier than that of the present, and that the youngest paleochannel was functioning during a climate more humid than that of the present.

The channel changes occurred not only because the water discharge increased or decreased, but also because climatic changes significantly altered the type of sediment load moved from the headwaters across the alluvial plain. At present, erosion is not a problem in the Murrumbidgee drainage basin. A good cover of vegetation protects the source area, and the river transports small quantities of sand, silt, and clay. An increase in precipitation will further improve the vegetation, and, although runoff will increase, the sediment yield will decrease. On the other hand, a decrease in precipitation will decrease the amount of runoff but will also greatly increase the yield of sediment from the drainage basin (Schumm, 1965, 1968). Calculations of the quantity of sand that could have been moved through the channels at bank-full discharge show that Paleochannel 2 was competent to move large quantities of sand (Table 5-5). The abandoned channel of Paleochannel 2 is filled with sand, whereas the abandoned channel of Paleochannel 1 is filled largely with silts and clays. This suggests that, although Paleochannel 1 could have transported relatively large quantities of sand, this type of sediment was available in large quantities only during the existence of Paleochannel 2.

As fascinating as the paleochannels of the Riverine Plain may be, they are of concern here only as an illustration of the types of river changes that can occur naturally. If, for simplicity, it is considered that the paleochannels represent changes from a channel that initially was like that of the modern Murrumbidgee River (Figure 5-34), we can discuss the channel changes that will occur if the present climate of southeastern Australia becomes wetter (Paleochannel 1) or drier (Paleochannel 2). An increase in precipitation in the Murrumbidgee River headwaters will result in increased annual discharge and increased mean annual flood, but only a small change in sediment concentration and in the type of sediment load moved through the channel. In response to this hy-drologic change, which is similar in effect to that described by Equation 5-22, the shape of the channel will not change, but it will become wider and deeper, and meander wavelength and amplitude will increase. The initial response will undoubtedly be severe channel erosion until the new dimensions are established. The result will be a relatively stable channel, but one larger than the modern river. On the Riverine Plain it is significant that, although deepening of the channel did occur, the increased discharge did not cause major incision. Gradient remained essentially constant.

On the other hand, a decrease in precipitation in the headwaters of the Murrumbidgee River will not only cause a decrease in annual discharge, but, through reduction of vegetation density, it will increase peak discharges and greatly increase the amount of sand moved through the channels. The result will be a complete transformation of the river system. To transport the increased sand load with less water, the channel will become wider and shallower. The greater slope required to transport this load will not be developed by deposition and steepening of the Riverine Plain, which would require movement of immense quantities of sediment; rather the channel pattern will be changed. The gradient of the channel will be doubled, without significant deposition, by a reduction of the sinuosity from about 2 to 1. These changes are in complete accord with Equation 5-29.

As noted previously, the events that occurred on the surface of the Riverine Plain were the reverse of the above sequence, with the wide, straight, steep channel changing under the influence of altered hydrologic conditions to a relatively deep and sinuous channel. In fact, the documented changes are in accord with those suggested by Equation 5-28.

The Riverine Plain paleochannels provide an example of adjustment of gradient by a major change of channel pattern. This supports the suggestion made earlier that, if unconfined, rivers may decrease their gradient by meandering rather than by major degradation. Therefore, modern bank erosion problems may be only the initial stage of river metamorphosis if a reduction of river gradient is required as a result of man-induced changes of river regimen.

DISCUSSION

The equations presented in this chapter indicate the significant influence that water and sediment discharge exert on channel morphology. Changes in the hydrologic character of Zone 1, for whatever cause, can result in river metamorphosis and a drastic change in the sediment moved to Zone 3. Over a much longer time similar hydrologic changes may accompany the erosional reduction of a landscape, causing major changes in the sedimentary characteristics of fluvial deposits. For example, as relief is decreased and the source area morphology changes through time, bed-load streams may dominate at the base of a deposit with mixed-load streams in the middle and suspended-load streams at the top.

A genetic classification of river channels has been presented based on channel stability and type of sediment load. No classification of rivers will ever be wholly adequate, but the differences in pattern and channel shape as identified can be of use in the interpretation of river behavior from aerial photography when no other data are available (Kellerhals et al., 1976), and the cross section and nature of its sediments can aid in the prediction of the nature of fluvial sedimentary deposits by the sedimentologist and exploration geologist.

The evaluation of the relative stability of a channel depends on the training and goals of the investigator and therefore the time span considered. While meander shift may be a catastrophe to a landowner and a challenge to the river control engineer, it may be the anticipated result of natural channel development to the geomorphologist, who would conclude that these natural changes should be permitted to occur. If a river is considered as an organism with a history, then its relative stability and propensity for change can be more fully comprehended. Therefore, much channel "instability" may, in fact, be a natural and predictable adjustment to geomorphic controls. This perspective hopefully has potential for the better understanding of and the management of rivers.

Two types of threshold conditions have been identified with regard to channel patterns. The extrinsic thresholds of sediment load (slope) and stream power (velocity) determine whether the river will be straight, meandering, or braided. The intrinsic geomorphic pattern threshold, when exceeded, results in a change from relatively high to relatively low sinuosity (Figure 5-23). The exceeding of a pattern threshold, which introduces a period of channel instability and high sediment transport, can provide an explanation for an increased rate of sedimentation in a fluvial deposit when none is warranted by climatic or other evidence.

The fact that such pattern thresholds exist provides the river manager with an approach to river control that involves an appreciation of river history. Intrinsic thresholds can be exceeded at any time but usually only for reaches of relatively high sinuosity during large floods.

The Chippewa River was used as an example to demonstrate how geomorphic thresholds and the innate variability of river patterns can be used to aid in planning for river control. In the Chippewa River, where the quantity of water and sediment brought to the braided reach is no more than that transported through the meandering reach upstream, the conversion of the braided channel into a more sinuous course by structural means could significantly reduce sediment contribution to the

Mississippi River. The situation may be analogous to that near position 2 on Figure 5-23; sinuosity of the lower Chippewa River should be about 1.3, but is in fact 1.06, which is an unusually low value under the circumstances and indicates pattern instability.

The empirical equations presented in this chapter have also been used to provide an estimate of the hydrology of ungaged channels and of paleochannels. For example, Brown (1971) determined that channel cross-sectional area provided good estimates of bank-full discharge for channels in Kentucky, Tennessee, and Minnesota with perennial flow. Hedman (1970) used low-water channel widths and depths to estimate annual runoff, and Schumm (1972) used width/depth ratio and width in a series of equations to estimate paleochannel discharge, gradient, and meander wavelength. Width/depth ratio alone provided an estimate of sinuosity (Equation 5-19). Cotter (1971) used these relations to estimate paleodischarge of a Cretaceous River with apparent success, but the great difficulty in applying these relations to paleochannels is clearly indicated by Leeder (1973).

The need to estimate meander wavelength and sinuosity in a mineral or petroleum exploration program leads logically to attempts to use the equations for this purpose. Nevertheless, the inherent variability of channel patterns introduces an unwelcome complexity that may confound efforts to locate a series of presumed equally spaced point-bar deposits in a meander belt. The apparent answer is a more expensive drilling program.

Finally, if, as suggested, rivers can be classified by the nature of their sediment load, then not only associated sedimentary deposits in Zone 2, but also the sedimentary deposits of Zone 3, will be closely related to the hydrology of Zone 1 (Table 5-1) and to channel character and behavior in Zone 2.

REFERENCES

Ackers, P., 1964, Experiments on small streams in alluvium: J. Hydrol. Div., Am. Soc. Civil Eng. Proc. HY4, pp. 1–37.

Ackers, P., and Charlton, F. G., 1971, The slope and resistance of small meandering channels: Inst. Civil Eng. Proc. Suppl. XV, 1970; Paper 73625.

Adams, R. M., 1965, Land behind Baghdad: University of Chicago Press, Chicago, 187 pp.

Ager, D. V., 1973, The nature of the stratigraphic record: Macmillan, London, 114 pp.

Alexander, C. S. and Nunally, N. R., 1972, Channel stability on the lower Ohio River: Ann. Assoc. Am. Geogr., v. 62, pp. 411–417.

Bagnold, R. A., 1966, An approach to the sediment transport problem from general physics: U. S. Geol. Surv. Prof. Paper 422-I, 37 pp.

Bareis, C. J., 1964, Meander loops and the Cahokia site: Am. Antiq., v. 30, pp. 89–91.

Bhamidipaty, S. and Shen, H. W., 1971, Laboratory study of degradation and aggradation: A. S. C. E., J. Waterways, Harbors Coastal Eng. Div., v. 97, pp. 615–630.

Bourcart, J., 1947, La sédimentation dans la Manche: La Géologie des Terrains Récents dan l'ouest de l'Europe: Session extradinaire Soc. Belges Géol., Bruxelles 1946, pp. 14–43.

Bray, D. I., 1973, Regime relations for Alberta gravel-bed rivers, in Fluvial processes and sedimentation: National Research Council of Canada; Ottowa, pp. 440–452.

Brown, D. A., 1971, Stream channels and flow relations: Water Resour. Res., v. 7, pp. 304–310.

Brown, L. F. Jr., Cleaves, A. W. II and Erxleben, A. W., 1973, Pennsylvanian depositional systems in north-central Texas: Bureau of Economic Geology, University of Texas at Austin, Guidebook 14, 122 pp.

Brush, L. M. Jr., 1961, Drainage basins, channels and flow characteristics of selected streams in central Pennsylvania: U. S. Geol. Surv. Prof. Paper 282-F.

Burkham, D. E., 1972, Channel changes of the Gila River in Safford Valley, Arizona 1846–1970: U. S. Geol. Surv. Prof. Paper 655-G, 24 pp.

Busch, D. A., 1959, Prospecting for stratigraphic traps: Am. Assoc. Pet. Geol. Bull., v. 43, pp. 2829–2843.

Butzer, K. W. and Hansen, C. L., 1968, Desert and river in Nubia: University of Wisconsin Press, Madison, 562 pp.

Campbell, D. A., 1945, Soil conservation studies applied to farming in Hawke's Bay, Part 2, Investigations into soil erosion and flooding: N. Z. J. Sci. Technol., Sect. A., v. 27, p. 147–172.

Chow, Ven Te, 1959, Open-channel hydraulics: McGraw-Hill, New York, 680 pp.

Colby, B. R., 1964, Discharge of sands and mean-velocity relationships in sand-bed streams: U. S. Geol. Surv. Prof. Paper 462-A, 47 pp.

Coleman, J. M., 1969, Brahmaputra River: channel processes and sedimentation: Sediment. Geol., v. 3, pp. 129–239.

Cornish, J. H., 1961, Flow losses in dry sandy channels: J. Geophys. Res., v. 66, pp. 1845–1853.

Cotter, Edward, 1971, Paleoflow characteristics of a late Cretaceous river in Utah from analysis of sedimentary structures in the Ferron Sandstone: J. Sediment. Petrol., v. 41, pp. 129–138.

Craig, L. C. et al., 1955, Stratigraphy of the Morrison and related formations, Colorado Plateau region, a preliminary report: U. S. Geol. Surv. Bull., 1009-E, pp. 125–166.

Culbertson, D. M., Young, L. E. and Brice, J. C., 1967, Scour and fill in alluvial channels: U. S. Geol. Surv. Open-File Report, 58 pp.

Daniel, J. F., 1971, Channel movement of meandering Indiana streams: U. S. Geol. Surv. Prof. Paper 732-A, 18 pp.

Davis, W. M., 1899, The geographical cycle: Geogr. J., v. 14, pp. 481–504.

Denson, M. E., 1956, Geophysical–geochemical prospecting for uranium: U. S. Geol. Surv. Prof. Paper 300, pp. 387–703.

Doeglas, D. J., 1962, The structure of sedimentary deposits of braided streams: Sedimentology, v. 1, p. 167–190.

Dury, G. H., 1964, Principles of underfit streams: U. S. Geol. Surv. Prof. Paper 452-A, 67 pp.

Edgar, D. E., 1973, Geomorphic and hydraulic properties of laboratory rivers: unpublished M. S. Thesis, Colorado State University, 156 pp.

Einstein, H. A., 1950, The bed-load function for sediment transportation in open channel flows: U. S. Dept. Agric. Tech. Bull. 1926, 71 pp.

Everitt, B. L., 1968, Use of cottonwood in the investigation of the recent history of a flood plain: Am. J. Sci., v. 206, pp. 417–439.

Fisk, H. N., 1944, Geological investigation of the alluvial valley of the lower Mississippi River: Mississippi River Commission, Vicksburg, Miss., 78 pp.

Fisk, H. N. and McFarlan, E. Jr., 1955, Late Quaternary deltaic deposits of the Mississippi River: Geol. Soc. Am. Spec. Paper 62, pp. 279–302.

Friedkin, J. F., 1945, A laboratory study of the meandering of alluvial streams: U. S. Army Corps Eng. Waterways Expt. Sta., p. 40.

Galay, V. J., Kellerhals, R. and Bray, D. I., 1973, Diversity of river types in Canada in Fluvial Process and Sedimentation: Proc. Hydrol. Symp., National Research Council of Canada, pp. 217–250.

Gessler, Johannes, 1970, Self-stabilizing tendencies of alluvial channels: A. S. C. E. J. Waterways Harbors Div., v. 96, p. 235–249.

Gilbert, G. K., 1917, Hydraulic mining debris in the Sierra Nevada: U. S. Geol. Surv. Prof. Paper 105, 154 pp.

Grant, H. P., 1950, Soil conservation in New Zealand: N. Z. Inst. Eng., Proc., v. 36, pp. 269–301.

Gupta, Avigit, 1975, Stream characteristics in eastern Jamaica: an environment of seasonal flow and large floods: Am. J. Sci., v. 275, pp. 825–847.

Hack, J. T., 1957, Studies of longitudinal stream profiles in Virginia and Maryland: U. S. Geol. Surv. Prof. Paper 294-B, pp. 45–97.

Hadley, R. F., 1960, Recent sedimentation and erosional history of Fivemile Creek, Fremont County, Wyonimg: U. S. Geol. Surv. Prof. Paper 352-A, 16 pp.

Hedman, E. R., 1970, Mean annual runoff as related to channel geometry of selected streams in California: U. S. Geol. Surv., Water-Supply Paper 1999-E, 17 pp.

Hickin, E. J., 1974, Development of meanders in natural river channels: Am. J. Sci., v. 274, pp. 414–442.

Hickin, E. J. and Nanson, G. C., 1975, The character of channel migration on the Beatton River, N. E. British Columbia, Canada: Geol. Doc. Am. Bull., v. 86, pp. 487–494.

Hjulstrom, F., 1935, Studies of the morphologic activity of rivers as illustrated by the River Fjris: Geol. Inst. Uppsala Univ. (Sweden) Bull., v. 25, pp. 293–452.

Jacob, A. F., 1973, Depositional environments of Paleocene Tongue River formation, western North Dakota: Am. Assoc. Pet. Geol., v. 57, pp. 1038–1052.

Jefferson, Mark, 1907, Lateral erosion on some Michigan rivers: Geol. Soc. Am. Bull., v. 18, pp. 333–350.

Karl, H. H., 1976, Depositional history of Dakota formation (Cretaceous) sandstone, southeastern Nebraska: J. Sediment. Pet., v. 46, pp. 124–131.

Keller, E. A., 1975, Channelization: a search for a better way: Geology, v. 3, pp. 245–248.

Kellerhals, Rolf, Church, Michael and Bray, D. I., 1976, Classification and analysis of river processes: J. Hydraul. Div., Am. Soc. Civil Eng., v. 102, pp. 813–829.

Kellerhals, Rolf, Neill, C. R. and Bray, D. I., 1972, Hydraulic and geomorphic characteristics of rivers in Alberta: Research Council of Alberta, River Engineering and Surface Hydrology Report 72-1, 52 pp.

Khan, H. R., 1971, Laboratory study of river morphology: unpublished Ph.D. Dissertation, Colorado State University, 189 pp.

Kolb, C. R., 1963, Sediments forming the bed and banks of the lower Mississippi River and their effects on river migration: Sedimentology, v. 2, pp. 227–234.

Krigström, A., 1962, Geomorphological studies of sandur plains and their braided rivers in Iceland: Geogr. Ann., v. 44, pp. 328–346.

Lacey, Gerald, 1930, Stable channels in alluvium: Inst. Civil Eng., Proc. v. 229, pp. 259–384.

Lane, E. W., 1955, The importance of fluvial morphology in hydraulic engineering: Am. Soc. Civil Eng. Proc., v. 81, No. 745, 17 pp.

Lane, E. W., 1957, A study of the shape of channels formed by natural sreams flowing in erodible material: M. R. D. Sediment Series No. 9, U. S. Army Engineer Division, Missouri River, Corps Engineers, Omaha, Nebraska.

Lathrop, D. W., 1968, Aboriginal occupation and changes in river channel on the central Ucayali, Peru: Am. Antiq., v. 33, pp. 62–79.

Leeder, M. R., 1973, Fluviatile fining-upwards cycles and the magnitude of Plaeochannels: Geol. Mag., v. 110, pp. 265–276.

Leliavsky, Serge, 1955, An introduction to fluvial hydraulics: Constable, London, 256 pp.

Leopold, L. B., 1951, Rainfall frequency: an aspect of climatic variation: Am. Geophys. Union Trans., v. 32, pp. 327–357.

Leopold, L. B. and Maddock, Thomas Jr., 1953, The hydraulic geometry of stream channels and some physiographic implications: U. S. Geol. Surv. Prof. Paper 242, 57 pp.

Leopold, L. B. and Wolman, M. G., 1957, River channel patterns: braided, meandering and straight: U. S. Geol. Surv. Prof. Paper 282-B.

Lewis, C. P. and McDonald, B. C., 1973, Rivers of the Yukon North Slope, in Fluvial processes and sedimentation: Proc. Hydrol. Symp. National Research Council of Canada, pp. 251–271.

Livesey, R. H., 1963, Channel armoring below Fort Randall Dam: U. S. Dept. Agr. Misc. Publ. 970, pp. 461–469.

Machida, Tadashi, 1960, Geomorphological analysis of terrace plains–fluvial terraces along the River Kuji and the River Ara, Kanto District, Japan: Sci. Rep. Tokyo Kyoiku Daigaku, Ser., v. 7, pp. 137–194.

Mackin, J. H., 1948, Concept of the graded river: Geol. Soc. Am. Bull., v. 59, pp. 463–512.

Milliman, J. D. and Emery, K. O., 1968, Sea levels during the past 35,000 years: Science, v. 162, pp. 1121–1123.

Mollard, J. D., 1972, Airphoto interpretation of fluvial features, in Fluvial processes and sedimentation: Research Council of Canada, pp. 341–380.

Moody-Stuart, M., 1966, High and low sinuosity stream deposits with examples from the Devonian of Spitsbergen: J. Sediment. Petrol., v. 36, pp. 1101–1117.

Nevins, T. H. F., 1965, River classification with particular reference to New Zealand: N. Z. Geogr. Cong., 4th, Proc., v. 4, pp. 83–90.

Northrup, W. L., 1965, Republican River channel deterioration: U. S. Dept. Agric. Misc. Publ. 970, pp. 409–424.

Peltier, L. C., 1962, Area sampling for terrain analysis: Prof. Geogr., v. 14, pp. 24–28.

Pemberton, E. L., 1976, Channel changes in the Colorado River below Glen Canyon Dam:

Third Federal Inter-agency Sedimentation Conf., Proc., Sediment. Comm., Water Resources Council, Washington, pp. 5-61 to 5-73.

Philips, Philip, Ford, J. A., Griffin, J. B., 1951, Archaeological survey in the lower Mississippi alluvial valley 1940–1947: Peabody Museum Papers, v. 25.

Popov, I. V., 1964, Hydromorphological principles of the theory of channel processes and their use in hydrotechnical planning: Sov. Hydrol., 1964, pp. 158–195.

Quraishy, M. S., 1944, The origin of curves in rivers: Curr. Sci., v. 13, pp. 36–39.

Richmond, G. M., 1962, Quaternary stratigraphy of the La Sal Mountains, Utah: U. S. Geol. Surv. Prof. Paper 324, 135 pp.

Rittenhouse, Gordon, 1944, Sources of modern sands in the middle Rio Grande Valley, New Mexico: J. Geol., v. 52, pp. 145–183.

Rubey, W. W., 1952, Geology and mineral resources of the Hardin and Brussels Quadrangles, Illinois: U. S. Geol. Surv. Prof. Paper 218, 179 pp.

Schatner, I., 1962, The lower Jordan valley: Publications of Hebrew University, Jerusalem, v. 11, 123 pp.

Schmudde, T. H., 1963, Some aspects of the lower Missouri River floodplain: Ann. Assoc. Am. Geogr., v. 53, pp. 60–73.

Schumm, S. A., 1960, The effect of sediment type on the shape and stratification of some modern fluvial deposits: Am. J. Sci., v. 258, pp. 177–184.

Schumm, S. A., 1961, Effect of sediment characteristics of erosion and deposition in ephemeral-stream channels: U. S. Geol. Surv. Prof. Paper 352-C, pp. 31–70.

Schumm, S. A., 1965, Quaternary paleohydrology, in H. E. Wright, Jr. and D. G. Frey, (editors) Quaternary of the United States: Princeton University Press, Princeton, New Jersey, p. 783–794.

Schumm, S. A., 1967, Paleohydrology: application of modern hydrologic data to problems of the ancient past: Int. Hydrol. Symp. (Fort Collins), Proc., v. 1, pp. 185–193.

Schumm, S. A., 1968, River adjustment to altered hydrologic regimen, Murrumbidgee River and paleochannels, Australia: U. S. Geol. Surv. Prof. Paper 598.

Schumm, S. A., 1972, Fluvial paleochannels: Soc. Econ. Paleontol. and Mineral. Spec. Publ. 13, pp. 98–107.

Schumm, S. A., and Beathard, R. M., 1976, Geomorphic thresholds: an approach to river management, in Rivers 76, v. 1, 3rd Symposium of the Waterways: Harbors and Coastal Engineers Division of the American Society of Civil Engineers, pp. 707–724.

Schumm, S. A., and Khan, H. R., 1972, Experimental study of channel patterns: Geol. Soc. Am. Bull., v. 83, pp. 1755–1770.

Schumm, S. A., Khan, H. R., Winkley, B. R. and Robbins, L. G., 1972, Variability of river patterns: Nature, Phys. Sci., v. 237, pp. 75–76.

Schumm, S. A. and Lichty, R. W., 1963, Channel widening and floodplain construction along Cimarron River in Southwestern Kansas: U. S. Geol. Surv. Prof. Paper 352-D, pp. 71–88.

Shrock, R. R., 1948, Sequence in layered rocks: McGraw-Hill, New York, 507 pp.

Shulits, S., 1941, Rational equation of river-bed profile: Am. Geophys. Union Trans., v. 22, pp. 522–631.

Simons, D. B. and Albertson, M. L., 1960, Uniform water conveyance channels in alluvial materials: J. Hydrol. Div., Am. Soc. Civil Eng. Proc. HY5, pp. 33–71.

Simons, D. B. and Richardson, E. V., 1966, Resistance to flow in alluvial channels: U. S. Geol. Surv. Prof. Paper 422-J.

Simons, D. B., Stevens, M. A. and Duke, J. H. Jr., 1973, Predicting stages on sandbed rivers: J. Waterways, Harbors, Coastal Eng. Div. Am. Soc. Civil Eng., v. 99, pp. 231–243.

Smith, H. T. U., 1940, Notes on historic changes in stream courses of wetern Kansas, with a plea for additional data: Kansas Acad. Sci., Trans., v. 43, pp. 299–300.

Speight, J. G., 1965, Meander spectra of the Anabunga River: J. Hydrol., v. 3, pp. 1–15.

Speight, J. G., 1967, Spectral analysis of meanders of some Australian Rivers, in Landform studies from Australia and New Guinea: Aust. National University Press, p. 48–63.

Stevens, M. A., Simons, D. B., and Richardson, E. V., 1975, Non-equilibrium river form: J. Hydral. Div., A. S. C. E. v. 101, pp. 557–566.

Thornbury, W. D., 1969, Principles of geomorphology: Wiley, New York, 594 pp.

Tiffany, J. B. and Nelson, G. A., 1939, Studies of meandering of model-streams: Am. Geophys. Union Trans., Pt. IV, August, pp. 644–649.

Volkov, N. G., Sokolovsky, I. L. and Subbotin, A. I., 1967, Effect of recent crustal movements on the shape of longitudinal profiles and water levels in rivers: Symp. River Mechanics, Int. Union Geodesy Geophys. (Bern) Publ. 75, pp. 105–116.

von Bandat, H. F., 1962, Aerogeology: Gulf, Houston, Texas, 350 pp.

Wallace, R., 1967, Notes on stream channels offset by the San Andreas fault: Proc. Conf. Geol. Problems San Andreas Fault System, Stanford Univ. Publ. Geol. Sci., v. 11, pp. 6–20.

Walters, W. H. Jr., 1975, Regime changes of the lower Mississippi River: unpublished M. S. Thesis, Department of Civil Engineering, Colorado State University.

Warren, G. K., 1867, Survey of the Upper Mississippi River: House of Representatives Executive Document 58, 39th Congress, 2nd Session, 166 pp.

Winkley, B. R., 1970, Influence of geology on the regimen of a river: Am. Soc. Civil Eng., Natl. Water Resour. Meeting (Memphis) preprint 1078, 35 pp.

Yang, C. T., 1972, Unit stream power and sediment transport: Am. Soc. Civil. Eng., J. Hydraul. Div., v. 98, pp. 1804–1826.

Zeuner, F. E., 1959, The Pleistocene period: Hutchinson, London, 447 pp.

CHAPTER SIX

Valleys and Valley Fills (Zones 1 and 2)

The previous discussion of channel morphology was necessary for an understanding of this chapter, which involves consideration of bedrock morphology, valley-fill sediments, terraces, and placers in valley sediments, because the character of the valley itself and the nature of the valley-fill sedimentary deposits, reflect the behavior of the river and the products of Zone 1 upstream.

Most valleys contain rivers flowing on alluvial valley-fill deposits. The morphology of the bedrock valley itself is, of course, obscured by the deposits. Therefore, it is difficult to obtain information on the configuration of the bedrock floor of a valley, and yet the configuration of the valley floor and the valley sides, as well as the character of the alluvium at depth, is important. Unlike stream channels that are visible and available for study, the valley fill and the valley floor can be studied only where penetrated by wells, where excavated at construction sites, quarries, and mines, or where studied by seismic methods.

VALLEY MORPHOLOGY

Dimensions

The frequent use of the term paleochannel for what appears to be a valley-fill deposit suggests that the apparently simple problem of distinguishing between ancient channels and valleys is a major one. Size is one criterion that can be used to distinguish between the two. For example, the largest river in the world today is the Amazon. It drains an area of 2.3 million square miles with an average annual precipitation of 80 inches. The width of the Amazon ranges from 1 to 3 miles and the depth from 20 to 300 feet along the lower 900 miles of its course. At Obidos, where the U. S. Geological Survey has made discharge measurements, the channel is 200 feet deep and about 7500 feet wide (Oltman et al., 1964).

In contrast, the Mississippi River, the world's fourth largest (Morisawa, 1968), is about 2000 feet wide and 60 feet deep at Vicksburg. These channels are enormous, as they need to be to transport an average flow of about 5.5 million and 0.6 million cfs, respectively. The Amazon, in fact, transports 15 percent of all the fresh water running into the oceans.

Information on the dimensions of some paleovalley deposits (Table 6–1) reveals that most are smaller than the Amazon and Mississippi rivers, but if they are assumed to be paleochannels they must have

TABLE 6-1. PALEOVALLEY DIMENSIONS

Channel	Width	Depth (ft)
J Channel (Harms, 1966)	1500	50
Rocktown channel (Rubey and Bass, 1925)	0.5 mi	25 (range 15–100 ft)
Indiana channels (Friedman, 1960)		
New Goshen	0.5 mi	40
Terre Haute	0.25 mi	40
Winslow	2600 ft	50
Englevale channel (Howard and Schowe, 1965)	0.5 mi	60
Prepennsylvanian channel (Siever, 1951)	3.75 mi	200+
Bush City channel (Charles, 1941)	1000–2000 ft	55
Tonganoxie channel (Lins, 1950)	14 mi	100

drained huge areas of high rainfall. In many instances such source areas did not exist. There can be little doubt that many "paleochannel" deposits are, in fact, valley-fill deposits composed of sediments deposited in a shifting and aggrading channel. For example, Harms (1966) stresses that the "J" sand, which is about 2400 feet wide and 60 feet deep, is a valley-fill deposit. (For other examples, see Rubey and Bass, 1925; Friedman, 1960; Howard and Schoewe, 1965; Siever, 1951; Charles, 1941; Lins, 1950.)

As with stream channels, the dimensions of a valley should reflect the quantity of water that has or is being moved through the valley. A relationship similar to that between meander wavelength and discharge (Figure 5-7) has been developed for valley meander wavelength and drainage area, which is an index of discharge (Dury, 1965).

If valley meanders are related to paleodischarge (Table 5-1), then valley width and depth also should be related to past discharges. Obviously, large rivers should occupy large valleys. There are exceptions, of course, dependent on the resistance of the bedrock to erosion and the geomorphic history of the river (capture, etc.) but, in general, major rivers occupy large valleys. However, a study of valley-floor width of Iowa rivers (Salisbury et al., 1968) shows that valleys are highly variable from place to place and that no more than 16 percent of the variability of valley width can be accounted for by modern stream discharge or drainage area. This demonstrates that a valley morphology is strongly controlled by variations in bedrock.

Suballuvial Morphology

Frequently, little is known about valley morphology below the alluvial deposit that obscures the valley floor, and therefore, when sketches of a valley profile or cross section are made, a relatively smooth-floored profile is usually drawn. The smoothness of the valley floor, as sketched, is usually a reflection of ignorance. For example, Figure 6-1 is a cross section of the James River Valley in southern North Dakota. Based on only three drill holes, the cross section of the James River Valley is highly generalized and provides little information on details of the bedrock floor of the valley.

The valley section as shown is interesting because the James River is located on the left side of the valley, where the depth of alluvium below the channel is very shallow. The deepest part of the valley does not lie directly beneath the river. Also, the bores reveal that the lowermost part of the valley fill is composed of the coarsest material. Above this is an intermediate zone of finer sand and gravel containing some silts and clays, and then at the top is a floodplain deposit composed of very fine sediments. The valley fill is a fining upward sequence of fluvial sediments.

Krylov (1971) makes the point that a river should not be expected to lie directly over the deepest part of its valley. He indicates that a channel shift can take place as a result of either tilting, which would shift a river from one side of its valley to the other, or high sediment production by tributaries, which force the river laterally to the opposite side of its valley. Experimental studies on the effect of tributary discharge and sediment load (Mosley, 1976) demonstrate clearly the lateral shift of the main channel that can be expected when tributary contributions are large (Figure 6-2). Mosley's observations help to explain the position of a river within its valley; for example, the upper Mississippi River between St. Louis, Missouri, and St. Paul, Minnesota, is strongly influenced by large tributaries that have pushed the main channel to opposite sides of the valley. The persistence of this effect may well create a marked assymmetry of the bedrock valley at such locations. These factors certainly can be important, but during normal meander development a river shifts from one side of its valley to the other.

Dury's (1965) work suggests that, if in the past a valley was completely occupied by flowing water, the configuration of the valley, particularly at bends, should resemble that of an alluvial channel; that is, the valley will

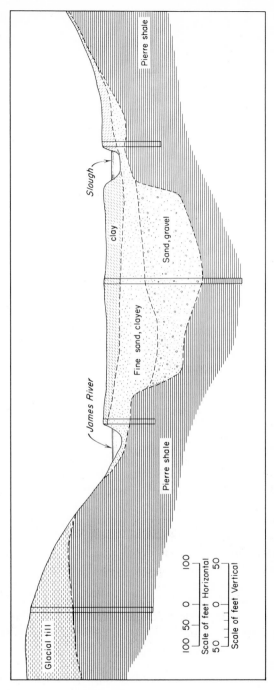

Figure 6-1 Cross section of James River valley at site of Jamestown Dam, North Dakota. (From U. S. Bureau of Reclamation, 1957.)

183

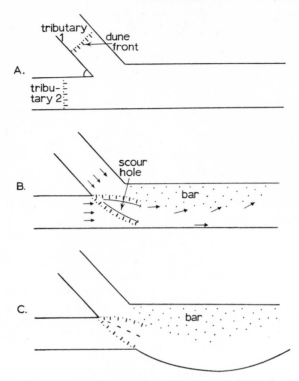

Figure 6-2   Effect of large tributary on position of main channel and channel scour during experimental study. (From Mosley, 1976.)

be deepest on the outside of bends. Palmquist (1975) indicates that, where the alluvium is not deep (no more than twice the bank height), scour of bedrock will occur during floods. Palmquist studied the position of rivers in their valleys and found that at a valley bend the river generally tended to be located on the outside of the bend. Therefore, it is probable that the bedrock floor of a valley will be asymmetrical at bends, with the deepest part of the valley floor on the outside of the bend. However, in a straight part of the valley the river is likely to be at any position within the valley.

An interesting example of valley-floor configuration and the contrariness of rivers is provided by the Mississippi River below its junction with the Missouri River at St. Louis (Figure 6-3). The form of the valley indicates that, as Mosely's experiments and common sense suggest, the river should occupy the east side of its valley where the maximum depth of alluvium is in excess of 160 feet. Instead, it is now flowing on bedrock

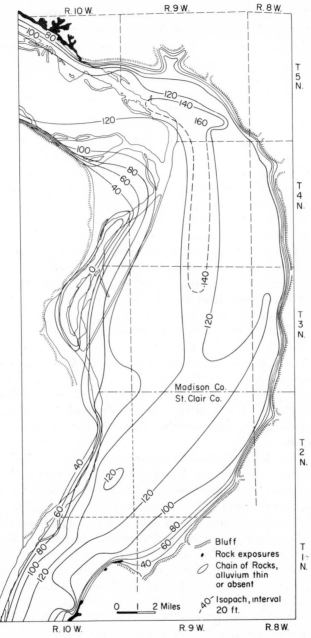

Figure 6-3 Thickness of Mississippi Valley alluvium, East St. Louis, Illinois. (From Bergstrom and Walker, 1956.)

at the Chain of Rocks on the west side of the valley. Note also the approximately 40-foot-deep and 2-mile-wide inner channel delineated by the 120-foot isopach that is cut in the bedrock of the valley floor. This must represent the position of the river when it was at the level of the valley floor. In addition, the valley floor is deepest just above the modern confluence of the Missouri with the Mississippi, indicating that the longitudinal profile of a valley probably will be irregular, depending in part on the effect of major tributary confluences.

An ancient example is the asymmetrical valley filled with the Berea Sandstone in Ohio (Figure 6-4). In this case it is unlikely that the asymmetry is due to scour through the overlying alluvium or to complete filling of the valley with water; rather it is probably due to progressive downward erosion with channel shift toward the outside of the bend, a not unusual condition. At some later time the valley-fill was deposited. Note the contours of the valley floor upstream and downstream from the quarry. These show that the deepest part of the valley floor is at the narrowest part of the valley, essentially at the cross section AA' (Figure 6-4). Below the bend the valley floor is broadly concave and relatively symmetrical, and downstream the depth of the valley is 100 feet less than that at the bend.

The work of Siever (1951) in delineating ancient valleys on the Mississippian–Pennsylvanian unconformity of southern Illinois provides additional examples of valley irregularity. Several hills are conspicuous in his cross sections, and he suggests that these are meander cores abandoned as bedrock meanders were cut off. He also identifies bedrock terraces at several levels in the valley. Obviously the morphology of valley floors is much more variable than the usual cross section (Figure 6-1) indicates.

Although an occasionally detailed valley cross section can be obtained, it is even rarer to find information on the longitudinal profile of valleys. The short segments of the Mississippi Valley and the Berea Sandstone valley (Figures 6-3 and 6-4) suggest that the long profile will not be smooth. For example, the shallow alluvial fill in a badland channel was probed with a metal rod to determine its total thickness. The results are shown in Figure 6-5. In this case the bedrock–alluvium interface is very irregular. Part of the irregularity may be due to the effects of tributary junctions, because Mosley's (1976) studies indicated that scour depths at tributary junctions increase with size of the tributary.

Another factor causing irregularity of a valley profile is diastrophism, and variations in the depth of bedrock in some valleys may reflect uplift or subsidence. Ancient valleys, of course, can be buried and subject to folding. For example, Harms (1966) describes a gently folded valley-fill

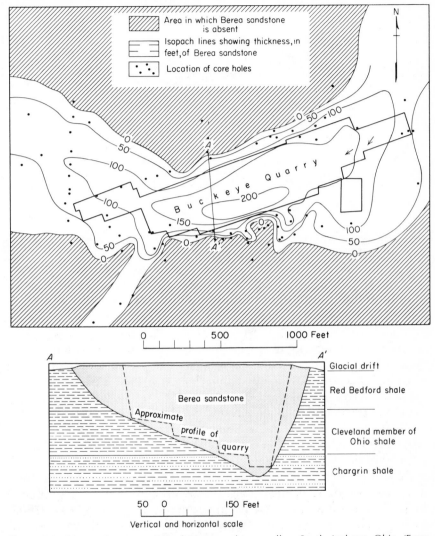

Figure 6-4 Map and cross section of Berea sandstone valley, South Amherst, Ohio. (From Pepper et al., 1954.)

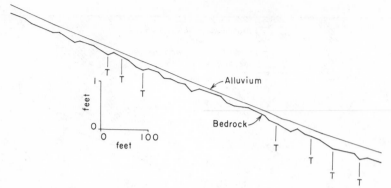

Figure 6-5   Longitudinal profile of alluvium and bedrock valley in badlands near Lusk, Wyoming. T designates tributary junction.

deposit, the J-sand of the Cretaceous age, which contains oil trapped at each high point of the deformed valley fill.

EXPERIMENTAL STUDIES OF VALLEY MORPHOLOGY

Although several types of erosive mechanisms and products can be investigated as they occur, the incision of a river into bedrock to form a valley is not amenable to observation. For example, the origin of incised meanders and the possibility of inheritance of their patterns from an erosion surface have long been a matter of discussion (Davis, 1893; Winslow, 1893), and the manner in which erosion progresses to develop incised meanders is not clearly understood (Leopold et al., 1964, p. 313). Therefore, valley formation may be one topic that, above all, can benefit from experimental investigation.

Experiments on valley development were performed using a 60-foot-long, 4-foot-wide steel and Plexiglas flume (Figure 6-6). The simulated bedrock was a fine-sand and kaolinite mixture. When mixed wet and then permitted to dry in the flume the material was uniform and sufficiently cohesive to permit erosion of the type required (Shepherd and Schumm, 1974).

Incision was studied in straight channels cut into the surface of the simulated bedrock. These troughs were about 1.3 feet wide and 0.1 foot deep, and erosion was initiated by increasing the slope of the flume. In two straight channels the same general sequence of erosional events was observed. This sequence is given in Figures 6-7 and 6-8, which show the transverse profiles and a plan view of part of the valley through time.

Figure 6-6 Experimental channel after 65 hours of incision into simulated bedrock (kaolinite–sand mixture). A narrow and deep inner channel formed in the straight initial channel, which was cut 1.3 feet wide and 0.10 feet deep in the sediment on the right side of the flume. The left side of the flume was occupied by the channel of a previous run. Discharge was 0.10 cfs and slope was 0.017. (From Shepherd and Schumm, 1974.)

After only a few hours of erosion, longitudinal lineations developed on the channel bed. These appeared as faint erosional streaks and shallow grooves (Figure 6-8a,b). With time the lineations enlarged into prominent longitudinal grooves (Figures 6-7e, f, g and 6-8c, d, e). Finally, one narrow and deep inner channel conveyed the entire flow (Figures 6-7h and 6-8f), leaving remnants of the previously scoured channel floor above the level of flow.

In summary, in the straight channels erosion and incision progressed through a sequence beginning with longitudinal lineations, potholes,

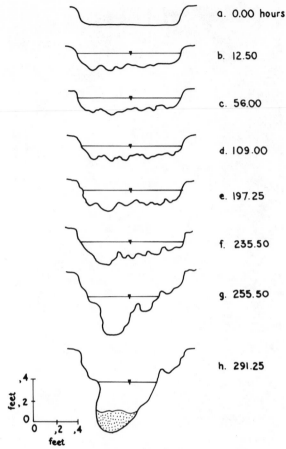

Figure 6-7   Series of transverse profiles measured as incision occurred in experimental channel. Elapsed run time is shown at each section. Initial flume slope was 0.0048. After 214 hours, erosion was still proceeding slowly, but then coarse sand was introduced at the rate of 25 g per minute. The sand-feed rate markedly influenced incision rates. Stippled pattern (h) shows extent of deposition at end of experiment. (From Shepherd and Schumm, 1974.)

and erosional ripples. The lineations enlarged into prominent grooves, and the sequence culminated in the development of a single inner channel that conveyed the entire flow. In some cases two grooves developed and an island was formed between two narrow and deep inner channels (Figure 6-6). The lineations and grooves appeared to form and enlarge in response to cells of secondary circulation (longitudinal vortices), whereas the erosional ripples and potholes owed their origin to irregularities on the bed and were associated with rollers and separated

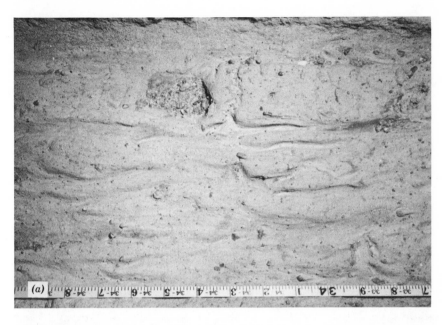

Figure 6-8   Bed-scour features through time in experimental channel. Scale in all photographs is in tenths of feet. Flow direction was to the right in all photographs. (a) Bed erosion after 12.5 hours, showing early stages of ripples, potholes, and grooves. (b) Longitudinal grooves becoming predominant; potholes present. Gravels are coarse fractions of bedrock (56 hours). (c) Scour

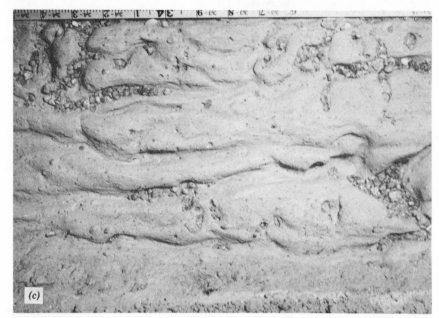

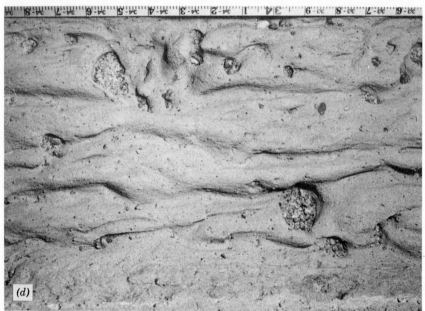

continuing, bed forms enlarging (129.5 hours). (*d*) Scour continuing, number of grooves decreasing (197.25 hours). (e) After the initial addition of sand to the flow (214 hours), the bed erosion increases significantly and a conspicuously large groove starts to become dominant

(lower-middle portion of the photo, 235.5 hours). (*f*) Final development of an inner channel with a low width/depth ratio (269.5 hours). The gradient is low enough to permit deposition on the inner channel floor. (From Shepherd and Schumm, 1974.)

flows, as discussed by Allen (1970, 1971). The experimental results support the conclusion that a valley floor may be morphologically far more complex than the usual transverse profiles suggest (Figure 6-1).

To investigate the development of incised meanders, a sinuous channel was excavated in the experimental material. Figure 6-9 shows the transverse profiles of the sinuous channel through time at two successive bends and at a crossing. The greatest erosion occurred initially at the inside or along the convex bank of each bend, but later, maximum erosion shifted towards the outside of the bend, and the concave bank was undercut. However, at the crossings between bends the channel incised almost vertically. With only minor variations this difference in the evolution of incision was observed at all bends and crossings, and scour was greatest at bends. The undercutting of the valley walls to produce overhanging "bedrock" valley walls appears unrealistic and a result of the experimental design, but, in fact, bedrock overhangs of this type have been observed (Logan, 1959). They are not as pronounced as those shown in Figures 6-9a, however.

Other laboratory studies of shear phenomena at bends in rigid boundary channels explain this apparently anomalous situation. For example, Ippen et al. (1962), Yen (1970), and Hooke (1975) conducted studies of boundary shear distributions in rigid, curved, trapezoidal channels. Their results indicate that the greatest shear stress occurs at

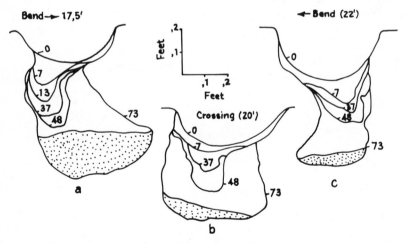

Figure 6-9   Transverse profiles of incised channel at two bends (a and c) and at a crossing (b). Arrows point to outside (concave bank) of bend. Distances along flume are given. Stippled areas represent sand deposition; elapsed time is shown at each profile. Sediment feed (fine sand) was increased after 27 hours. (From Shepherd, 1972.)

the inside of a bend. It is possible that these conditions exist only at relatively high velocities, when the maximum flow velocity and bed-load transport occur on the inside of a meander bend across the point bar.

Another significant factor in this seemingly anomalous localization of scour in bends is the influence of sediment deposition. Sand was entrained while scour occurred at the inside of bends, but later sediment was deposited on the bottom of the channel as the gradient was progressively decreased by scour. Irrigation engineers have long known that a diversion channel branching from a stream on the inside of a bend aggrades more rapidly than a diversion channel placed elsewhere. This occurs because a large percentage of bed load is carried around the inside of the bend. The bed load was also concentrated at the inside of the bends in the experimental channel, and therefore, erosion of the channel bottom was enhanced by abrasion in this area of highest shear stress. However, as the gradient of the channel was steadily decreased by this continued erosion, a condition was reached at which deposition began, and then maximum erosion shifted to the outside of the bend.

In summary, the location of maximum erosion in an incising bend depends on sediment load and velocity, which determines whether transportation or deposition of the sediment load occurs at the bend. When the load is fully entrained and velocity is high, incision occurs on the inside of the bend. After deposition begins with reduced velocity or increased sediment load, erosion shifts to the outside of the bend. The form of incised meanders apparently depends on the amount of load entrained by the incising stream. The significance of these observations is that the deepest part of a valley need not be on the outside of a bend, as the studies of Palmquist (1974) and Dury (1965) suggest, because scour can occur on the inside of a bend.

Longitudinal Profile. To collect information on variations in the long profile of incising experimental channels, a series of profiles of each channel floor and water surface was measured during the previously described experiments. The water and bed surface profile of channel 1 after 255.5 hours of elapsed run time is shown in Figure 6-10. At this time the channel was incising in the upper 30 feet of the flume, and three bedrock scour lows are present there. Scour also occurred below baselevel along the lower 25 feet of the profile.

During this experiment another important aspect of channel morphology was noted: the channel was markedly narrower and deeper at the scour lows and wider and shallower at the scour highs. Therefore, channel morphology varied both vertically and horizontally along the channel. The straight channel, while incising, exhibited relatively regu-

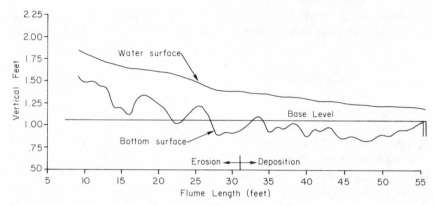

Figure 6-10   Water-surface and bed longitudinal profiles of experimental channel after 255 hours into the experiment. (From Shepherd and Schumm, 1974.)

lar changes of width/depth ratio and relatively uniform spacing of scour lows while maintaining a generally smooth water-surface profile. The changes in the bottom profiles of channel 2 through time are shown in Figure 6-11. Deposition was induced in this channel by a decrease of flume slope after 75 hours.

At 64.75 hours of elapsed run time, the flow was entirely conveyed within an inner channel, and the profile shown is a bedrock profile (Figure 6-11). Deposition was then induced by a slope decrease. After deposition the channel floor was excavated, and the final bedrock profile under the alluvial deposit was recorded (Figure 6-11). The earlier profile (64.75 hours) had more regularly spaced scours than did the final one.

The difference between the earlier and final profiles may be explained by the relative scour associated with the amount of load entrained. The earlier profile developed when essentially all the sediment load was entrained, and the scour apparently developed a regular pattern. However, when deposition began it occurred first in the lows, and scour was concentrated at the bedrock highs. As some of the highs were reduced by scour, the final profile under the alluvial deposit did not display a regular scour pattern.

In summary, these results suggest that the bedrock profiles of valleys probably exhibit irregular scour patterns, unless deposition was very rapid and deep enough to protect the valley floor. Actively incising channels may have regular scour patterns, but bedrock type, structure, and the influence of tributaries have complicating effects on the longitudinal profile of a bedrock valley. Contrary to expectations, incision

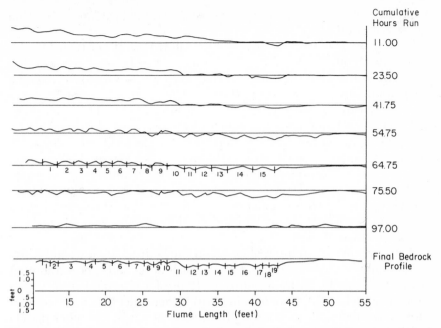

Figure 6-11   Bed profiles of experimental channel. Scour lows are indicated on incised "bedrock" profile (64.7 hours) and on final bedrock profile after aggradation. (From Shepherd and Schumm, 1974.)

did not occur uniformly over the width of the valley floor during the experiments. Rather, with water flowing bank-full in the straight trapezoidal channels, narrow and deep inner bedrock channels formed. The occurrence of scour below baselevel in the experimental channels suggests that considerable depths of alluvium can exist upstream from local baselevels in natural rivers.

Field Analogs

That inner channels and bedrock highs and lows exist beneath the alluvium of valleys is an interesting possibility, but one that is obviously difficult to confirm. Nevertheless, some information is available that supports the conclusions reached from experimentation. For example, Bretz (1924) presents a topographic map showing a prominent inner channel in basalt at Five Mile Rapids of the Columbia River near The Dalles, Oregon. The topography is remarkably similar to that which developed in the experiments. In addition, Bretz states that the Columbia River has eroded 115 feet below sea level at a point 192 river miles from the ocean, and this provides a spectacular field example of erosion below baselevel.

A cross section taken at the location of Hoover Dam (Figure 6-12) shows a well-developed inner channel flanked by bedrock terraces. Excavation of the dam site for the Prineville Dam in Oregon revealed a narrow and deep "inner gorge" (Logan, 1959, p. 2) averaging 70 feet in width and with a depth as great as 60 feet (Figure 6-13). The inner gorge contained overhanging cliffs, potholes, and narrow and steep-sided interconnecting trenches. The Trinity Dam site in California also has a prominent inner bedrock channel that had to be excavated before dam construction could proceed, and multiple inner channels were revealed at the Grand Coulee Dam (Flint and Irwin, 1939). Inner channels have been observed by river engineers, but often they have been interpreted as ancient low-flow channels, which, according to experimental results, is probably not the case.

The existence of an inner channel on the bedrock floor of an incised valley could be a potential area for the localization and concentration of heavy minerals by hydraulic sorting. If the location and trend of an inner channel could be determined, in either paleofluvial deposits or Holocene valleys, the exploration for gold, diamonds, and other placers would be facilitated. A field study of Tertiary age gravel-filled valleys in northern California revealed that some contain a "gut" (Figure 6-14) similar to the experimentally developed inner channels. Not all the paleochannels have a gut, but where present, the gut may contain rich gold deposits (Peterson et al., 1968).

Inner channels probably will not be found in all bedrock valleys, but their existence should be anticipated when planning for dam construction, alluvial aquifer exploration, and other engineering and geologic endeavors in alluvial valleys.

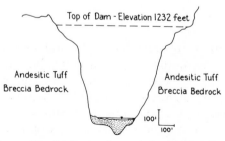

Figure 6-12   Transverse profile of bedrock valley and alluvial fill, Colorado River near Hoover Dam. (After Wilbur and Mead, 1933.)

Figure 6-13   Inner channel in bedrock at Prinville Dam site, Oregon. (U. S. Bureau of Reclamation photograph.)

Incised Meanders

During the experimental investigation of bedrock incision, alluvial meanders developed in a sand cover placed over the simulated bedrock, but in every case when the slope of the flume was increased to induce incision, the alluvial meanders were destroyed and a relatively straight channel incised into bedrock. From these observations it is difficult to

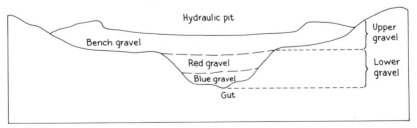

Figure 6-14   Diagrammatic section across an idealized Tertiary channel in Nevada County, California, showing the presence of a "gut" or inner channel. (From Peterson et al., 1968.)

accept the hypotheses that symmetrical incised meanders in nature inherited their patterns from an alluvial channel superimposed from a
warped peneplain. However, another way in which incised meanders
can form is by baselevel lowering or essentially vertical uplift. Gardner
(1975) showed by additional experimentation that when a bedrock surface is horizontal, a lowering of baselevel causes headward incision up
the meander pattern. Following rejuvenation, a nickpoint will migrate
upstream and will follow the the existing channel pattern to form incised
meanders in the underlying bedrock. However, as headward erosion
progresses along a given meander, the downstream limb of the meander
encounters bedrock first, and it is then locked in position. The upstream
limb of the meander, still on alluvium, continues to shift downstream as

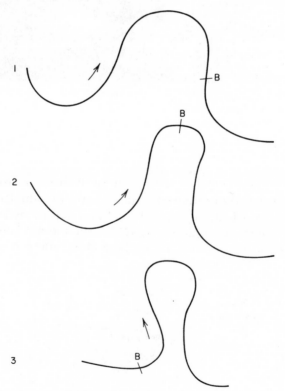

Figure 6-15 Development of deformed incised meander when downstream limb is fixed by
bedrock. The letter B indicates the location at which the channel enters bedrock. Upstream the
channel is in alluvium.

part of a normal downvalley sweep of the meander pattern, and the meander loop is deformed. By the time the upstream limbs of the experimental meanders became fixed in bedrock, a very deformed meander usually had developed (Figure 6-15). This appears to be an explanation of deformed incised meanders of the type that is typified by the Goosenecks of the San Juan River (Figure 6-16).

Hunt (1969) has observed that in the Colorado Plateau incised meanders exist upstream from the axis of folds but not downstream from them (Figure 6-17). Experiments provide an explanation of this phenomenon (Gardner, 1975). When a river incises from an alluvial cover onto a broad anticline or monocline, upstream from the structural axis the channel incises into bedrock, and headward erosion up the channel preserves the meandering pattern, although the meanders may be deformed (Figures 6-15 and 6-16). Downstream of the fold axis, the stream flows down the dip of the strata, and before it can incise into bedrock the increased gradient destroys the alluvial meander patterns. The effect is similar to tilting of the flume with meander destruction.

Figure 6-16   Incised meanders of Goosenecks of San Juan River. Deformed incised meanders are characteristic of many rivers of the Colorado Plateaus.

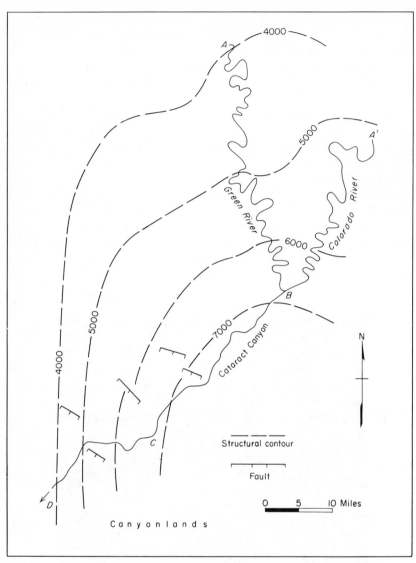

Figure 6-17   Sketch map showing distribution of incised meanders in Canyonlands area of Utah. Structural contours (feet above sea level) are drawn on top of the Chinle Formation. The Green and Colorado rivers flow upstructure between locations A-A'and B, on the structure between B and C, and down the structural dip between C and D. (From Gardner, 1975.)

THE VALLEY FILL

Valley bedrock morphology is only one aspect of this component of the fluvial system. The other major component is the valley-fill deposit. In general, this is a fining upward sequence of sediment (Figure 6-1). The coarsest sediment lies at the base of the valley fill, and the finest sediments are at the top. Of course, much depends on the nature of rocks underlying the sediment source area. If the product from Zone 1 is sand, then the valley will be filled with sand. If Zone 1 is composed of a variety of sediments, then the coarsest material will be deposited at the bottom of the valley, but with reduction of gradient and an increase of weathering, progressively finer sediments will be transported from the Zone 1. If the drainage basin is entirely underlain by fine-grained deposits, then the river will transport primarily suspended load, and the valley fill will be fine grained. Based on the relationships between type of sediment load and channel morphology discussed in Chapter Five, a difference in the sediments produced by Zone 1 will be reflected in the valley-fill sedimentology and stratigraphy. However, it is unlikely that a valley will be filled without interruption, and variations from a fining upward sequence of sediment can be expected as a result of climate change and diastrophisms.

The actual process of valley filling can take place in three ways, depending on the nature of the control that is causing deposition. First, there can be a change in baselevel that will reduce gradient in the lower end of the valley. This downstream control will initiate a progressive backfilling of the valley (Figure 5-28). If there is uplift in the source area or a change in climate such that a great increase in sediment production results, aggradation will again result. The effect of the upstream control, in contrast to the backfilling of the valley, will be a progressive downfilling as the coarse sediment load is progressively deposited farther down the valley. On the other hand, there can also be a vertical filling of the valley by a great increase in production of sediment from numerous tributaries. Under these conditions there is a uniform raising of the level of the valley floor.

With backfilling the coarsest material will be deposited first on the floor of the channel and finer sediments will be deposited downstream (Figure 5-28). This downstream and vertical similarity in the sediment sequence conforms to Walther's law of sediment deposition.

With downfilling the first sediments to reach a downstream point will be the finest, with the coarsest deposited upvalley. At a midvalley position, sediments being deposited will coarsen upward as deposition progresses downstream.

With uniform filling of the valley by major tributary contributions, there will be great local variation depending on the nature of the sediments contributed from the tributaries. In all cases the variability of sediment on the valley floor and in the alluvial valley fill will be large.

Modern examples of downfilling result from hydraulic mining (Gilbert, 1917) and agricultural activities (Trimble, 1975). Sandurs and glacial outwash plains, which are constructed by deposition of large amounts of glacial debris, are formed in this way (Krigstrom, 1962; Church, 1972). An interesting aspect of the modern sandurs is that they frequently are incised near the glacier. This may be due to variations in sediment load and discharge, or, as suggested by Church (1972, pp. 79, 109), it may be a normal feature of sandur development as sediment is stored and remobilized at the head of the deposit. The geomorphic threshold concept probably applies to this type of depositional situation. If so, recurrent incision and remobilization and reworking of sediments will produce a complicated sequence of valley sediments (Church and Gilbert, 1975, Figure 46).

Classification of Valley-Fill Deposits

A classification of valley sedimentary deposits by Happ (1971) is presented in Table 6-2 and in Figure 6-18. Of course, not all these types of sediments will be identifiable in every valley or paleovalley deposit, and the nature of the sediments will vary depending on type of sediment load.

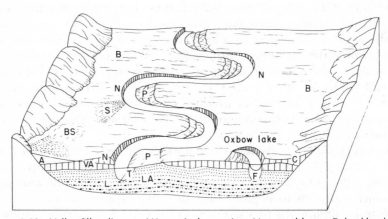

Figure 6-18   Valley-fill sediments. VA, vertical accretion; N, natural levee; B, backland; BS, backswamp; LA, lateral accretion; P, point bar; S, splay; A, alluvial fan; T, transitory bar; L, lag deposit; F, channel fill; C, colluvium (From S. C. Happ, 1971, Genetic classification of valley sediment deposits: A.S.C.E. J. Hydraul. Div., v. 97, pp. 43–53.)

TABLE 6-2. CLASSIFICATION OF VALLEY SEDIMENTS (FROM HAPP, 1971)

Place of deposition (1)	Name (2)	Characteristics (3)
Channel	Transitory channel deposits	Primarily bed load temporarily at rest; part may be preserved in more durable channel fills or lateral accretions
	Lag deposits	Segregations of larger or heavier particles, more persistent than transitory channel deposits, and including heavy mineral placers
	Channel fills	Accumulations in abandoned or aggrading channel segments; ranging from relatively course bed load to fine-grained oxbow lake deposits
Channel margin	Lateral accretion deposits	Point and marginal bars that may be preserved by channel shifting and added to overbank floodplain by vertical accretion deposits at top
Overbank flood-plain	Vertical accretion deposits	Fine-grained sediment deposited from suspended load of overbank floodwater; including natural levee and black-land (backswamp) deposits
	Splays	Local accumulations of bed load materials, spread from channels onto adjacent floodplains
Valley margin	Colluvium	Deposits derived chiefly from unconcentrated slope wash and soil creep on adjacent valley sides
	Mass movement deposits	Earthflow, debris avalanche, and landslide deposits commonly intermix with marginal colluvium; mudflows usually follow channels but also spill overbank

Considerable post-depositional modification of valley-fill sediments can take place when incision of the deposits initiates slumping along the sides of the new channel or when incising and widening produce another valley within the fill. Slumps are readily recognized in modern sediments, but in limited exposures or in drill cores, the steeply dipping bedding of the slumped block may cause consternation among those whose job it is to interpret the puzzle. Flint and Irwin (1939, Plate 1) recognized slumping in the Pleistocene sediments in the Columbia River Canyon, and Williams et al. (1965) cite examples of Paleozoic slumps in paleovalleys of western Pennsylvania.

In Fisk's diagrams (Figure 5-33), which show the filling of the Mississippi Valley, it is obvious that the vertical difference in sediments reflects deposits from very different types of rivers ranging perhaps from bed load to mixed load. Just as channel morphology and channel fill deposits differ (Figures 5-27 and 5-29), depending on the type of sediment load moved through the channels, so do valley-fills differ. The diagrammatic cross sections of Figure 6-19 suggest how valley-fill deposits of the three river types might appear in section.

The valley-fill stratigraphy of a bed-load channel (Figure 6-19) is based upon changes that have occurred along the bed-load streams of Kansas and Texas (Schumm and Lichty, 1963) where, during years of low peak discharge, a veneer of fine sediments is deposited over the thick deposit of cross-bedded sand and gravel to form a floodplain. The result is a flat-topped sand body capped by a relatively thin deposit of fine alluvium. This floodplain may be destroyed periodically by major floods, when the fine sediment is carried away in suspension. In the valley of the Canadian River of northern Texas, borings by the Bureau

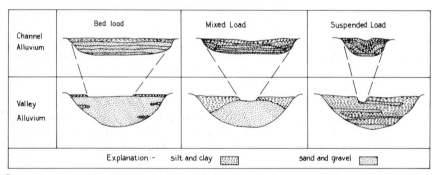

Figure 6-19   Idealized cross sections showing nature of channel and valley-fill deposits associated with the three types of rivers. (From Schumm, 1968a.)

of Reclamation at the site of the Sanford Dam show a veneer of a few feet of fine sediment over 150 feet of clean sand and fine gravel.

The valley-fill stratigraphy of a mixed-load channel is based partly upon borings into the prior-stream channels adjacent to the Murrumbidgee River (Figures 5-34 and 6-20). The mixed-load valley fill of Figure 6-19 is essentially a lens-shaped deposit of cross-bedded sand. The base of the deposit is composed of sand and some gravel, and the upper part is sand flanked by silt, sand, and clay. As aggradation progressed more of the fine suspended-load sediments were deposited along the flanks of the channel to form a well-developed floodplain.

The valley-fill stratigraphy associated with a suspended-load channel is based upon information obtained from bores into the Murrumbidgee River and its floodplain. Lateral migration of this suspended-load channel leaves a sheet of channel sand that is overlain by point-bar deposits of lateral accretion and overbank deposits (Figure 6-21).

The results of aggradation by bed-load and suspended-load streams on an alluvial plain are not unlike the braided- and meandering-stream depositional models of Allen (1965b). Further, according to the classification of sand bodies proposed by Potter (1963), some pods and

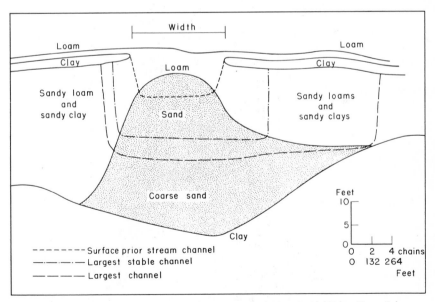

Figure 6-20   Cross section of paleochannel, Riverine Plain, New South Wales. (From Schumm, 1968b.)

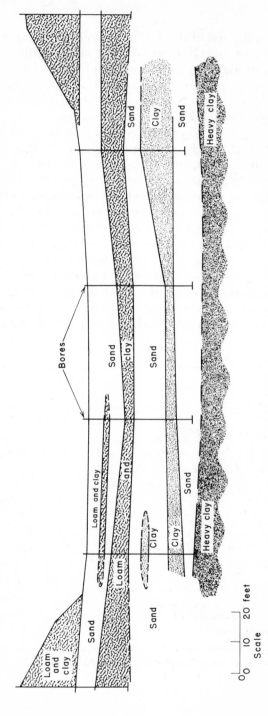

Figure 6-21   Cross-section of channel, Murrumbidgee River, New South Wales, and associated valley-fill sediments. (From Schumm, 1968b.)

ribbon deposits may be discontinuous sand bodies deposited by suspended-load rivers, whereas the dendroids and belt deposits may have been deposited by mixed- and bed-load channels. Sheet deposits can be formed by all three river types. Thin sheet deposits can be formed by a meandering suspended-load or mixed-load channel, whereas a thick fluvial sheet deposit can be the result of bed-load channel deposition over an alluvial plain.

Of the examples cited previously, the Berea Sandstone valley fill is an example of deposition by a bed-load channel (Figure 6-4). A sandstone channel described by Lins (1950, Figure 2) appears to be a mixed-load valley fill with a cross section similar to that of Figure 6-20. Suspended-load valley fills are more likely to be located in near-shore coastal plain, piedmont (Martin, 1966), or deltaic environments, where, of course, estuarine sediments may comprise a part of the total accumulation (Upson and Spencer, 1964).

Bed-load and sandy mixed-load valley fills are sufficiently permeable to permit the migration of uranium-bearing fluids and to form stratigraphic traps for petroleum, whereas the finer suspended-load and silty mixed-load deposits are not. However, fine channel-fill deposits can act as impermeable barriers to form oil fields (Berg, 1968; Martin, 1966). In the Fall River Sandstone Reservoir of northeastern Wyoming oil is held in point-bar sandstones by, according to Berg's (1968) interpretation, abandoned channel or oxbow lake deposits. When the channel fill is updip of the point bar, oil is trapped against it and held in the point-bar sands. A similar situation apparently exists in the Hughenden area, Alberta, Canada, where a meandering clay-filled channel acts as a barrier to oil migration in a sandy valley-fill deposit, and the oil is held in the updip edge of a meander (Martin, 1966).

Needless to say, if oil is trapped in valley fills, it is important to be able to identify the total drainage pattern as a guide to further exploration (Martin, 1966; Stapp, 1967). Stapp (1967) provides a map of a Cretaceous drainage network or valley pattern that was subsequently filled with sediments that now contain oil. A drainage network that developed on a flat surface was incised sufficiently to form a valley network, which in turn was filled with sandstone. In the southern or headward part of the drainage system, sediments were fine grained, but to the north tributaries draining from areas underlain by the Dakota Sandstone produced coarse sediments that formed valley-fill sediments of sufficient permeability for petroleum migration. Therefore, oil is found in the downvalley part of the valley network as a result of differences in the nature of sediment moved and deposited in the valley. Recently,

Coneybeare (1976) has summarized the literature of oil fields located in fluvial deposits.

Floodplains and Terraces

A floodplain is usually composed primarily of lateral-accretion deposits with an overlay of fine vertical-accretion flood deposits (Wolman and Leopold, 1957). This model is based on studies of deposition in the channel and on the floodplain of meandering rivers (Figure 6-18). However, studies of active floodplain construction, for example, in the Cimarron River valley of Kansas, reveal that vertical accretion can be the dominant process (Schumm and Lichty, 1963).

The floodplain of the Cimarron River was destroyed by large floods during the 1930s. After a major flood in 1942, the floodplain began to reform and it was built almost entirely by a vertical accretion of sediments, which occurred in two ways: firstly, by island formation in the channel with subsequent attachment of the island to one bank by channel abandonment, and secondly, by deposition on and build up of areas not occupied by the low-water channel.

In most cases patches of floodplain in the most sheltered parts of the channel formed first. These patches coalesced and joined the islands and abandoned channels to form a composite floodplain. A floodplain, however, can be built simultaneously over large areas. The new floodplain is composed of sedimentary units deposited by overbank floods. A deposit of sand is overlain by a thin mud layer, which was deposited during recession of floodwaters.

After the floodplain has been formed by vertical accretion, the stream may begin to meander and form point bars. This reworking of the floodplain alluvium by lateral migration of the stream forms a floodplain composed predominantly of lateral-accretion deposits, as described by Wolman and Leopold (1957) and by Adler and Lattman (1961). A floodplain may be formed by both processes, but after a meandering stream has migrated from one side of the valley to the other, the stratigraphic evidence for vertical accretion will have been destroyed. Therefore, the identification of lateral accretion deposits, as a major part of a floodplain, may not mean that it was initially formed by point-bar construction and meander migration.

The manner of floodplain formation is of far more than academic interest because it is at the core of most litigations concerning boundaries. If a floodplain is constructed by lateral accretion and a stream shifts by erosion of one bank and point-bar deposition on the other, the boundary shifts with the stream. However, if the channel shift is abrupt, by

avulsion, the boundary remains fixed. The description of the establishment of the boundary between Texas and Oklahoma in the Red River
valley indicates the difficulty courts have in obtaining understandable
and pertinent scientific testimony upon which a decision can be based
(Bowman, 1923). If geomorphic evidence is to be used in such a case it
must be supported by hydrologic, sedimentologic, botanical, and historical information. A general description of channel types and their presumed behavior is background information only, and an expert opinion,
to be creditable, must be based on evidence from the area of dispute.

Incision of a floodplain produces a terrace. Terraces border most
valleys, and where the valley has been filled with alluvium it is logical to
assume that buried terraces may lie beneath the alluvial floor of the
valley. The influence of climate, baselevel change (Table 5-3), and tectonics on rivers and terrace formation is discussed in Chapter Three
and, of course, most major terraces can be attributed to these causes.
However, because terraces form an integral part of valley morphology
and of valley-fill alluvium, further discussion of them is appropriate
here. Figure 6-22 shows diagrammatically several different stratigraphic
and morphologic situations that can occur within a valley.

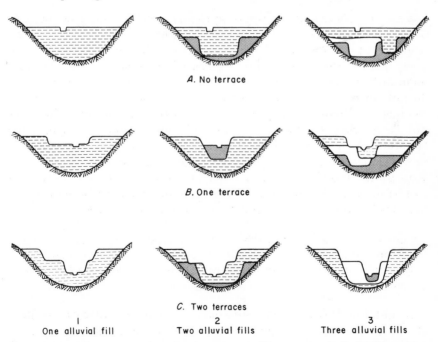

Figure 6-22   Valley cross sections showing some possible terrace and alluvial fill combinations. (From Leopold and Miller, 1954.)

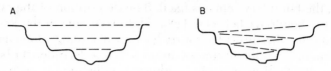

Figure 6-23   Paired and unpaired terraces.

Figure 6-23 shows the difference between paired and unpaired terraces. Paired terraces are commonly attributed to episodic incision as a result of climate or tectonic events, whereas unpaired terraces are generally explained as a result of progressive downcutting with lateral shift of the channel.

The importance of identifying the separate fills and terraces in a valley is, of course, that each represents a change in the behavior of the river system (Table 5-5). In addition, terrace surfaces may represent periods of sediment reworking and therefore may contain heavy mineral concentrations. Alluvium normally contains heavy minerals, but, without reworking of the deposit they may be distributed uniformly through the sediment and, therefore, have no economic value.

Complex Response.   River response to changed climatic, tectonic, and baselevel conditions is considered in Chapter Five as is the complex response of the drainage basin and channel to rejuvenation (Figure 4-12). During the experimental studies of drainage network development and response to rejuvenation, terraces formed as sediment production increased beyond that of the transporting capability of the channel and then decreased again. Therefore, although major terraces can be attributed to climate, baselevel, and tectonic change, some Holocene terraces may be the result of the crossing of a geomorphic threshold coupled with a complex response. These two concepts can assist in the development of an explanation of terrace- and alluvial fill correlation problems in the southwestern United States where the situation has beem described as follows (Kottlowski et al., 1965):

> Late recent time is represented by epicycles of erosion and alluviation in the canyons and valleys of the southwest; however the number, magnitude, and duration of the events differ from basin to basin and along reaches of the same stream.

In addition, Haynes' (1968) summary of extensive radiocarbon dating of alluvial deposits in the southwestern United States demonstrates that, during the last 5000 years of record, there is significant temporal overlap among the three most recent alluvial deposits. This indicates that, as the above quotation states, deposition was not in phase everywhere and that apparently deposition did not occur in response to a single event. Part of the complexity, at least as related to the most recent events, may be explained by the threshold concept, with erosion occurring as described for the Piceance Creek area when a geomorphic threshold is exceeded. However, within one region not all valleys will achieve the threshold at the same time, and so the dates will not be consistent.

Some degree of inconsistency of this type probably is inherent in all stratigraphic correlations, but it is insignificant over the long periods of geologic (cyclic) time; however, the problem becomes major when continental deposits of the last few thousand years are studied.

Both experimental (Figure 4-12) and field studies (Schumm and Hadley, 1957) reveal that when sediment production is high, deposition inevitably follows. Such a sequence of events may be underway in Rio Puerco, a major arroyo in New Mexico, as well as in other Southwestern channels. For example, the dry channel of Rio Puerco, although previously trenched to depths of 13 m, is now less than 4 m deep near its mouth. This is due to deposition caused by very high sediment loads produced by the rejuvenated drainage system (Schumm, 1973; Barsch and Royce, 1972). In fact, where long-term observation of arroyos has been made, the evidence indicates that they are aggrading (Emmett, 1974), as would be expected from a complex response. The time period between rejuvenation and deposition depends on the size of the drainage basin and probably climatic conditions, thereby insuring that correlations cannot be precise.

The complex response may therefore be an explanation of some valley-fill deposits customarily attributed to climate change. An example is the work of Vita-Finzi (1969) in Libya. Based on dates of Roman dams and artifacts he was able to establish that following bedrock incision valleys were filled with sediment during Pleistocene time. Caliche layers in the fill indicate that the filling was not continuous. In Preroman times the valley floors were trenched and the Romans constructed dams in these washes. Sediment then filled the reservoirs and the dams were left as a record of past channel history. Since dam construction, the valley was trenched, a younger fill was deposited during the Middle Ages, and this in turn was trenched in recent times. These last two events can be due to climatic fluctuations, land use, or a complex response of the drainage systems to failure of the valley floor. There is no clear evidence of an external influence, and, in fact, the response of this drainage system to failure of the valley floor and the dams is very similar indeed to the effect of baselevel lowering in the REF.

A further modern example is provided by the Thompson Creek basin in Iowa. Figure 6-24 shows the interpretation by Daniels and Jordan (1966) of the relatively recent events in this basin. Before 1719 the Mullenix fill was trenched from 10 to 25 feet, and following this incision the Turton fill was deposited in 1850. The Turton fill itself was trenched about 1880, and, based on this history, it is predicted that a new fill will eventually be deposited in the trench.

The situation in the Thompson Creek watershed and elsewhere in western Iowa leads Daniels and Jordan (1966, p. 38) to conclude that:

> The alluvial history of these watersheds indicates that landscapes do not develop through continuous slow erosion and alluviation but through periods of erosion and alluviation, probably followed by a period of stability. The resulting landscape is not one in which every part is the same age but consists of many geomorphic surfaces of different ages.

This idea has been stated before by other workers in semiarid and subhumid regions (Thornthwaite et al., 1942, p. 89; McGee, 1891, pp. 261, 262; Schumm and Hadley, 1957).

A further interesting suggestion regarding terraces and gullies in small arid watersheds is that the terraces are temporary and were formed by the flushing action of a "superflood" (Schick, 1974). There seems to be little doubt that such can be the case, but of course a superflood may have only a minor impact unless the valley fill is susceptible to scour, which requires a gradient at which erosion will occur under the given flood conditions. Nevertheless, Schick's suggestion is an advance over the assumption that every terrace, no matter how fragmentary the evidence, is related to climate or baselevel change.

The concept of complex response and episodic erosion provides a new perspective for the interpretation of Holocene events in many valleys. In addition, it becomes very clear that attempts at channel stabilization will be most successful when there is a tendency for aggradation to occur within the channel. If geomorphic criteria can be established to identify the most favorable time for the application of conservation techniques, presumably when there is a tendency toward deposition, then the chance of success will be much greater than when the channel is actively eroding (Schumm, 1961; Daniels and Jordan, 1966).

Episodic Erosion.   It has been suggested that erosion in high relief areas or during the early part of the erosional evolution of a landscape can

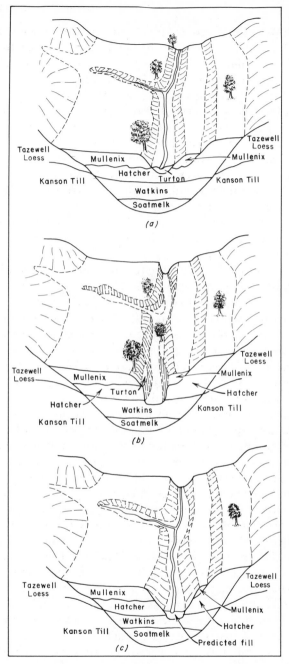

Figure 6-24 Valley floor conditions in Thompson Creek, Iowa: (a) circa 1850, (b) present condition of valley, (c) future conditions. (From Daniels and Jordan, 1966.)

proceed in pulses by episodic erosion (dynamic metastable equilibrium, Figure 1-2). Evidence for such incisions should appear in valley walls and in alluvial valley-fill deposits. If uplift is rapid or relief is great, downcutting probably will not be able to keep pace because of increased sediment delivery from upstream. Therefore, vertical incision into bedrock probably will be interrupted by pauses in incision and, perhaps, even by short periods of aggradation. For example, Miser (1925) states that in the canyon of the San Juan River, Utah, (Figure 6-18) there were pauses during canyon cutting as indicated by the presence of gravel-floored benches or terraces. These are found in comparatively few places, and their small size suggests that the river paused at these levels for short periods only. The benches occur at several levels, up to 600 feet above the river, and they are covered with up to 100 feet of gravel. Of course, benches of this type also form as a result of episodic changes of baselevel or episodic uplift.

To test the possibility that these features might be a result of episodic erosion, another experiment was performed in the REF (Figure 4-3). In this case baselevel was lowered 0.6 m, a considerable amount for a drainage basin that was only 8 m long. The cross sections of Figure 6-25 show the response of the channel to rejuvenation. Incision into the sediment was rapid, and several pauses during incision and the formation of small terraces were observed, but they were quickly destroyed by the impact of raindrops and by channel migration (Figure 6-25). However, after 45 minutes incision ceased, apparently as a result of extremely high sediment production from upstream. At 60 minutes the channel incised again, leaving behind a "bedrock" terrace. As incision and valley widening continued, much of the terrace was destroyed, but remnants were still preserved at the end of the experiment at 120 minutes. Although high-level terraces or benches of small size may be the result of external influences, the experiment suggests that they can also be a natural result of major valley incision (Weaver and Schumm, 1975).

A further example of episodic erosion is the terrace sequence in Douglas Creek, which drains an area of 1070 km² in northwestern Colorado. Multiple unpaired terraces flank the Douglas Creek channel (Figure 6-26). A small building on the old valley floor above the terraces indicates that they may postdate settlement of the area (Figure 6-27).

The terraces bordering Douglas Creek vary in number at any location from 1 to 7, including the highest surface or valley floor upon which the old building rests. The surfaces are small (2 to 20 m wide and 10 to 150 m long), discontinuous, and, for the most part, unpaired, but they provide a unique record of channel behavior in this valley. Based on the testimony of early settlers incision below the valley floor began after

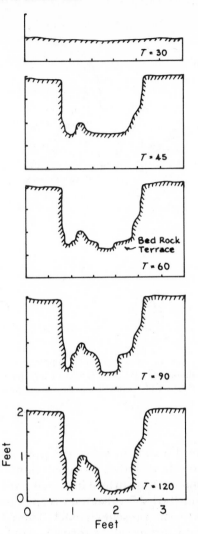

Figure 6-25 Development of bedrock terraces during experimental valley incision. T is time in minutes from lowering of baselevel.

about 1882. Overgrazing resulting from the introduction of 27,000 cattle in 1885 may have initiated incision of the alluvial floor of the valley (Womack and Schumm, 1977).

At one cross section (Figure 6-26) there are six terraces. The upper two, which were present in 1882, are the valley floor and a lower surface, perhaps a floodplain, and are composed of the oldest alluvium. A boxelder tree germinated on the fourth terrace in 1907 according to a tree-ring count. The tree is now buried by about 2 m of recent alluvium.

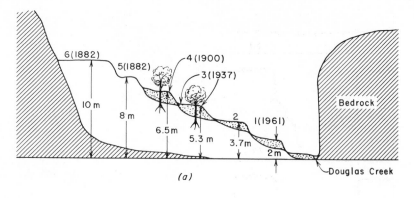

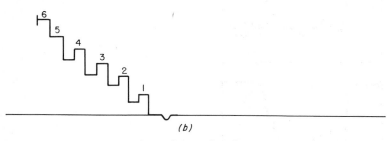

Figure 6-26 (a) Cross section of Douglas Creek valley. Terraces 5 and 6 represent the pre-1882 valley floor and probably the old floodplain of Douglas Creek. Terraces 1 through 4 were formed after 1882. (b) Diagrammatic representation of channel behavior at this cross section. (From Womack and Schumm, 1977.)

By 1937 the channel eroded to a level 3 to 4 m above the present channel (the base of the third terrace level), as shown on aerial photographs of that date. A saltcedar growing on this surface has been partially buried. Aerial photographs taken in 1961 show that the stream was at the first terrace level, about 2 m above the present channel. Therefore, between 1937 and 1961 the second terrace (T 2) formed. After 1961 the channel cut off and abandoned a large meander loop at the first terrace level, and it incised to its present position.

The cross sections along Douglas Creek vary greatly, indicating a different erosional–depositional history at various locations in the valley. These differences may be due partially to destruction of some terraces by lateral erosion, but, nevertheless, the variations are so great that it is impossible to identify periods of cutting and filling that affected the entire valley at one time.

Because of the relatively short period of time during which incision

Figure 6-27   Cabin on edge of Douglas Creek arroyo in 1975. Terraces *1* through *4* (Figure 6-26) were formed below the valley floor surface on which the building was constructed.

and terrace formation have occurred in Douglas Creek, the fact that the terraces are discontinuous, unpaired, and cannot be readily traced throughout the valley, plus the lack of similar terraces in adjacent valleys, indicates that the sequence of events in Douglas Creek cannot be attributed to external influences such as climate, land-use, and baselevel change. Certainly the depositional and erosional events since 1882 as shown in Figure 6-26*b* would require a very complex series of climatic fluctuations.

It appears, therefore, that the controls are inherent to the Douglas Creek geomorphic system, although the initial period of erosion is likely the result of the overgrazing in the 1880s. The explanation of the multiple terraces in Douglas Creek is a modification of the complex response sequence described in Chapter Four. In a typical complex response, incision takes place to some level and then there is aggradation followed by renewed minor incision. In Douglas Creek the incision was episodic and probably resulted from the very large quantities of sediment delivered from the steep tributaries, which temporarily overwhelmed the channel's ability to transport it.

The large quantities of sediment entering Douglas Creek from rejuvenated tributaries caused local deposition and oversteepening of the valley floor. Such accumulations, when repeatedly trenched, produced the flights of terraces that persist for only short distances along the stream. However, some variation in the number of terraces was also observed even along reaches dominated by the influence of a single major tributary, so that tributary influence alone cannot explain every episode of deposition and erosion. Adding complexity to the situation are meander cutoffs, which cause local steepening and channel scour with consequent downstream deposition.

It appears that the unpaired, discontinuous terraces of Douglas Creek have been formed through a complex response of the watershed to initial arroyo cutting and perhaps to local events, including flood deposition and erosion, meander cutoffs, and rejuvenation of tributaries. Because lateral erosion by the channel will gradually destroy these terrace remnants, it is possible that within 50 years only a few terrace remnants will remain as evidence of the manner in which Douglas Creek incised. As it exists today, however, Douglas Creek provides a good example of the short-term channel adjustment to high-sediment loads produced by rejuvenation. This suggests that perhaps the flights of terraces that form where large quantities of stored glacial and alluvial sediments are being removed from a valley are also the result of the complex response or episodic erosion mechanism (e.g., Howard, 1960, p. 91; Alden, 1953, pp. 181, 188) rather than a response to climatic fluctuations, and so forth.

During another experiment in the REF, a small baselevel lowering resulted in some vertical incision and significant lateral shift of the channel. The progressive shift of the channel permitted preservation of terraces on one side of the valley, and during a half-hour period three small terraces formed as the channel aggraded and water and sediment spread widely over the valley floor. Following each period of aggradation renewed incision formed a small terrace of the Douglas Creek type.

The Douglas Creek situation appears to conform to the observations of Born and Ritter (1970), who have mapped six discontinuous and unpaired terraces at the mouth of Truckee River, where it enters Pyramid Lake in Nevada. A reduction of the water level in Pyramid Lake reduced the base level of the lower Truckee River, but instead of simple downcutting commensurate with the lowering of the baselevel, the channel in fact paused as many as six times.

Gage (1970) cites an example of rapid deposition that caused aggradation of from 19 to 80 ft in the Waiho River of New Zealand. This glacier-fed river then proceeded to clear the deposited sediment over a period of a few weeks. The erosion produced a flight of 10-foot terraces. Gage attributed this and similar events to 10-year weather patterns, and he cautioned that if some of these terraces were preserved they could easily be mistaken for surfaces of considerable antiquity. For other examples, see Thornthwaite et al. (1942) and Small (1973).

Episodic erosion is an additional type of complex response. Simply stated, when relief and sediment production are high and downcutting is significant, pauses in incision can be expected as the fluvial system adjusts internally to drastic change.

PLACERS

A discussion of fluvial placers in valleys has been deferred to this point, although they might have been considered earlier, because placer formation is dependent on conditions and events in the sediment source area, the valley, and the channel, and this background information was considered to be a necessary prerequisite to a discussion of these economic deposits.

Placers can be found at any location within a valley from the top of the divide to the bedrock base of the valley fill (Figure 6-28). Within a valley,

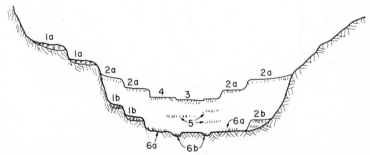

Figure 6-28   Classification of fluvial placers. (1) Bedrock terrace: (a) high level, (b) buried; (2) alluvial terrace: (a) high level, (b) buried; (3) channel lag; (4) floodplain, point bar; (5) lag in valley fill; (6) bedrock: (a) surface, (b) inner channel.

placers may be found on high or low terraces above the modern valley floor. These benches may be composed of bedrock with only a veneer of gravel, or they may be a remnant of valley alluvium preserved high above the modern channel. Following a brief discussion of channel and floodplain placers (Figure 6-28, *3* and *4*), the occurrence of placers on the bedrock valley floor and in valley-fill deposits are reviewed.

Channel and Floodplain Placers

In streams that are actively forming concentrations of heavy minerals, placers are found normally on the upstream part of point bars (Figure 6-29) or midchannel bars that form at wide reaches of the channel. As a meander increases in amplitude and shifts downstream, these local concentrations become elongated "pay streaks" in the floodplain sediments (Figure 6-30).

Because a placer represents a process of deposition, reworking, and concentration, major placer deposits are related to reworking of previously deposited sediments and, depending on the size of sediment and the velocity of flow, this could occur either in high- or low-velocity reaches of the channel. In the Tertiary channels of California, wherever the velocity of a stream was reduced, placer deposits formed (Figure 6-31);

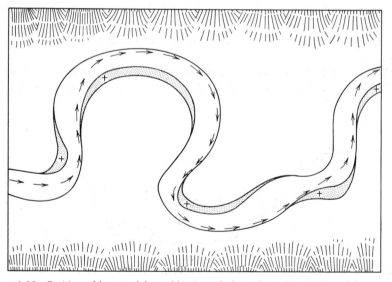

Figure 6-29 Position of bars and favorable sites of placer formation, indicated by crosses. (From Spurr and Goodrich, 1889.)

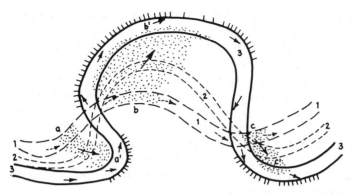

Figure 6-30   Gravel deposition and formation of pay streaks in rapidly flowing meandering stream, in which meanders migrate laterally and downstream. Stream arrows represent point of cutting: (1) original position; (2) intermediate position; and (3) present position of stream. Deposits formed at a, b, c, or inside meanders of stream 1 become extended downstream and laterally in direction of heavy arrow growth to a', b', c' on present stream, and buried pay streaks result. (From Bateman, 1950.)

the factors controlling deposition in these valleys were bends, pools, and variation of stream width (Crampton, 1937).

It is logical that deposition will occur where velocities are reduced, but placers need not form at these locations unless the velocity reduction is such that only heavy minerals and equivalent grain sizes of coarse sediments are deposited. The finer fraction of the sediment must continue or the deposit will not be economic.

The previous discussion of river types and the degree to which the morphology of a channel changes as hydrologic and sediment-load

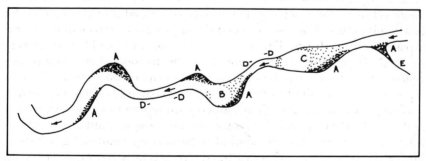

Figure 6-31   Gold concentrations in Tertiary channel Nevada County, California: (A) at bends, in lee of valley bend; (B) at wider section of channel; (C) in scour pools, at entry and at outlet; (D) in rapids, only very coarse gold deposited; (E) at tributary mouth. (From Crampton, 1937.)

variables change indicate that if a bed-load or a mixed-load channel is forming placers, the change from a bed load to a mixed load, or to a suspended-load channel will change the nature of the sedimentary deposits and the placer-forming tendencies. In short, it is possible that a modern river that shows no evidence of placer formation may, in fact, be obscuring the bed-load or mixed-load channel placers that lie beneath the more recent floodplain sediment. The modern character of the stream may differ greatly from the character of the streams that deposited the bulk of the valley-fill sediments. Therefore, a lack of placers at the surface may be a result of greatly altered hydraulic conditions and the search for placers should be conducted beneath the fine-grained suspended-load channel deposits.

It is possible that the equations relating channel dimension, type, and sinuosity to discharge and type of sediment load (Chapter Five) can be used to estimate paleochannel morphology, which in turn may aid in the prediction of placer locations.

Valley-Fill Placers

Because of the great age of most valleys, instead of a uniformity and regularity of concentration of heavy minerals at favorable points, placer deposits invariably show evidence of many stages of deposition and erosion (Kartashov, 1971). In short, there is a great deal of variability in the concentration of heavy minerals in all three dimensions, vertically, transversally, and longitudinally, in a valley fill. As a further complication, Jenkins (1964) has noted that, because of recent climate changes in the Great Basin of the western United States, there are Pleistocene stream placers buried beneath alluvial fans.

The distribution of gravel and heavy minerals in a vertical section reflects the erosional history of the drainage basin and any changes in baselevel or tectonic activity. If deposition is rapid and continuous the heavy minerals will be disseminated throughout the alluvial deposit, and a placer will not form. The alluvium must be reworked before placers develop. Depending on the extent of the incision that accompanies rejuvenation, there may be reworking of gravel down to bedrock or to some intermediate depth where an armor of coarse alluvium may form.

Changes of climate and their influence on sediment yield (Figure 3-1) and river behavior (Table 5-2) must also play a significant role in placer formation. For example, in tropical regions, deep weathering is favorable for release of heavy minerals, but dense vegetative cover prevents the movement of this material into the valleys (Krook, 1968). However, with a climate change to drier conditions, erosion will remove and concentrate the heavy minerals.

Another explanation of placers is that they formed when erosion reached the gold-bearing bedrock. This is certainly a suitable explanation for the appearance of gold in a fluvial deposit, but the formation of a placer usually involves a more complicated sequence of events. For example, one can envision a landscape of low relief that has been subjected to weathering and denudation for very long periods. Under such conditions the heavy minerals are concentrated near the surface with other resistant minerals and rock fragments, and if they are large they could form an armor similar to a desert pavement. Even with low relief and gentle slopes these minerals would slowly creep into depressions and swales to form high local concentrations. With rejuvenation of the area this concentration of heavy minerals would move into the larger streams to form placers. Rich concentrations of diamonds and gold could form in this fashion, and some of the diamond deposits south of the Orange River, South Africa, may be of this type.

Interruptions of denudation by baselevel, tectonic, or climatic change influence the position of placer formation. A lowering of baselevel, uplift, or a climate change from wet to drier will increase erosion and stored sediments will be remobilized and reworked. Therefore, placer deposits along coasts, for example, may reflect climatic conditions that permit movement of the heavy minerals downvalley to a new site of deposition. Table 5-2 suggests under what climatic conditions and where within the fluvial system stored sediments will be eroded. For example, a climate change from arid to semiarid will move sediments off interfluve areas and out of low-order channels downstream to higher-order channels. A further increase of precipitation and runoff will cause erosion and reworking of these deposits, formation of placers in major valleys, and movement of the finest heavy minerals long distances downvalley and perhaps to the coast.

The complex response of a drainage system may also be a significant mechanism for the concentration of placers. Without any major change of baselevel or climate, periodic reworking of the deposited alluvium will flush out the lighter mineral grains and concentrate the heavier. For example, during an experimental study of alluvial fan growth, which is discussed in Chapter Seven, a valley fill was deposited in the sediment source area as the fan grew and raised the baselevel at the mouth of the small experimental drainage basin. Deposition in the valley was not continuous, however, and the valley sediments were eroded periodically and reworked. A small quantity of magnetite was uniformly distributed throughout the sediment comprising the drainage basin, and this was concentrated in the valley alluvium by reworking. When the fill was sectioned to reveal its internal stratigraphy, the magnetite was found to be concentrated on the bedrock floor of the valley, and concentrations were also found to be distributed vertically throughout the valley-fill deposit.

The concentration of magnetite was greatest where the channel maintained a preferred position within the valley. The valley was essentially straight, and where the flow shifted in an unrestricted fashion, magnetite was distributed throughout the deposit. However, where the flow was maintained in one position because of a valley bend or because of a tributary influence (Figure 6-32), magnetite was concentrated in the valley fill at a location where the channel persisted. Therefore, there may be preferred positions of placers in alluvial fills, but an understanding of the channel history and the factors controlling deposition of the fill in each reach of the valley must be comprehended before predictions of placer locations can be made.

One of the difficulties with the location of placers in an alluvial valley fill, as stated by Crampton (1937), is that the generally accepted theory that the greatest concentrations of gold will occur close to the center of the trough or in the streambed is not correct. Also, the assumption that an entire deposit will carry good concentrations of heavy minerals is, in his words, an "absurd premise." Only in rare and exceptional cases will a deposit be uniform. Usually if there is a uniform distribution the sediments have not been reworked and the placer is not economic. In Crampton's (1937) words, "each placer deposit, whether modern or ancient, exposed or buried, affords its individual and peculiar problem," and it is necessary to determine the character and dynamics of the stream that deposited the sediments.

Bedrock Concentrations.   Important concentrations of heavy minerals occur on the floor of valleys, on or near bedrock (Yeend, 1974). In fact, Cheney and Patton (1967) state that the concentration of heavy minerals within or near bedrock or a false bedrock is axiomatic. However, the deposition of barren material such as volcanic ash, mudflow deposits, and barren fluvial sediments produces a "false bottom" above the true valley floor (Raeburn and Milner, 1927), which may mislead the miner into ceasing his efforts when, in fact, rich placers lie below the false bottom. Gold may occur within inner channels on this bedrock floor or it may be concentrated on bedrock benches (terraces) flanking the valley floor (Figure 6-28). Above the bedrock there are concentrations of heavy minerals in lag gravels, which formed as a result of pauses in aggrada-

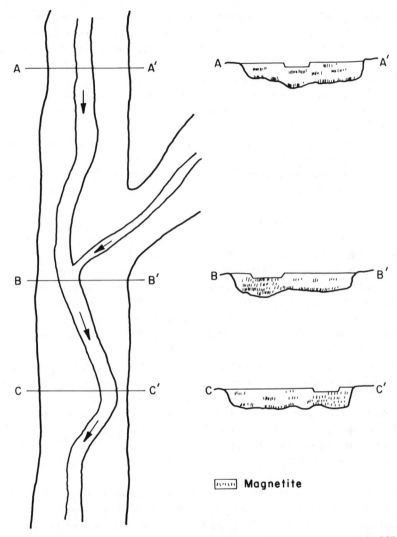

Figure 6-32 Magnetite concentrations in valley fill formed during experiments in REF. At section A-A' stream shifted position and numerous small concentrations were distributed throughout the deposit. At section B-B' a major concentration formed on the left side of the valley, as the tributary maintained the channel at that position. At section C-C' the channel maintained itself in a preferred position on the right side of the valley, and a major concentration formed there.

tion and reworking of sediments. The heavy minerals concentrated in benches and terraces obviously result from reworking of sediment at a level above that to which the stream eventually cut. These benches may be themselves buried in more recent alluvium or preserved at consider- able elevation above the modern stream channel.

There has been considerable discussion concerning the origin of the concentrations of heavy minerals on the bedrock valley floor under tens of feet of sediment. Cheney and Patton (1967) suggest that the bedrock values were concentrated by reworking during the infrequent floods of unusually large magnitude. They cite evidence from stream gaging stations that indicate considerable scour during large floods. This, of course, is the idea advanced by Dury (1964) and Palmquist (1975) con- cerning the origin of the deepest part of a valley floor. However, no one explanation is completely adequate to explain all concentrations of heavy minerals on the bedrock floors. Gunn (1968) suggests simply that agitation of sediments during flow permits downward movement of the heavy minerals. Tuck (1968) concludes that the river, during a period of downcutting, concentrated the heavy minerals on the bedrock floor, and these concentrations were buried during aggradation. In addition, during and following changes of baselevel, there is scour and redeposition of sediments, so through time any change of baselevel will cause reworking of gravels and heavy mineral concentration.

An understanding of the behavior of Zone 1 and valleys that drain it provides an explanation of the bedrock concentrations. During the normal progress of erosion, deposition will usually occur as sediment production from the headwaters exceeds capacity of a channel to convey it (Figure 4-12). Even during scour of the bedrock, a thin veneer of the coarsest sediment will form a lag gravel on the valley floor. This material will be composed of the most resistant, heaviest, and largest fragments in the valley.

The coarsest materials may be relatively stable and may not move downvalley, but at very high velocities they may vibrate in place (Schumm and Stevens, 1973) without appreciable downvalley move- ment. Under these conditions the void spaces between the coarse gravel could be filled with smaller particles, and heavier minerals will accumu- late there. If this situation persists for a long time, the natural attrition of the large particles will indeed cause downstream movement of some of them, and so there will be movement and replacement, at least of the upper layers of the lag, with continual reworking of the deeper materials during large floods.

The lag gravels will act as a trap for finer and heavier sediments moving through the system. Eventually, however, sediment loads deliv- ered from upstream will be so high that deposition will become relatively rapid, thereby inhibiting reworking of deposited material. Under these conditions the formation of concentrations of heavy minerals on the bedrock floor will cease.

During the previously described experimental studies on channel incision (Shepherd and Schumm, 1974), in at least two cases, when incision of the channel reached maximum depth, aggradation was induced by either increasing sand feed at the head of the flume or by raising baselevel. In the first case deposition occurred first in the upper parts of the channel. The gradient was steepened there, and sediment moved progressively downstream. In the second case deposition occurred first at the lower end of the flume, and the channel then was backfilled. In both cases a sediment containing 0.38 percent magnetite was moving through the flume, and the coarsest particles plus the magnetite formed a lag on the channel floor. As aggradation progressed, the magnetite concentration was buried and preserved on the floor of the valley. Above this bedrock concentration a valley-fill deposit that had not been reworked contained magnetite but not in noticeable concentrations. Deposition was not uniform over the bedrock floor of the channel, but magnetite concentrations occurred on both the low and the higher points of the bedrock floor. In the pools the heavy material was trapped and concentrated with the coarsest material, but where the valley floor was high, channel width was also greatest and flow velocities were locally reduced, thereby causing deposition of the coarser and heaviest sediment at these locations also. Thus there was no regular pattern of heavy material deposition in the flume such as that described by Wertz (1949). The experimental observations seem to conform to information obtained during the hydraulic mining of the gold-bearing channels in California, which shows gold concentrations on the higher parts of the floor of a Tertiary channel in the Sierra Nevada Mountains (Lindgren, 1911).

In summary, in rivers draining from rocks that contain heavy minerals of any type, concentrations of heavy minerals should be expected on the bedrock floor of the valley as a natural consequence of valley formation. The position of the concentrations depends on channel history and valley morphology.

Examples of Placers

The physical characteristics of fluvial placers are rarely described in sufficient detail to permit evaluation of the concepts and hypotheses presented herein, but a few examples exist and they are described briefly.

On the flat plain near Lichtenburg, South Africa, there are discontinuous troughs that once contained gravels and diamonds (duToit, 1951). The gravels have been mined and the diamonds removed, so the explanation for the bedrock troughs is academic; however, the only possible explanation for these features is that they are remnants of an old, irregular valley floor. For example, if most of the bedrock channel shown in Figure 6-10 was destroyed by erosion, only the deepest scour features would remain. The Lichtenburg gravels are found in depressions in dolomite and some effects of solution are certain, but other channel remnants in diabase cannot be explained by solution. The linear character of the Lichtenburg channels indicates a fluvial origin, with subsequent solutional modification of the depressions.

An interesting example of episodic erosion that had economic implications occurred in the Pioneer Placer District of Montana (Pardee, 1951). At one location in Pioneer Gulch there are six terraces that were worked for placer gold (Figure 6-33). The terraces were cut in a bedrock compose of easily eroded Tertiary lake and ash deposits. Only at one location are the six terraces preserved, and it may be they did not form elsewhere. Based on a limited description presented by Pardee, it is possible to suggest that at this location, which is below the merging of three high gradient streams, sediments were stored and periodically reworked to produce the terraces and gold concentrations, perhaps in a manner analogous to the formation of the Douglas Creek terraces (Figure 6-26). Note the convex part of the longitudinal profile of Pioneer Gulch below the junction of the three channels (Figure 6-33a). This may reflect the high sediment contribution from the three tributaries, and it is a likely site for channel incision, and local terrace and placer formation. Episodic reworking of the alluvium concentrated the gold to produce a rich placer deposit at this favorable locality.

The Manhattan Gulch placers near Manhattan, Nevada, provide an excellent example of the effect of Quaternary history on placer development (Ferguson, 1924). A generalized cross section of Manhattan Gulch is presented in Figure 6-34. Over a distance of 18,000 feet the gravels and bedrock floor of Manhattan Gulch have been closely scrutinized. There have been several stages of erosion. The oldest gravels, which are coarse (4-8 inches), occur in patches along the valley sides. In the Gulch proper the deepest channel is from 40 to more than 100 feet below the present alluvial surface, but several benches (or buried terraces) are found at higher levels. The benches are not continuous and the complexity of the bedrock floor is further illustrated in Figure 6-35. Multiple channels and islands are present, as many as three benches are preserved, and the bedrock floor of tributaries are not accordant with the deep inner channel. The gravel of the benches is less

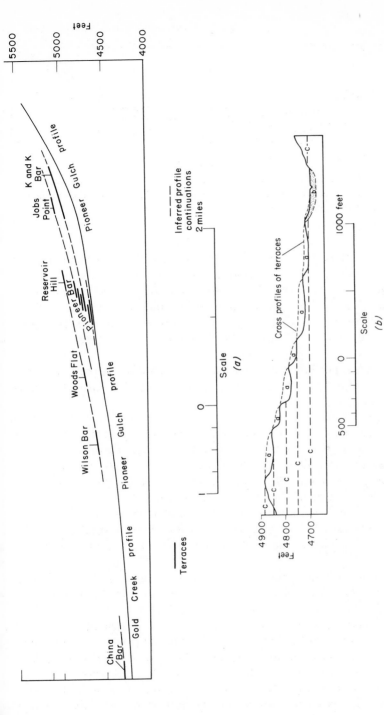

Figure 6-33 Pioneer Gulch, Montana (from Pardee, 1951). (a) Longitudinal profile showing placer locations. (b) Cross section showing terraces at Pioneer Bar.

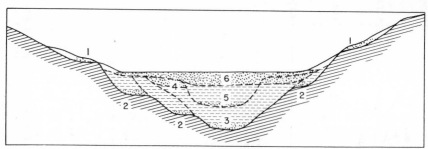

Figure 6-34   Cross section of Manhattan Bulch, Nevada, showing the results of several periods of stream deposition from the oldest (1) to the youngest (6). (Ferguson, 1924.)

valuable than that of the inner channel and probably reflects the time of concentration of gravels and gold at the different levels.

Pleistocene fossils were found in the basal gravel, and Ferguson believes that erosional events in Manhattan Gulch are related to Pleistocene climate changes. The diagrammatic cross section of Figure 6-34 shows the sequence of events to be as follows:

1. A long period of Prepleistocene erosion formed the upper part of the valley of Manhattan Gulch and deposited gravel 1 that is found in patches at high levels.
2. Increased rates of incision produced an inner valley that runs from 40 to 100 feet deep. The incision was not continuous as the location of the benches and gravel 2 attests. Gravel 3 was deposited on the bedrock floor at the level of deepest incision.
3. The inner valley was filled with gravel 4 as sediment loads increased or as the capacity of the channel decreased.
4. Rejuvenation eroded gravel 4 and deposited gravel 5.
5. The gulch was filled to its present level and gravel 6 was deposited by floods of the magnitude of those that occur at present.

Incision of the inner valley may be related to increased runoff when large pluvial lakes occupied valleys in Nevada and Utah, although the rejuvenation may also be the result of faulting.

The detailed study by Ferguson is unique in the information provided on valley morphology, and it clearly indicates that placer deposits can be found at several locations in a sediment-filled valley. The bedrock floor is always a favorable site, but terraces or benches also should provide placer minerals because they apparently represent a pause in downcutting, when sediment deposition and the reworking of sediments produce heavy mineral concentrations.

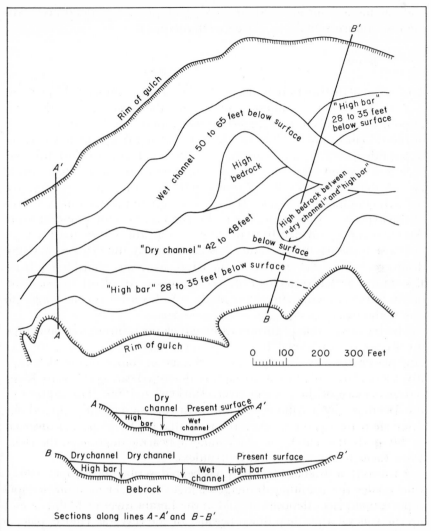

Figure 6-35   Sketch map and sections of parts of Manhattan Gulch showing benches and deep channel. (From Ferguson, 1924.)

Sigov et al. (1972) conclude from a study of heavy mineral concentrations in the Ural Mountains, U. S. S. R., that during major periods of uplift or subsidence, placers are not formed. This is because at these times erosion and deposition are too rapid, and significant reworking and concentration of the deposits cannot occur. However, during long periods of crustal stability, the normal processes of weathering, erosion, and sediment transport with reworking of previously deposited sediments produce significant placer accumulations.

River Capture

The regional distribution of placers can be strongly influenced by stream capture. Capture is a common event during the erosional evolution of a region, and the result from an economic point of view is that the source of the valuable minerals may be abruptly isolated from the downstream depositional area. A simple example is shown in Figure 6-36. In this case sediment eroded from the upper right part of the block diagrams is initially delivered to a valley draining to the lower left, but after capture the sediment moves to a valley at the lower right of the diagram. Capture of this type is very common, but it also can occur on the grandest scale. An example is provided by Wilhelmy (1969), who shows that the easternmost tributary of the Indus was captured by the Ganges, and the drainage from a large area of the Himalayas was transferred from Pakistan to India in geologically recent times. An effort to trace the origin of certain sediments in the modern Indus River system would fail unless the drainage changes were recognized.

The reconstruction of former drainage patterns through geomorphic investigations of regional drainage patterns may lead to the discovery of new placer deposits. For example, a change in course of the Delaware River left a large amount of precapture ilmenite-bearing Delaware River sediments east of the present river (Markewicz, 1969). The capture of the Delaware by a tributary of the Schuykill significantly altered the drainage patterns and, unless it is known that the Delaware was diverted to the south, the search for heavy-mineral-bearing deposits of the Delaware River to the east would be fruitless.

A reversal of drainage by uplift has been described by Ruppel (1967), who relates the resulting drainage changes to placer location. Ruppel reports that placer deposits of gold in the Lemhi River of Idaho extend up the valley rather than down because of the reversal. Hence, placers may be found on the drainage divide but not in the lower valley of a reversed river. An understanding of the geomorphic history of drainage pattern development and change appears to be a necessary prerequisite for the search for fluvial placers.

DISCUSSION

Although the morphology of modern alluvial rivers is largely the result of the water and sediment moving through the channels, the

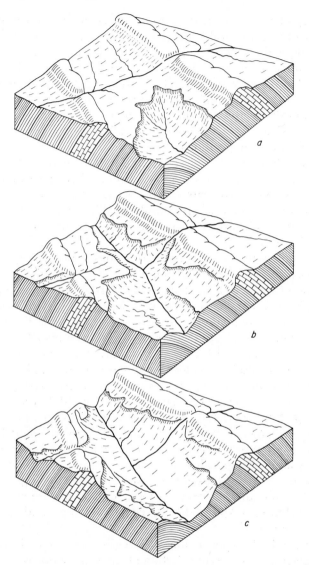

Figure 6-36 Three successive stages in stream piracy. The stream cutting back at the lower elevation beheads and captures the stream flowing at a higher level. (From Jenkins, 1964.)

morphology of valleys is more closely related to the resistance of the materials forming the walls and floor of the valley and the Tertiary history of the region. One thing is clear from the information assembled on valley morphology, and that is that the valley floor will be characterized by the presence of inner channels and bedrock highs and lows. The position of these irregularities can be anticipated to some extent by variations in valley width and the position of tributary junctions, but few generalizations can be made about the valley floor without an understanding of past river positions.

The valley-fill alluvium will reflect the nature of the sediment load transported from Zone 1, and a very different valley-fill stratigraphy will be related to deposits associated with suspended-load, mixed-load, and bed-load channels. The valley fill should be a fining upward deposit, but climate changes can produce very different sediment loads and channel deposits (Figure 5-27).

All the complexities of the history of Zones 1 and 2 are reflected in valley-fill deposits and the reworking of valley-fill sediments to form placers. Therefore, it appears that any standard or inflexible exploration model will be inadequate, because it is the complexity of geomorphic history and the complex response that are responsible for placer development. The several placer deposits at both Pioneer Gulch (Figure 6-33) and Manhattan Gulch (Figure 6-34) are illustrations of this fact.

If morphologic and hydrologic changes are too great, placers may not form or they may be obscured. For example, Jenkins (1964) has pointed out not only how placers can be preserved by burial, but also how they can be hidden and rendered more difficult to detect because of burial. In California, placers have been hidden beneath landslides and mudflows, lake deposits, volcanic ash, lava, glacial deposits, and alluvial fans and by alluvial deposition at the base of fault scarps. In addition, river metamorphosis will completely alter the morphology of a valley and possibly obscure placers formed under different hydrologic conditions. Hence, a knowledge of climatic change and geomorphic history is essential.

According to both experimental and field results the bedrock surface beneath bench gravels (Figure 6-28) and the valley floor is an irregular surface both transverse to and parallel to flow direction. Inner channels and up-and-down long profiles are probably characteristic of the bedrock valley floor (Figure 6-10). The question is then, where on the bedrock are the highest placer concentrations? In the Tertiary channels of California and in other valleys for which observations are available, concentrations are greatest in inner channels or in longitudinal depressions in bedrock. Therefore, the prospector must search for the buried inner channels. If lithologic and structural variations are not significant, then in a straight reach, the inner channel is most likely near the center of the valley (Figure 6-32). During incision, there can be bedrock scour and inner channel formation at the inside of valley bends (Figure 6-9), but another bedrock low may form at the outside of the bend if scour, during floods, penetrates the alluvium that covers the valley floor (Palmquist, 1975). Subsequent aggradation of the valley may preserve the greatest concentration, where the channel persisted longest prior to and during aggradation (Figure 6-37).

Another location in a valley fill, where placers should be found, is at junctions of major tributaries. At such places the main channel is frequently forced to the opposite side of the valley, with the result that scour and placer formation in the main channel is most active opposite and downstream from the tributary junctions (Figure 6-2). In addition, if tributary sediment contributions are large, repeated steepening and incision of the sediment below the tributary junction may produce a series of lag deposits or terraces similar to those formed in Pioneer Gulch (Figure 6-33) and Douglas Creek (Figure 6-26).

River capture and the geomorphic history of drainage patterns also provide an interesting geomorphic challenge. If, through time, drainage changes are important, for example, if a slight warping permits major river capture, then there will be valleys with high level placers but little heavy mineral in the modern channel. Other valleys that captured the source stream may have barren high-level terraces but rich bedrock and alluvial fill placer deposits. Abandoned valley remnants and, of course, meander cutoffs are the likely place to prospect for small placers. These placer remnants could be located by aerial photograph interpretation and by careful study of drainage patterns and gravel sources, in short, by a thorough geomorphic analysis of the present drainage pattern and the possible paleodrainage systems.

The terrace sequence that forms in the valley-fill alluvium invariably reflects a complicated erosional and depositional history. This can be further confused by episodic erosion and sedimentation.

Episodic erosion, as described in the Douglas Creek Valley, is another type of complex response (Schumm, 1976). Instead of incision to a maximum depth followed by deposition and minor incision at about the same level (Figure 4-12), episodic erosion is part of a major change of level that cannot, because of high sediment loads, be accomplished by progressive incision. Data on the variation in sediment yield from Douglas Creek during the past 100 years would be of considerable interest. The storage and flushing of sediment from the valley must have delivered greatly different quantities of sediment to the White River from decade to decade.

Although complex response and episodic erosion may appear to be

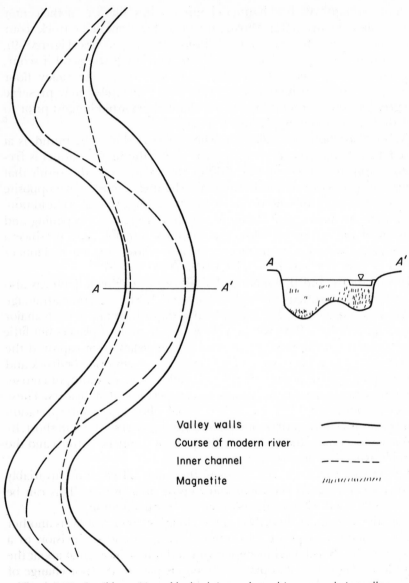

Figure 6-37   Possible position of bedrock inner channel in a meandering valley.

just another set of problems that the Quaternary stratigrapher must overcome, in fact, they simplify his problem. That is, the lowest Holocene terrace and the most recent Holocene alluvial deposit need not now be considered the result of a minor climatic change; rather they can be due to the normal workings of the fluvial system. The recognition that deposition inevitably follows channel incision should also be of assistance to the agricultural engineer and soil conservationist. For example, if it is possible to anticipate and wait for natural deposition (Figure 6-24), then healing of a gully by deposition can be accomplished by working with the channel's natural tendency rather than by forcing deposition during the erosional phase of gully development. This philosophy is the same as that expressed in the preceding chapter when the Chippewa River problem was discussed.

REFERENCES

Adler, A. A. and Lattman, L. H., 1961, Flood plain sediments of Halfmoon Creek, Pennsylvania: Miner. Ind. Exp. Sta. (Pa. State Univ.) Bull. 77, pp. 1–11.

Alden, W. C., 1953, Physiography and glacial geology of Western Montana and adjacent areas: U. S. Geol. Surv. Prof. Paper 321, 200 p.

Allen, J. R. L., 1965a, Fining-upwards cycles in alluvial successions: Geol. J. (Liverpool and Manchester), v. 4, pp. 229–246.

Allen J. R. L., 1965b, A review of the origin and characteristics of recent alluvial sediments: Sedimentology, v. 5, pp. 89–191.

Allen, J. R. L., 1970, Physical processes of sedimentation: George Allen and Unwin, London, 248 pp.

Allen, J. R. L., 1971, Transverse erosional marks of mud and rock: their physical basis and geological significance: Sediment. Geol., v. 5, pp. 167–385.

Bergstrom, R. E. and Walker, T.R., 1956, Groundwater geology of the East St. Louis area, Illinois: Illinois State Geological Survey Report of Investigations 191, 44 pp.

Barsch, Dietrich and Royce, C. F. Jr., 1972, A model for development of Quaternary terraces and pediment terraces in the southwestern United States of America: Z. Geomorphol., v. 16, pp. 54–75.

Bateman, A. M., 1950, Economic mineral deposits, 2nd ed.: Wiley, New York, 916 pp.

Berg, R. R., 1968, Point-bar origin of Fall River sandstone reservoirs, northeastern Wyoming: Am. Assoc. Pet. Geol. Bull., v. 52, pp. 2116–2122.

Born, S. M., and Ritter, D. F., 1970, Modern terrace develoment near Pyramid Lake, Nevada, and its geologic implications: Geol. Soc. Am. Bull., v. 81, pp. 1233–1242.

Bowman, Isaiah, 1923, An American boundary dispute: Geog. Rev., v. 13, pp. 161–189.

Bretz, J. H., 1924, The Dalles type of river channel: J. Geol., v. 24, pp. 129–149.

Charles, H. H., 1941, Bush City Oil Field, Anderson Co. Kansas, in Stratigraphic type of oil fields: American Association of Petroleum Geologists, Tulsa, pp. 43–56.

Cheney, E. S. and Patton, T. C., 1967, Origin of bedrock values of placer deposits: Econ. Geol., v. 62, pp. 852–860.

Church, Michael, 1972, Baffin Island sandurs: a study of Arctic fluvial processes: Geol. Surv. Can. Bull. 216, 208 pp.

Church, Michael and Gilbert, Robert, 1975, Proglacial fluvial and lacustrine sediments: Soc. Econ. Paleontol. Mineral. Spec. Pub. 23, pp. 22–100.

Coneybeare, C. E. B., 1976, Geomorphology of oil and gas fields in sandstone bodies: Elsevier, Amsterdam, 341 pp.

Crampton, F. A., 1937, Occurrence of gold in stream placers: Mining J., v. 20, pp. 3–4, 33–34.

Daniels, R. B. and Jordan, R. H., 1966, Physiographic history and the soils, entrenched stream systems, gullies, Harrison County, Iowa: U. S. Dept. Agric., Tech. Bull. 1348.

Davis, W. M., 1893, The Osage River and the Ozark Uplift: Science, v. 22, pp. 276–279.

Dury, G. H., 1964, Subsurface exploration and chronology of underfit streams: U. S. Geol. Surv. Prof. Paper 452-B, 56 pp.

Dury, G. H., 1965, Theoretical implications of underfit streams: U. S. Geol. Surv. Prof. Paper 452-C, 43 pp.

duToit, A. L., 1951, The diamoniferous gravels of Lichtenburg: Geol. Surv. of S. Afr., 50 pp.

Emmett, W. W., 1974, Channel aggradation in western United States as indicated by observations at Vigil Network sites: Z. Geomorphol. Suppl. Bd. 6–32 21, pp. 52–62.

Ferguson, H. G., 1924, Geology and ore deposits of the Manhattan District, Nevada: U. S. Geol. Surv. Bull. 723, 163 pp.

Flint, R. F. and Irwin, W. H., 1939, Glacial geology of Grand Coulee Dam, Washington: Geol. Soc. Am. Bull., v. 50, pp. 661–680.

Friedman, S. A., 1960, Channel-fill sandstones in the Middle Pennsylvanian rocks of Indiana: Indiana Geol. Surv., Rep. Progr. 23, 59 pp.

Gage, M., 1970, The tempo of geomorphic change: J. Geol., v. 78, pp. 619–625.

Gardner, T. W., 1975, The history of part of the Colorado River and its tributaries: an experimental study: Four Corners Geol. Soc. Guidebook, 9th Field Conf., Canyonlands, pp. 87–95.

Gilbert, G. K., 1917, Hydraulic mining debris in the Sierra Nevada: U. S. Geol. Surv. Prof. Paper 105, 154 pp.

Gunn, C. B., 1968, Origin of the bedrock values of placer deposits: Econ. Geol., v. 63, p. 86.

Happ, S. C., 1971, Genetic classification of valley sediment deposits: A. S. C. E. J. Hydraulics Div., v. 97, pp. 43–53.

Harms, J. C., 1966, Stratigraphic traps in a valley fill, western Nebraska: Am. Assoc. Pet. Geol. Bull., v. 50, pp. 2119–2149.

Haynes, C. V., 1968, Geochronology of late-Quaternary alluvium, in H. E. Wright, and R. B. Morrison, (editors), Means of correlation of Quaternary successions: Salt Lake City, University of Utah Press, pp. 591–631.

Hooke, R. L., 1975, Distribution of sediment transport and shear stress in a meander bend: J. Geol., v. 83, pp. 543–566.

Howard, A. D., 1960, Canozoic history of Northeastern Montana and Northwestern North Dakota with emphasis on the Pleistocene: U. S. Geol. Surv. Prof. Paper 326, 107 pp.

Howard, L. W. and Schoewe, W. H., 1965, The Englevale channel sandstone: Kansas Acad. Sci. Trans., vl. 68, pp. 88–106.

Hunt, C. B., 1969, Geological history of the Colorado River: U. S. Geol. Surv. Prof. Paper 669, pp. 59–130.

Ippen, A. T., Drinker, P. A., 1962, Boundary shear stresses in curved trapezoidal channels: Am. Soc. Civil Eng., Proc. J. Hydraul. Div. v. 88, pp. 143–179.

Jenkins, O. P., 1964, Geology of placer deposits: Calif. Div. Mines Bull. 135, pp. 147–216.

Kartashov, I. P., 1971, Geological features of alluvial placers: Econ. Geol., v. 66, pp. 879–885.

Kottlowski, F. E., Cooley, M. E. and Ruhe, R. V., 1965, Quaternary geology of the Southwest, in H. E. Wright and D. G. Frey (editors), Quaternary of the United States: pp. 287–298.

Krigstrom, Arne, 1962, Geomorphological studies of sandur plains and their braided rivers in Iceland: Geografis. Annder, v. 44, pp. 328–346.

Krook, Leendert, 1968, Origin of bedrock values of placer deposits: Econ. Geol., v. 63, pp. 844–846.

Krylov, I. I., 1971, Geological factors in the course changes of a system of river valleys in mountainous regions: Soviet Hydrol., No. 6, pp. 562–565.

Leopold, L. B. and Miller, J. P., 1954, A postglacial chronology for some alluvial valleys in Wyoming: U. S. Geol. Surv. Water-Supply Paper 1261, 90 pp.

Leopold, L. B., Wolman, M. G. and Miller, J. P., 1964, Fluvial Processes in Geomorphology: Freeman, San Francisco and London, 522 pp.

Lindgren, Waldemar, 1911, Tertiary gravels of the Sierra Nevada of California: U. S. Geol. Surv. Prof. Paper 73, 226 pp.

Lins, T. W., 1950, Origin and environment of the Tonganoxie sandstone in northeastern Kansas: Kansas Geol. Surv. Bull. 86, pp. 105–140.

Logan, M. H., 1959, Field trip report to Prinville Dam, Sept. 8-11, 1959: U. S. Bureau of Reclamation, Geology Open-File Report, Denver, Colorado, 15 pp.

McGee, W. J., 1891, The Pleistocene history of northeastern Iowa: U. S. Geol. Surv., 11th Ann. Rep., Pt. 1, pp. 199–577.

Markewicz, F. J., 1969, Ilmenite deposits of the New Jersey coastal plains, in Geology of Selected Area of New Jersey and Eastern Pennsylvania: Rutgers University Press, New Brunswick, pp. 363–382.

Martin, R., 1966, Paleogeomorphology and its application to exploration for oil and gas (with examples from western Canada): Am. Assoc. Pet. Geol. Bull., v. 50, pp. 2277–2311.

Miser, H. D., 1925, Erosion in San Juan Canyon, Utah: Geol. Soc. Am. Bull. v. 36, pp. 365–378.

Morisawa, M., 1968, Streams, their dynamics and morphology: McGraw-Hill, New York, 175 pp.

Mosley, M. P., 1976, An experimental study of channel confluences: J. Geol., v. 84, pp. 535–562.

Oltman, R. E., Sternberg, H. O'R, Ames, F. C. and Davis, L. C. Jr., 1964, Amazon River investigations reconnaissance measurements of July 1963: U. S. Geol. Surv. Circ. 486, 15 pp.

Palmquist, 1975, Preferred position model and subsurface symmetry of valleys: Geol. Soc. Am., Bull. v. 86, pp. 1392–1398.

Pardee, J. T., 1951, Gold placers of the Pioneer District, Montana: U. S. Geol. Surv. Bull. 978C, pp. 69–99.

Pepper, J. G., DeWitt, Wallace Jr. and Demarest, D. F., 1954, Geology of the Bedford Shale and Berea Sandstone in the Appalachian Region: U. S. Geol. Surv. Prof. Paper 259, 109 pp.

Peterson, D. W. et al., 1968, Tertiary gold-bearing channel gravel in northern Nevada County, California: U. S. Geol. Surv. Circ. 566, 22 pp.

Potter, P. E., 1963, Late Paleozoic sandstones of the Illinois basin: Illinois Geol. Surv. Rep. Invest. 217, 92 pp.

Raeburn, Colin and Milner, H. B., 1927, Alluvial prospecting: Van Nostrand, New York, 478 pp.

Rubey, W. W. and Bass, N. W., 1925, Geology of Russell County, Kansas: Geol. Surv. Kansas, Bull. 10, pp. 1–86.

Ruppel, E. T., 1967, Late Cenozoic drainage reversal, east-central Idaho, and its relation to possible undiscovered placer deposits: Economic Geol., v. 62, pp. 648–663.

Salisbury, N. E., Knox, J. C. and Stephenson, R. A., 1968, The valleys of Iowa-1, Iowa Studies in Geography No. 5: University of Iowa, 107 pp.

Schick, A. P., 1974, Formation and obliteration of desert stream terraces—a conceptual analysis: Z. Geomorphol., Suppl. Bd. 21, pp. 88–105.

Schumm, S. A., 1961, Effect of sediment characteristics on erosion and deposition in ephemeral stream channels: U. S. Geol. Surv. Prof. Paper 352-C, pp. 31–70.

Schumm, S. A., 1968a, Speculations concerning paleohydrologic controls of terrestrial sedimentation: Geol. Soc. Am. Bull. v. 79, pp. 1573–1588.

Schumm, S. A., 1968b, River adjustment to altered hydrologic regimen—Murrumbidgee River and paleochannels, Australia: U. S. Geol. Surv. Prof. Paper 598, 65 pp.

Schumm, S. A., 1973, Geomorphic thresholds and complex response of drainage systems, in M. Morisawa (editor), Fluvial geomorphology, Publications in Geomorphology: State University of New York, Binghamton, pp. 299–310.

Schumm, S. A., 1976, Episodic erosion: a modification of the geomorphic cycle, in R. Flemal and W. Melhorn, (editors), Theories of landform development; Publications in Geomorphology: State University of New York, Binghamton, pp. 69–85.

Schumm, S. A., and Hadley, R. F., 1957, Arroyos and the semiarid cycle of erosion: Am. J. Sci., v. 255, pp. 161–174.

Schumm, S. A. and Lichty, R. W., 1963, Channel widening and flodplain construction along Cimarron River in southwestern Kansas: U. S. Geol. Surv. Prof. Paper 352-D, pp. 71–88.

Schumm, S. A. and Stevens, M. A., 1973, Abrasion in place: a mechanism for rounding and size reduction of coarse sediments in rivers: Geology, v. 1, pp. 37–40.

Shepherd, R. G., 1972, Incised river meanders: evolution in simulated bedrock: Science, v. 178, pp. 409–411.

Shepherd, R. G. and Schumm, S. A., 1974, Experimental study of river incision: Geol. Soc. Am. Bull., v. 85, pp. 257–268.

Siever, Raymond, 1951, The Mississippian–Pennsylvanian unconformity in southern Illinois: Am. Assoc. Pet. Geol., Bull. v. 35, pp. 542–581.

Sigov, A. P., Lomayer, A. V., Sigov, A. V., Storozhenko, L. Y., Khrypor, V. N. and Shub, I. Z., 1972, Placers of the Urals, their formation, distribution and elements of geomorphic prediction: Sov. Geogr. v. 13, pp. 375–387.

Small, R. J., 1973, Braiding terraces in the Val D'Herens, Switzerland: Geography, v. 58, pp. 129–135.

Spurr, J. E. and Goodrich, H. B., 1889, Geology of the Yukon gold district: U. S. Geol. Surv. Annu. Rep. (1886–1987) Part 3, pp. 87–392.

Stapp, R. W., 1967, Relationship of lower Cretaceous depositional environment of oil accumulation, northeastern Powder River Basin, Wyoming: Am. Assoc. Pet. Geol. Bull., v. 51, pp. 2044–2055.

Thornthwaite, C., Sharpe, C. F. S. and Dosch, E. F., 1942, Climate and accelerated erosion in the arid and semi-arid Southwest, with special reference to the Polacca Wash drainage basin, Arizona: U. S. Dept. Agric. Tech. Bull. 808.

Trimble, S. W., 1975, Denudation studies: can we assume stream steady state?: Science, v. 188, pp. 1207–1208.

Tuck, Ralph, 1968, Origin of bedrock values or placer deposits: Econ. Geol. v. 63, pp. 191–193.

Upson, J. E. and Spencer, C. W., 1964, Bedrock valleys of the New England coast as related to fluctuations of sea level: U. S. Geol. Surv. Prof. Paper 454-M, 44 pp.

U. S. Bureau of Reclamation, 1957, Technical Record of Design and Construction Johnstown Dam: Denver, Colorado, 86 pp.

Vita-Finzi, Claudio, 1969, The Mediterranean Valleys: Cambridge University Press, Cambridge, 140 pp.

Weaver, W. E. and Schumm, S. A., 1975, The development of multiple erosional terraces during channel incision: Geol. Soc. Am. Abstr. with Program, v. 7, pp. 1312–1313.

Wertz, J. B., 1949, Logarithmic pattern in river placer deposits: Econ. Geol., v. 44, pp. 193–209.

Wilbur, R. L. and Mead, Elwood, 1933, The construction of Hoover Dam: U. S. Government Printing Office, Washington, D. C.

Wilhelmy, H., 1969, Das Urstromtal am Ostrand der Indusbene und das Sarasvati Problem: Z. Geomorphol. Suppl. 8, pp. 76–93.

Williams, E. G., Guber, A. L. and Johnson, A. M., 1965, Rotational slumping and the recognition of disconformities: J. Geol., v. 73, pp. 539–547.

Winslow, A., 1893, The Osage River and its meanders: Science, v. 22, pp. 31–32.

Wolman, M. G. and Leopold, L. B., 1957, River flood plains: some observations on their formation: U. S. Geol. Surv. Prof. Paper 282-C, pp. 87–107.

Womack, W. R. and Schumm, S. A., 1977, Terraces of Douglas Creek, northwestern Colorado: an example of episodic erosion: Geology, v. 5, pp. 72–76.

Yeend, W. E., 1974, Gold-bearing gravel of the ancestral Yuba River, Sierra Nevada, California: U. S. Geol. Surv. Prof. Paper 772, 44 pp.

Yen, Chin-lien, 1970, Bend topography effect flow in a meander: Am. Soc. Civil Eng. Proc., J. Hydrol. Div., No. HY1, pp. 57–73.

CHAPTER SEVEN

Piedmont (Zone 3)

The piedmont, as the name implies, is located favorably for the rapid accumulation of sediment from an adjacent source area (Zone 1). Characteristic depositional features of the piedmont are alluvial fans, which may coalesce along the base of a mountain range to form a bajada. The sedimentologic and morphologic character of an alluvial fan depends almost entirely on the nature of Zone 1, its geology, geomorphology, and hydrology. However, fans are found in a variety of environments and the primary requisite for fan formation is a large sediment supply and a lowland to which the sediment is delivered. When sediment delivery to the piedmont is relatively low the landform that appears is the pediment, an erosion surface mantled with several feet of fluvial gravel.

In this chapter these two typical piedmont landforms are considered because each provides information on the manner in which erosion progresses. In addition, large quantities of uranium and placer minerals are found in piedmont deposits. This fortunately provides an unusual amount of stratigraphic and sedimentologic information on ancient piedmont deposits that can be considered in relation to modern fan morphology and depositional history.

FAN MORPHOLOGY

Fans can be of two types, dry or mudflow fans formed by ephemeral stream flow, and wet fans formed by perennial stream flow. Both depend on a large sediment supply from Zone 1. The dry fan is prevalent today, but during the geologic past the wet fan was much more common, as the conclusions of Chapter Three indicate.

Dry (Alluvial) Fans

Bull (1968) has graphically summarized his observations on modern dry fans and he recognizes two different conditions of fan morphology (Figure 7-1). The first situation occurs when deposition is near the mountain front and the fan surface is undissected. The second situation occurs when deposition is at the toe of the fan and water and sediment move to this location through a fan-head trench. A logical explanation for these differences is a change of an external variable, such as climate and tectonism, and land-use. Another explanation was offered by Eckis (1928), who suggested that trenching of fans will take place, as sediment yields from the source area decrease through time, during the normal

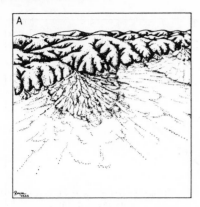 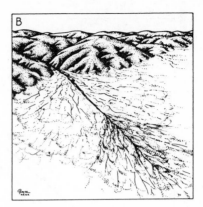

Figure 7-1 Diverse morphology of alluvial fans: (A) area of deposition at fan head, (B) fan-head trench with deposition at fan toe. (From Bull, 1968.)

progress of the erosion cycle. However, in that case the trenching should be deeper and more extensive. In fact, the progressive accumulation of sediment at a fan head could create a situation analogous to sediment accumulation in the valley of Piceance Creek basin with eventual incision and reworking of the deposit.

Anstey (1965) presents a detailed comparison of fans in the Great Basin of the western United States and in Baluchistan, Pakistan. He demonstrates from a sample of almost 2000 fans that the greatest number of modern fans have radii between 1.0 and 5 miles. The largest fan in his sample has a radius of 16 miles. Modern fans, therefore, are relatively small features. This is in marked contrast to ancient fanlike deposits, which are very large.

Modern alluvial fans have been studied sufficiently so that quantitative relations have been developed between fan size and slope and the size, relief, and geology of Zone 1. For example, a large source area produces large quantities of sediment and, therefore, fan size should be significantly related to size of the sediment source area. Bull (1964) provides an example of a relationship of this type from the Fresno, California, area (Figure 7-2). He shows that a good relationship exists between fan area and drainage basin area, and that geology also influences fan area. For a given drainage area, fans constructed of sediments from basins underlain primarily by sandstone have a smaller area than fans associated with drainage basins underlain by mudstone and shale, because the highly erodible mudstone and shale drainage basins produce more sediment. Also, there is an inverse relation between drainage basin area and fan slope (Figure 7-2).

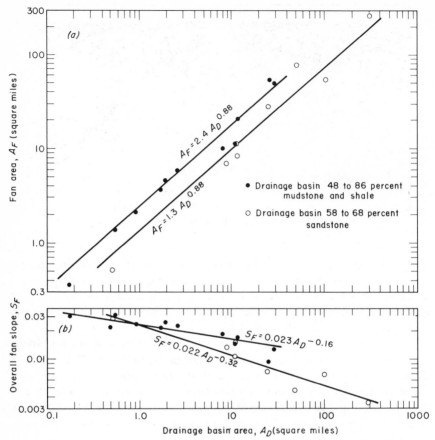

Figure 7-2   Relation between drainage basin area and (A) fan area and (B) fan slope. (From Bull, 1964.)

Ryder (1971) has made a detailed morphological analysis of fans located in five valleys in British Columbia. These fans are termed paraglacial because they formed during deglaciation and their development was dependent on the temporary abundance of glacial debris. They are all trenched because of relatively rapid depletion of the erodible glacial debris and subsequent reduction of sediment loads from the drainage basins. This is an example of the Eckis-type trenching. Ryder found a relation among drainage basin area, fan area, and gradient similar to that of Figure 7-2, but she also found that the greater the ruggedness or average slope of the drainage basin the greater is the gradient of the fan (Figure 7-3). The differences in the regression equations are probably a function of basin size, climate, and geology.

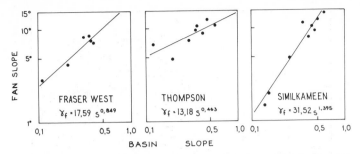

Figure 7-3 Relation between drainage basin slope and fan slope. (From Ryder, 1971. Reproduced by permission of the National Research Council of Canada from Canadian Journal of Earth Sciences, v. 8, 1971, pp. 1252–1264.

The relations among fan slope, fan area, and drainage basin characteristics are not surprising. What is surprising is the variation in fan surface morphology within a given region; that is, the presence or absence of fan-head trenches. A series of fan maps prepared by Hunt and Mabey (1966) show the great differences in fan morphology in Death Valley, California (Figure 7-4). These differences have been attributed to tilting and to the obvious tectonic activity in the Death Valley area, but they are similar to fan differences elsewhere that have been attributed to climate change (Williams, 1973). The patterns of recent gravel distribution on the Trail Canyon, Hanaupah Canyon, and Johnson Canyon fans illustrate these morphologic differences. The Trail Canyon map shows that Holocene fan gravel is widely dispersed on the fan in a number of distributary channels. This is true also of the Hanaupah Canyon fan, although the distribution of channels and recent gravel is less extensive and the most recent gravels are at the fan toe. In contrast, the Johnson Canyon fan shows one main channel leading from the canyon mouth to the toe of the fan. Distributaries branch from this channel, but over most of the fan smaller channels, which seem to have formed locally and independently of the main channel as a result of local precipitation and drainage, are the dominant feature.

The fans appear to form a series similar to that shown in Figure 7-1. For example, on Trail Canyon's fan the modern sediments are being distributed widely over the fan. At the other extreme the sediments are delivered to the distal end of the Johnson Canyon fan, with perhaps only minor deposition and minor reworking of the sediments at the head of the fan.

Another interesting comparison of this type can be made along the foot of the San Gabriel Mountains east of Los Angeles (U. S. Geological Survey, Ontario, California, quadrangle). Fans have developed along

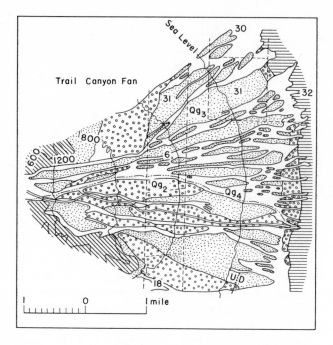

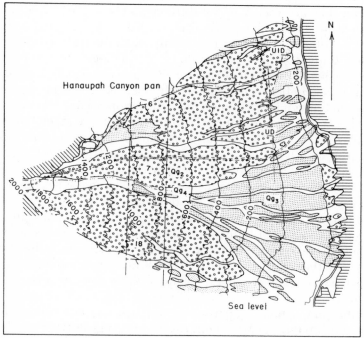

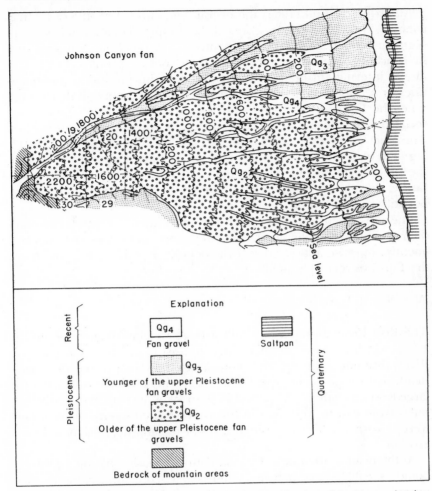

Figure 7-4   Morphology and gravel distribution on Death Valley fans. (From Hunt and Mabey, 1966.)

the south side of the San Gabriel Mountains, and the Cucamonga fan at the mouth of Cucamonga Canyon has a very spectacular trench running the length of the fan. The adjacent fan to the east, the Deer Canyon fan, is very different in that it has no trench. The trenching of the Cucamonga fan has been attributed by Eckis (1928) to reduction in sediment delivered from the mountains through geologic time, but this might be expected also of the adjacent Deer Canyon fan. Within one geographical area, alluvial fans show considerable variation of morphology.

According to Bull (1964) the overall longitudinal profile of a fan is concave. However, this concavity may be composed of a series of straight segments. Bull has described segmented fans from the Fresno area, and he concluded that there are two types of concave profiles. The first is due to intermittent uplift of the mountains; this produces large quantities of sediment and builds a steep fan head. Progressively through time, the fan head steepens and each major episode of uplift is associated with a steeper fan-head segment; the end result is a concave fan. The other case is due to trenching and the building out of a low, flatter segment of recent alluvium at the toe of the fan. This is the reverse of the preceding situation in that the most recent material is deposited farther down the fan on gentler slopes (Figure 7-1). The result is a flatter but still concave profile.

The fans discussed above have formed under dry conditions, and their streams are ephemeral. Mud flow and debris flow deposits frequently comprise a large part of the deposit. For this reason, perhaps, dry fans are relatively small.

Wet (Fluvial) Fans

The Kosi River in India has built a large wet fan (Gole and Chitale, 1966), which provides an interesting contrast to the dry fans. The Kosi River, draining from the high Himalayas, delivers a tremendous sediment load to the Ganges piedmont area, where it has constructed the large Kosi fan. During the period 1736 to 1964 the Kosi River shifted 70 miles from east to west, and in this process 3500 square miles of land were reworked and laid waste as a result of sand deposition and bank erosion.

At the head of the fan, at Chatra (Figure 7-5), the channel consists of boulders, cobbles, and pebbles. These coarse sediments are rarely transported downstream for more than 9.5 miles from Chatra, where the coarse material practically disappears. The river widens downstream of Chatra, and braiding is characteristic from Belka downstream where interlacing channels are spread over a width of approximately 4 miles. From the head of the fan, the gradient decreases from 5 to about 1 foot per mile. At the lower gradients, the river divides into several channels that spread over an area 10 miles wide.

The shift of the Kosi River to the west is shown in Figure 7-6. The difference between this and the arid fans discussed above is that this is a wet, alluvial fan of considerable magnitude. The almost random distribution of erosion and deposition patterns on the arid fan (Figure 7-4) is replaced by a progressively shifting channel. Comparison of the posi-

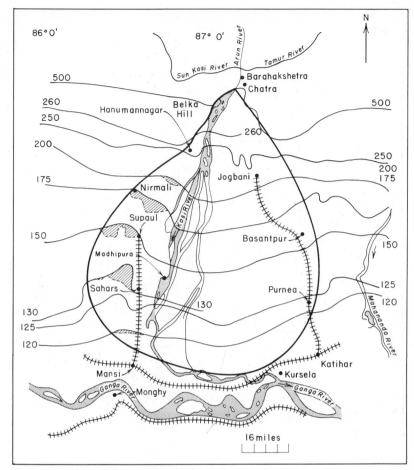

Figure 7-5   Kosi River fan. Solid contours show fan configuration in 1936. Dashed contours are based on 1957 survey. Shaded areas show contour straightening due to deposition on west side of fan between surveys. (From C. V. Gole and S. V. Chitale, 1966, Inland delta building activity of Kosi River: Am. Soc. Civil Eng. J. Hydraul. Div. HY-2, pp. 111–126.)

tion of the contours on Figure 7-5 shows that between 1938 and 1957 the river moved westward by avulsion into a low area which was then built up by deposition. This movement of the river to the west could have been anticipated by the concavity of the 1938 contours. The shaded areas of Figure 7-5 represent the areas where deposition has smoothed the surface and straightened the contours. If this progressive shift of the Kosi River to the west is not due to tilting to the west, then the possibility

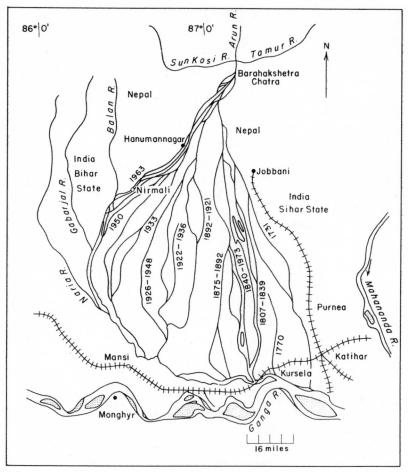

Figure 7-6   Courses of Kosi River, 1731 to 1963. (From C. V. Gole and S. V. Chitale, 1966, Inland delta building activity of Kosi River: Am. Soc. Civil Eng. J. Hydraul. Div. HY-2, pp. 111–126.)

that the river will soon begin migrating to the east is worthy of consideration. However, it is equally possible that, if there is a low area on the east
side of the fan at present, the channel might shift to that position by
avulsion.

Sedimentology.   The lack of extensive exposure prevents sampling of
modern alluvial fans except at the surface and in gullies; therefore the
most complete information on grain-size and mineralogical variations

comes from studies of ancient fans that contain economic deposits of gold and uranium. Normally the coarsest sediments are found at the fan head (McPherson and Hirst, 1972). However, when fan-head trenching occurs there is reworking and flushing of the sediment farther downstream. Sometimes this results in a slight increase in the size of sediment along the fan radius (Denny, 1965). Of course the shifting patterns of deposition on an alluvial fan will result in considerable sediment variability (Lustig, 1965, Figure 113). A further complicating factor is the frequent occurrence of mudflows on dry fans. These deposits are found interbedded with fluvial sediments.

The variability of sediment size on the fan surface is also encountered at depth; however, the overall vertical change in sediment size should be from finest at the base to progressively coarser as the fan grows up and out from the canyon mouth (Ryder, 1971), but then grain size should decrease as erosion reduces the source area. A fan deposited by perennial stream flow, such as the Kosi fan, should, of course, show better-defined stratification and less sediment-size variability.

EXPERIMENTAL STUDY OF ALLUVIAL FANS

Alluvial fans are ideal subjects for experimentation because the conditions required for fan growth are very easy to simulate. For example, Hooke's (1967, 1968) experimental studies provided new information on the growth of mudflow fans. Hooke concluded that some fan-head trenches occur as debris and stream flows alternate. That is, a water flow, following a series of debris flows, will cause trenching. Hence, certain types of channels at the fan head may be temporary and related simply to the concentrations of sediment in the water delivered from the sediment source area.

Experimental studies of mudflow fans performed in the REF reproduced this process (Weaver, 1976). In this series of experiments, unlike those described in Chapter Four, the upper half of the REF was the sediment source area, and the lower half was the depositional area. Precipitation was applied to the source, and the sediment and water moved out onto the piedmont where the coarser sediments were deposited (Figure 7-7). A wooden wall was constructed to separate the source area from the depositional area, and discharge moved through a slot in the wall, which was fixed in position. Thus the flow could not migrate laterally until it exited from the canyon mouth. The experimental design therefore included both Zones 1 and 3.

Figure 7-8 shows a small experimental fan formed primarily by

Figure 7-7   Rainfall-erosion facility (REF) and fluvial fan. When the fan essentially filled the lower half of REF it was contained by gravel, which was analogous to adjacent fan growth. Numbered plastic squares in source area were placed on surface to reduce erosion and to produce an Eckis-type tranch. (From Weaver, 1976.)

mudflows. The mudflows were formed by applying bursts of high-intensity precipitation to the sediment source area. The mudflow and stream-flow episodes constructed a steep fan with an irregular surface composed of mudflow lobes. The sediment in the source area was a silty sand with a small percentage of granules and fine gravel. In addition, the sediment contained a small portion of magnetite (0.05%). Because there was little or no reworking of the mudflow deposits the magnetite was distributed almost uniformly throughout the deposit (Figure 7-9), although both magnetite concentration and sediment size did decrease in a down-fan direction.

Although there is probably a continuum of alluvial fan types, with the mudflow fan at one extreme, only one other fan, a wet fan, was studied experimentally. It was formed by flow from the steep, high-sediment-yield source area to which precipitation was applied at about 5 cm per hour for 1- and 2-hour periods. At the end of each run data were collected on fan growth and the changes in Zone 1. Under these conditions runoff from the source area was uniform, and it was assumed that sediment production would also be almost constant. Sediment samples were collected every 15 minutes during each run.

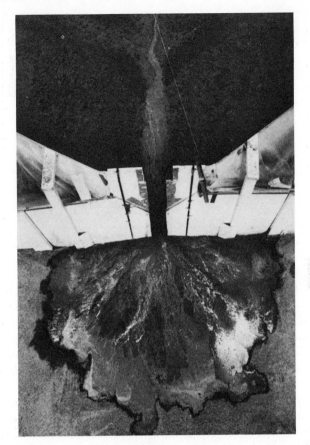

Figure 7-8   Mudflow fan developed during experiments in REF. Note irregular outline of fan and lobate deposits on fan surface. (From Weaver, 1976.)

Before data collection began on the fan, it was necessary that the source area channel and the fan surface be accordant. Therefore, the first few applications of precipitation permitted some incision of Zone 1 channels. The eroded sediment was deposited rapidly on the flat piedmont surface, but as the source-area channel cut down, the protofan was built up until the channel and fan profiles were accordant. At this stage data collection began.

It soon became apparent that the diverse fan morphologies noted in the field (Figure 7-4) were being reproduced through time on the experimental fan. For example, as the fan grew to a radius of about 6 m, it alternated between two very different morphologic and hydraulic

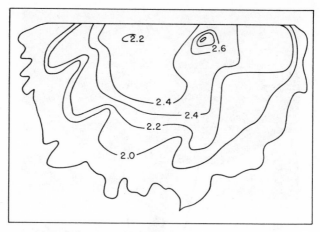

Figure 7-9   Magnetite distribution in mudflow fan. Contours are log of magnetite concentration in percent multiplied by 100. (From Macke, 1976.)

conditions. First, water issued from the "canyon" and spread in a sheet at the fan head (Figure 7-10a). Farther down fan the flow subdivided into many shifting braided channels (Figure 7-10b). This expected runoff configuration was interrupted periodically by fan-head trenching (Figure 7-11a), when the water issued from Zone 1 and continued down fan in a trench that conveyed water and sediment to the distal part of the fan (Figure 7-11b).

Following development of a fan-head trench the source-area channel was rejuvenated, and increased sediment delivery aided the backfilling of the trench and restoration of the smooth fan-head configuration (Figure 7-10a).

This sequence of events can be explained by changes at the fan head. Water leaving the upper part of the REF and spreading over the fan was slowed, and the velocity decrease caused sediment deposition at the fan head. This continued until a threshold slope was achieved at the constant discharge, and thus trenching and reworking of the fan head occurred.

Figure 7-12 shows the changes at the fan head during one such cut and fill cycle. Note that the profile of the upper part of this fan changes from straight to convex during incision and then is restored by deposition to a straight profile before the next trenching event.

The alluvial fan grew progressively with time, but growth at the fan head was episodic, being interrupted by periods of incision, sediment reworking, and down-fan distribution of sediment.

Remember that precipitation intensity and, therefore, discharge were constant during the experiments. However, sediment yield did vary, but the greatest variations were related to fan-head trenching and aggradation. With fan-head trenching the baselevel of the source area was lowered by the incision. Alluvium in the valleys of the source area was flushed out and terraces appeared along the valley sides (Figure 7-11a). This increased sediment discharge accelerated the filling of the fan trench, which in turn raised the baselevel at the fan head, thereby reducing sediment delivery to the fan. The situation is portrayed diagrammatically in Figure 7-13.

The wet-fan experiment shows that under the conditions of the study geomorphic (slope) thresholds controlled fan growth, which was episodic. Hence, the wet-fan growth resembled in reverse the incision of alluvium in the Douglas Creek Valley. Again the dynamic metastable equilibrium model seems to apply in situations of high sediment transport.

Although fan-head trenches were the most spectacular, other trenches developed on the lower fan. These usually formed on the lower midfan, and then eroded upfan. Surprisingly, these trenches rarely affected the fan head. As they approached the fan head, the increasing sediment loads delivered to these trenches caused them to aggrade, so they never became conveyors of large quantities of Zone 1 sediment to the lower fan. Nevertheless, the mid and lower fan were repeatedly incised by these small channels when water was spread over the fan (Figure 7-10b).

Figure 7-14 is a series of maps showing the different patterns of fan deposition that occurred during several different experimental runs. Obviously a fluvial fan depositional unit may take on a very irregular configuration and in some cases it may appear to be completely isolated from the sediment source (Figure 7-14e) if a fan-head trench was active.

At the end of the experiment sediment yields from Zone 1 were artificially reduced by means of plastic squares that were placed randomly in the source area (Figure 7-7). These reduced the effects of raindrop impact and surficial runoff. Nevertheless, this reduction of sediment from hillsides was compensated for by erosion of valley alluvium. Not until about 40 percent of the source area was covered with plastic did the sediment yield decrease sufficiently for a deep Eckis-type trench to form (Weaver, 1976).

Wet-Fan Sedimentology

Upon completion of the experimental study of wet-fan morphology, sediment samples were taken of the upper 10 cm of the deposit and the fan was dissected to reveal its stratigraphy. In contrast to the dry

Figure 7-10   Wet alluvial fan, deposition at fan head: (a) water spread at fan head, (b) water distribution on fan, during growth of fan head. (From Weaver, 1976.)

mudflow fan, two striking differences were apparent. First, there was an increase in grain size downfan, and second, the magnetite that was distributed throughout the source and dry fan was concentrated at several stratigraphic levels on the wet fan.

Observation of fan growth during the experiment permits an explanation of these wet fan anomolies. It was noted earlier that other studies showed a downfan increase of surface grain size, at least at the proximal part of the fan (Denny, 1965; Lustig, 1965). On the experimental fan, as water spread over the fan head deposition there was rapid, but at the same time the increase in height of the fan head reduced the gradient of

(b)

the channel feeding it, and as a result, fan-head growth was by deposition of sediment that became finer grained. Upon trenching, the coarse sediment stored in the valley of the source area was remobilized, and it moved through the trench to the midfan or distal fan area. In this way along a given fan radius there was an increase in grain-size downfan in the upper 10 cm of the deposit.

Another factor of significance, however, is that much of the suspended sediment-load removed from the source area continued out of the REF with the water; therefore, it was not deposited at the most distal part of the fan. Hence the experimental fan can be considered to be only the proximal and midfan areas of what would have been a much larger wet fan if all the sediment and water had been delivered to a closed basin. Therefore, the down-fan increase of sediment size is restricted to the upper fan.

The repeated reworking of the fan head produced a significant concentration of magnetite at that position (Figure 7-15). Within the source-area sediment plus magnetite moved from the slopes, through low-order tributaries, and into the main channels. Local channel scour reworked the sediment to form valley placers. Fan-head trenching caused reworking of at least the deposits in the lower part of Zone 1, and in this way twice-reworked magnetite was then deposited at the fan head and in the fan-head trench. Renewed fan-head trenching further concentrated the heavy minerals. The result is a striking concentration of

Figure 7-11   Wet alluvial fan, fan-head trench: (a) fan-head trench, (b) water distribution on trenched fan. (From Weaver, 1976.)

heavy minerals at the fan head and at the base of backfilled channels. This condition is obviously very different from that of the dry alluvial fan.

In addition, the contrast between the earlier rapidly deposited sediment at the fan base and the upper reworked sediment above this basal deposit was marked. The rapidly deposited, poorly sorted sediment contained the same amount of magnetite, but it was not concentrated. However, in the upper part of the fan that was reworked by fan-head trenching, both sediment sorting into fine and coarse strata and the concentration of magnetite into miniature placers occurred. Magnetite

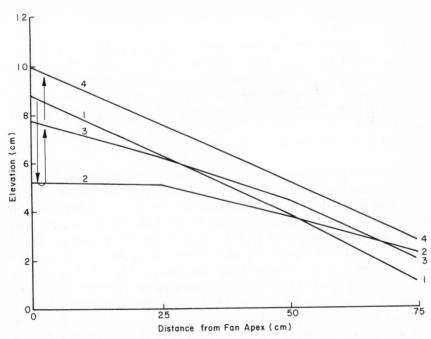

Figure 7-12   Profiles of wet fan during fan-head trenching cycle. (From Weaver, 1976.)

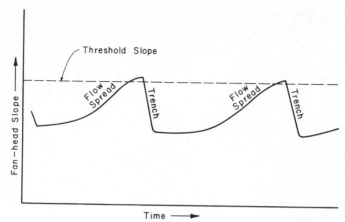

Figure 7-13   Changing slope at fan head leading to fan-head trenching.

was concentrated in the channels as they were cut and backfilled. Later migration of the channels produced a thin sheet of magnetite.

FIELD EXAMPLES

Piedmont deposits are well known from the ancient rocks, and they have been identified by many authors. Several examples are cited here; some are considered in more detail not only because they contain important concentrations of economic minerals, but also because these deposits have been studied in detail. A final example of a modern fluvial fan, the Riverine Plain area of Australia, is described because it bears some analogy to a distal fan deposit.

Some ancient piedmont deposits very closely resemble the modern and experimental fans described above, for example, the Devonian fans described by Miall (1970), the upper Cretaceous–lower Tertiary fans from southwestern Montana described by Wilson (1970), and the very thick, coarse conglomerate deposits of northwestern Wyoming of Cretaceous and Tertiary ages. Because of the coarseness of these materials they seem to be associated with the proximal facies of large fans. Lindsey (1972) made a detailed investigation of the Harebell and Pinyon conglomerates in Wyoming primarily because they contain small quantities of fine-grained gold. In spite of the coarseness and alluvial-fan character of these conglomerates, he concluded that the sediments were deposited in a relatively warm, humid environment. Almost 10,000 feet

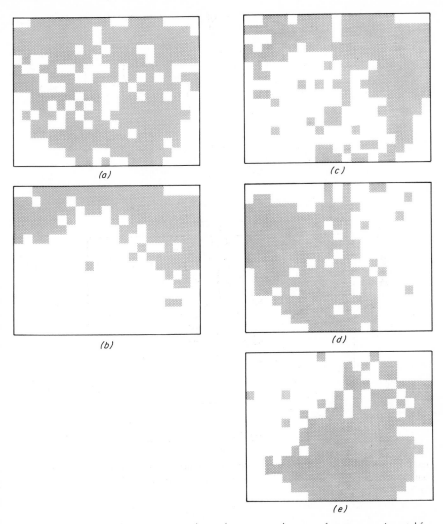

Figure 7-14 Depth of deposition on 18 by 21 foot rectangular area of upper experimental fan during 2-hour runs. Arrow designates outlet from source area. Each square represents deposition on 1 square foot of fan surface. (a) Widespread deposition period characterized by flow that spread widely over fan. (b) Deposition concentrated in upper part of fan. Flow persisted on upper right and then shifted to left, as fan head channels changed position. (c) Deposition concentrated on upper right and at fan head with minimum deposition on lower fan. Note fan-head trench, white rectangle at arrow, that formed just before termination of run. (d) Deposition at lower left. Sediments conveyed to lower fan by fan-head trench and persistence of flow to lower left. (e) Deposition at lower center. Fan-head trenching moved large quantities of sediment to lower fan. (From Weaver, 1976.)

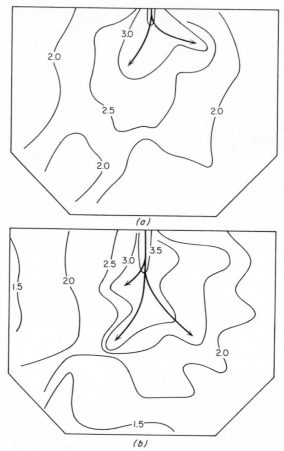

Figure 7-15 Magnetite distribution in wet experimental fan. Contours are log of magnetite concentrations in percent multiplied by 100: (a) 0- to 5-cm depth, (b) 5- to 10-cm depth. (From Macke, 1976.)

of sediment are contained within these two depositional units, composed predominantly of quartzite pebbles, cobbles, and boulders set in a sandstone matrix.

Lindsey (1972) suggests that these conglomerates and associated materials have been transported by streams for as much as 100 to 200 miles from sources in Idaho and Montana. He concludes that the conglomerate facies of the Harebell and Pinyon conglomerates were deposited as fans of coarse alluvial detritus on the eastern margin of the ancestral Teton Range. The coarseness of the sediment and the poor concentration of heavy minerals suggest limited reworking and rapid accumulation of this sediment. It is likely that under these circumstances the finer sediments and fine gold, which are the hydraulic equivalent of finer sediment fractions, were deposited much farther downfan and certainly not at the fan head.

Van Horn Sandstone.   A very complete picture of an alluvial fan complex of Precambrian age is provided by McGowen and Groat (1971) through their detailed study of the Van Horn sandstone. The Van Horn sandstone crops out in westernmost Texas, east of El Paso. Sediments ranging in size from boulders to silt were transported southward by high-gradient mountain streams. To the south there is a marked change in the nature of the sediments deposited, and three facies have been identified as follows: proximal facies of gravel, midfan facies of alternating gravel and coarse sand, and the distal facies of coarse sand.

Figure 7-16 shows the Van Horn paleogeography and the three facies. The Van Horn is wholly a fluvial deposit that, because of its age, must have been deposited in prevegetation times. The climate was probably wet, and large quantities of sediment were flushed from the sediment

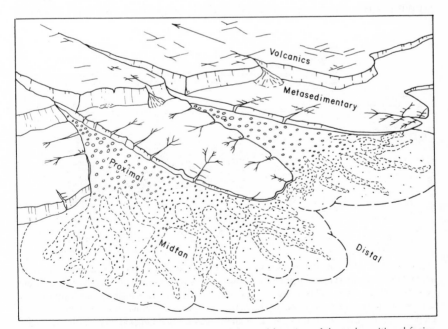

Figure 7-16   Van Horn Sandstone paleogeography and location of three depositional facies. (From McGowen and Groat, 1971.)

source area without any influence of vegetative cover (McGowen and Groat, 1971).

There is a decrease in sediment size from fan head to fan toe, and at a given cross section, the sediment becomes finer upward. Figure 7-17 shows a cross section near the fan head. The details of distal fan sediments are shown in Figure 7-18. Note the gravel layers that may be gravel lag or armor layers of the type formed by scour and sediment reworking below dams (Chapter Five). There seems to be no preferential concentration of heavy minerals in the upper portion of the fan. In fact, the gold and other heavy minerals found in this deposit are the hydraulic equivalents of coarse sand, and, therefore, they were moved to the distal part of the fan, where small concentrations of gold and other heavy minerals are found.

The Van Horn sandstone is up to 1200 feet thick in the northern outcrops, and it thins irregularly to about 100 to 200 feet near its southernmost outcrops over a distance of about 20 to 25 miles. Gravel is confined primarily to the northern outcrop area and stratigraphically to the lowermost section of the Van Horn sandstone. Beds containing boulder-size material and gravel tend to be massive, and sediment size decreases upward in this section, as well as toward the south. Accompanying a decrease in grain size is a decrease in bedding thickness and

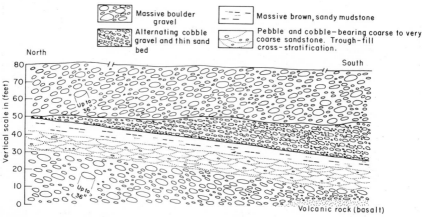

Figure 7-17   Diagrammatic cross section of Van Horn Sandstone showing character of proximal facies. Lowermost massive gravel has clasts up to 36 inches in diameter. Five feet of trough cross-bedded gravelly sand lie above basal gravel. Massive sandy mudstone comprises the next unit. Above the mudstone is a sequence of alternating sand and gravel units, which have been eroded to produce the discordant contact with the uppermost boulder gravel. Shifting flows and scour at the fan head can be expected to produce this type of deposit. (From McGowen and Groat, 1971.)

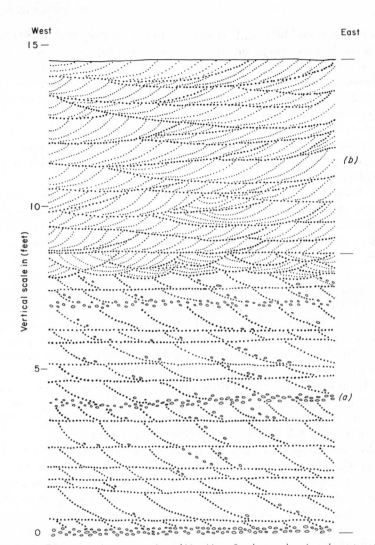

Figure 7-18   Diagrammatic cross section of Van Horn Sandstone showing character of distal facies. The lower unit (a) at this location is composed of muddy coarse sand and gravel. The unit was deposited during three depositional events. At the base of each of these units is a gravel layer 1 to 2 pebbles thick. The uppermost unit (b) is a trough cross-bedded coarse sand. (From McGowen and Groat, 1971.)

frequency of gravel beds and an increase in the number and thickness of sand beds. For example, the base of the fan, which is dominated by gravel in the north, is replaced to the south by alternating gravel and sand beds. At some moment in time, the Van Horn surface displayed the following features from north to south: (1) thick massive boulder beds, (2) alternating thick, horizontally stratified cobble-to-boulder beds, and thin, massive, or parallel laminated sand beds, (3) alternating thin-to-thick pebble-to-cobble beds and thin-to-thick sand beds, (4) coarse-to-very-coarse sand, and (5) coarse-to-very-coarse sand and muddy coarse sand (McGowen and Groat, 1971).

The Van Horn sandstone is predominantly fluvial. Therefore it is not a dry alluvial fan, but because of the coarseness of the sediments it is not identical to the wet fluvial fan that was produced experimentally. The Van Horn fan is probably intermediate in character between the dry and wet fans described above.

Witwatersrand Gold Fields. The Witwatersrand Basin was filled with about 14,000 meters of sediments and volcanics between 2.5 and 2.8 billion years ago. It ranks as one of the greatest mining fields of the world; about 55 percent of all the gold ever mined has been obtained from it. In 1970, 1000 metric tons of gold were mined from this basin. These figures indicate why so much emphasis has been placed on developing an understanding of these ancient alluvial deposits. Mining has reached a maximum depth of 3600 meters in certain sections of the basin, and some stratigraphic horizons have been mined out for 70 k along strike and for 8 k down dip (Pretorius, 1974a).

Within the basin there are six major goldfields (Figure 7-19). The Klerksdorp, East Rand, and West Rand fields were discovered through surface outcrops. The remaining three goldfields were located beneath a younger sedimentary cover that is up to 3000 thick. During deposition of the fan sediments, there was active warping of the basin as well as active faulting. The situation therefore was ideal for deposition of piedmont deposits.

The gold fields and their sedimentary deposits are not entirely fluvial; the lower end of each deposit has been reworked by the longshore drift of currents in a lake or a shallow sea. For example, the East Rand fan extends for 40 km, at which point it merges with sediments deposited in a lacustrine environment. The midfan portion is 50 km wide, and the fan base section is 90 km wide.

The coarser sediments of the fan exhibit a typical braided stream pattern. Most of the Witwatersrand channels are shallow, with a high width/depth ratio. Generally the channels are less than 0.7 m deep. The

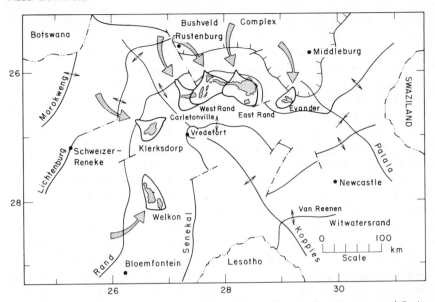

Figure 7-19 Index map showing gold fields and fluvial fans in the Witwatersrand Basin. Arrows indicate sediment transport directions. (From Pretorius, 1974a.)

largest channels are found in the western lobe of the East Rand fan, where two parallel channels are filled with heavy pyritic sand and minor amounts of gravel. One channel has a maximum width of 1000 m and a maximum depth of 35 m, whereas the other channel is up to 750 m wide and 85 m deep. Both channels have been traced for distances of over 8 km in the mine workings. These may represent major trenches of the Eckis-type.

The fans are composed of a large number of cycles of sedimentation, each separated by unconformities. They fine upwards and seem to be related to tectonic adjustments along the boundary fault. Movement along the boundary faults uplifted the fan-head sediments, and they were then reworked and incorporated into the basal sediments of the next cycle.

The gold and uranium mineralization occurs in or immediately adjacent to bands of conglomerate that are preferentially developed at or near the base of each cycle of sedimentation. These are the reefs of the mining industry. The number of reefs mined in a particular fan varies from a minimum of 1 in the Evander goldfield to a maximum of 10 in the Klerksdorp and West Rand goldfields. The average per fan is between 5 and 6. Considering the great thickness of sediments involved, conditions favorable to the concentration of the heavy minerals were rare.

Within the Witwatersrand, fine gold (0.035 mm) and uranium (0.065 mm) occur in the fluvial sediments (1) in the matrix of conglomerate, (2) in pyritic sand, which usually fills erosion channels, the gold lying on the forsets of the cross-bedded sand, and (3) on sand along the plains of unconformity which separate two cycles of sedimentation.

In situation 1 it appears that the gold is trapped in previously deposited conglomerates. In situation 2 the heavy minerals concentrated as the channels backfilled. In situation 3 the heavy minerals are concentrated as a result of reworking of the sediment before deposition of the next layer of gravel. As might be expected, the gold content of the reef is highly variable from point to point both laterally and vertically.

Pretorius (1974b) summarizes the characteristics of a Witwatersrand goldfield as follows: the weight of evidence that has been gathered indicates that each goldfield is a fluvial (wet) fan or fan delta developed where a major river discharged into a shallow lake or inland sea. The basin was fault-bounded on the northwestern edge, and it was shrinking progressively with time. Repeated tectonic adjustments took place along the active northwestern margin. The uplift of basin-edge materials led to many cycles of reworking of previously deposited sediments, and this recycling was an important factor in the gradual concentration of gold and uranium.

Each cycle started with a high-energy pulse of sedimentation, as a result of tectonic adjustment along the basin edge. Material was delivered from the source area and distributed over the surface by a system of braided-stream channels. The interlacing of these channels frequently gives the impression of a continuous sheet of gravel. The higher gold and uranium concentrations normally occur within these channels.

The best developed fan in the Witwatersrand basin is that of the East Rand. It is the largest known, and it is the one that has been mined most extensively. Figure 7-20 shows the main components of this typical gold- and uranium-bearing alluvial fan. The apex was located in a synclinal downwarp between two granite domes. The fan was also contained between domes of basement granite, which continued to rise during sedimentation, thereby influencing the geometry of the fan. Two main lobes formed, and on each lobe numerous channels assumed a braided pattern radiating out from the apex of the fan. The channels contain higher concentrations of heavy minerals, and they constitute the pay shoots that are preferentially mined. However, the concentrating process came into operation on less than 20 occasions during the deposition

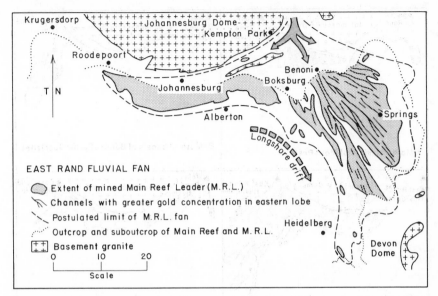

Krugersdorp
Johannesburg Dome
Kempton Park
Roodepoort
T N
Benoni
Boksburg
Johannesburg
Springs
Alberton
Longshore drift

EAST RAND FLUVIAL FAN

Extent of mined Main Reef Leader (M.R.L.)
Channels with greater gold concentration in eastern lobe
Postulated limit of M.R.L. fan
Outcrop and suboutcrop of Main Reef and M.R.L.
Heidelberg
Basement granite
Devon Dome
0   10   20
Scale

Figure 7-20   Sketch map of typical Witwatersrand fluvial fan. The asymmetry of the fan is typical, because of the influence of clockwise longshore currents. The western lobe forms part of the Central Rand Goldfield and the eastern lobe forms the whole of the East Rand Goldfield. The original fan covered at least 1300 km². (From Pretorius, 1974a.)

of more than 8000 m of sediment over a period of 100 to 250 million years.

The major fans are relatively close together, and the margin of one fan merges almost imperceptively into the margin of the other. The best example of this is the West and East Rand fans. The western lobe of the East Rand fan overlaps the eastern rim of the West Rand fan in the vicinity of Johannesburg to give the appearance of continuous deposition. This area of the intermingling of the two lobes is the Central Rand gold field. Figures 7-21 and 7-22 show the periods of activity of adjacent fans. During Main Reef deposition the areas involved were about the same on both fans. Two lobes were forming in the West Rand fan, but only the western lobe of the East Rand fan was active. When the Banded Pyritic Quartzites were being formed, the East Rand fan was subjected to the most deposition. Both lobes were being constructed, but only one lobe of the West Rand fan was active. During Main Reef Leader times all activity was focused on the East Rand fan, with both lobes building out to a very marked extent. The West Rand fluvial system does not seem to have been very active at this time. When the South Reef was being

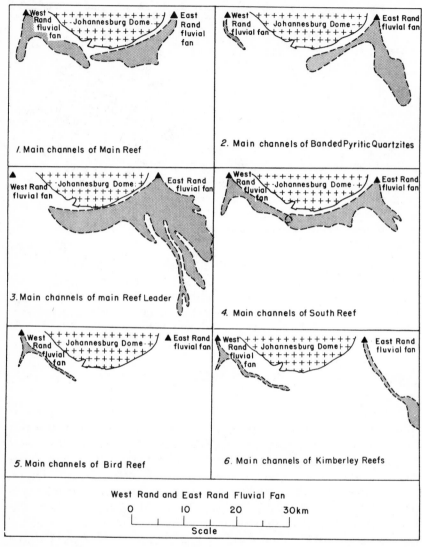

1. Main channels of Main Reef

2. Main channels of Banded Pyritic Quartzites

3. Main channels of main Reef Leader

4. Main channels of South Reef

5. Main channels of Bird Reef

6. Main channels of Kimberley Reefs

West Rand and East Rand Fluvial Fan

0   10   20   30km

Scale

Figure 7-21 The relative amounts of coarser sediments deposited on the adjacent West Rand and East Rand fluvial fans during Main Reef, Banded Pyritic Quartzites, Main Reef Leader, South Reef, Bird Reef, and Kimberly Reef times. (From Pretorius, 1974a.)

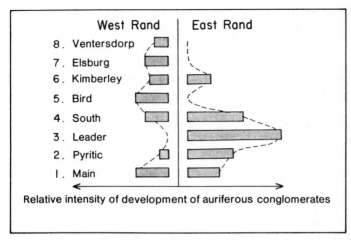

Figure 7-22   Sketch based on Figure 7-21 showing relative deposition of gold-bearing conglomerates on West and East Rand fluvial fans. (From Pretorius, 1974a.)

deposited the East Rand fan was much less active than during Main Reef Leader times, but the West Rand depositional processes were once again operative. The East Rand fan appears to have received no coarse sediments during Bird Reef times, and the West Rand fan received only a relatively small volume. In Kimberley time the East Rand fan was reactivated, and the sedimentation on it was of greater importance than that on the West Rand fan. The variations in relative activity of the two fans are depicted in Figure 7-22. The East Rand fan received a greater amount of sediment overall, and the period of active sedimentation on each fan seems to have been out of phase. Whenever coarse sediments, which now contain gold and uranium, were brought down to one fan, the transportation and depositional activity on the other fan was markedly diminished in importance. This has been attributed to nonuniform tectonic disturbances in the source area. In addition, the patterns of activity (Figure 7-21) indicate that there were two types of sediment distribution: (1) broad sheets of gravel spread extensively over the fan surface and (2) linear deposits. These are the two extremes of alluvial fan activity, as noted during experimentation. It is not surprising that the systems are out of phase considering the behavior of the experimental fan and the morphologic differences among modern arid fans (Figure 7-4).

The bilobate nature of the Rand fans maybe a result of warping of the depositional basin, because the experimental studies show that as a result of the momentum of the water leaving the source area, major deposition and conception of heavy minerals should be in the central areas of the fan; however, the maps of fan deposition (Figure 7-9) indicate that almost any pattern can be expected for at least short periods of time.

Pretorius (1974b) has attempted to summarize the data collected on Witwatersrand fan growth and gold concentration to develop a model for this type of goldfield. He views the Witwatersrand fans as high-energy fluvial systems, but it appears that the Witwatersrand-type goldfields developed at periods of neither minimum nor maximum energy, which seems to concur with the results of the experimental studies. For example, with rapid uplift of the source area large quantities of poorly sorted sediment were dumped at the basin edge with no concentration of the heavy minerals; however, as elevation of the source and the energy of the system began to decrease, sediment production from the source area decreased, and there was reworking of the sediments stored in the valleys of the source area and of the fan-head sediments; this produced concentrations of heavy minerals. As the energy of the system further decreased in the Witwatersrand Basin, there was relatively little downfan movement of heavy minerals or coarse sediment, but gold was concentrated at the distal part of the fan by wave action. With renewed uplift, the stored sediments and the weathered materials of the source area were flushed out of Zone 1. Fan-head trenching took place, and reworking of the sediment and concentration of the heavy minerals during the period of increasing basin elevation and energy occurred. However, at the time of maximum energy in this second cycle, sediment production was very great and sorting and reworking of the sediments was minimal, with the result that gold concentration ceased.

The Pretorius model is clearly understandable in view of the experimental results, and it is supported by the history of placer formation in the Ural Mountains (Sigov et al., 1972), which shows that during periods of tectonic activity (late Triassic–early Jurassic), heavy minerals were disseminated through the sedimentary deposits. However, during late Jurassic time, a period of stability and peneplanation, placers were formed, primarily in streams. During the Cretaceous and early Tertiary ages, a time of maximum regional subsidence, existing placers were buried, and the heavy minerals were not concentrated in the rapidly deposited sediment. In the Midtertiary age, there was another period of tectonic stability and erosion when placers were formed. The Russian studies show that major heavy mineral concentrations do not form during periods of rapid erosion and deposition.

There are some interesting similarities between the broader features of the Witwatersrand goldfields and the experimental wet fans described previously. The similarities may be more apparent than real because the major features of the Witwatersrand fans are probably related to tectonic activity; however, lower-order cycles of sedimentation may be the result of threshold behavior of these large wet fans.

Tarkwaian of Ghana. The Precambrian conglomerates of the Tarkwaian Series are also gold-bearing alluvial fan deposits (Sestini, 1973). Variations of thickness, facies, and cross-bedding direction indicate four coalescing fans with dispersal from the east and southeast. The Tarkwaian Series is up to 2400 m thick and has been divided into four formations, each of which has considerable vertical and lateral variability.

The Banket Formation is of most interest because it contains at least three gold-bearing conglomerate layers. In spite of the variability of the deposition in the Banket, at least three conglomerate units are persistent, the Breccia Reef, Middle Reef, and Basal Conglomerate. The Breccia Reef so named after the tabular angular pebbles of schist and phyllite that are abundant in this deposit, is 2 to 10 m thick. The Middle Reef is 1.5 to 15 m thick on the west side of the syncline, and it thins rapidly to the east in an upfan direction, where it wedges out or merges with the Basal Conglomerate. It frequently includes 2 beds of conglomerate and, in places, up to 5. In the Basal Conglomerate, the number of beds varies from 2 to 10, being more abundant in the west or in the distal portion of the fan.

The occurrence of gold in the conglomerate bands provides a means of correlation. The most gold is in the Basal Conglomerate, and it occurs in progressively decreasing quantities in the Middle and Breccia Reefs. The Banket Formation, in addition to the conglomeratic zones, is actually composed mainly of fine- to medium-grained quartzite. Sestini, as noted above, concludes that the sediments of the Tarkwa area were deposited in a piedmont environment and that the sediments represent coalescent alluvial fans. This is strongly supported by the fact that the gold-bearing conglomerates are continuous over a distance of at least 25 km laterally, across the direction of transport. Sestini (1973) says that his environmental interpretation is supported by three additional facts: (1) a concentration of gold near the eastern margin outcrop or fan head, with a rapid decrease westward, (2) a rapid westward, downfan, increase of the thickness of the conglomerate zone accompanied by a pinching and swelling in the northeast–southwest direction, (3) a radiating pattern of current direction, similar to that described for arid alluvial fans.

Item 2 above is interesting because it suggests that there is an increase in the number of conglomerate beds and an increase in the thickness of the conglomerate zone away from the apex of the fan. This would seem to be contrary to most of the assumptions regarding deposition on alluvial fans; nevertheless, it conforms to the wet-alluvial-fan sedimentology described previously.

The rapid upcurrent thinning of the Middle Reef could arise from partial erosion of the upstream fan head. In modern alluvial fans the greatest thickness of sediment is toward the apex, but this is also the area at which major erosion and reworking of sediment begin. Erosion and reworking of the fan head could account for the absence of the Middle Reef near the eastern margin of outcrop.

Reworking could also be the cause of the thinner and better-sorted auriferous conglomerates. The gold occurs mainly in the lower part of the conglomerate units and in the lower 25 to 50 c of the Basal Reef. In fact, the lower 20 cm of the Basal Reef contain two to six times more gold than the entire reef. Ore concentrations in the gravels are very narrow and lenticular, and they occur about 200 to 500 m apart. They are 50 to 150 m wide and 200 to 500 m long. The pattern results from the shifting braided channels of an alluvial fan.

Sestini (1973) has also studied in some detail a cross section of a channel (Figure 7-23) where gold concentrations are highest. Beyond the channel the reef is thicker, and about 70 percent is cross-bedded quartzite with scattered pebbles. In the channel the Basal Reef is thinner and it contains up to four thin conglomerate layers. These appear to be the result of reworking and concentration of the gravels as armors at several levels in the channel.

Morrison Formation, U. S. A.   The Morrison Formation of the late Jurassic age consists of approximately 9200 cubic miles of continental alluvial and paludal (marshy) sedimentary rocks. In the region of study,

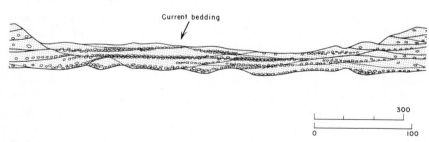

Figure 7-23   Cross section of paleochannel on Tarkwa fans. Note gravel layers formed by reworking of sediment in channel. (From Sestini, 1973.)

it is divided stratigraphically into four members, which are, from bottom to top, Salt Wash, Recapture, Westwater Canyon, and Brushy Basin. The Salt Wash is present in the northern two-thirds of the region, the Recapture and Westwater Canyon in the southern half, and the Brushy Basin throughout almost the entire region. Sediments that comprise these units were transported north and east across the region of study. The Morrison Formation contains, by volume, 48 percent light-colored, cross-bedded irregularly lensing sandstone and conglomeratic strata, 51 percent claystone, siltstone, and mudstone strata, and 1 percent limestones and other miscellaneous rocks. Half of the sandstone is in the Salt Wash Member, which comprises 40 percent of the formation, and 60 percent of the mudstone, claystone, and sandstone is in the Brushy Basin Member, which comprises 33 percent of the formation (Craig et al., 1955, p. 106).

Detailed studies of the stratigraphy and sedimentology of the Morrison Formation have been carried out because it is one of the main sources of uranium in the United States. The Salt Wash Member has been described in detail by Mullens and Freeman (1957). The isopachs of Figure 7-24 show that it was deposited as a fan with the apex in south central Utah. The fan is not completely symmetrical, as there is a thinning of the beds to the southeast. In this area the Salt Wash overlies the Bluff sandstone, which is predominantly aeolian. Its occurrence suggests that in this area there was a large dune field during the deposition of the Salt Wash. If the Bluff sandstone were absent, the Salt Wash Member would be a very large, essentially symmetrical fan-shaped piedmont deposit, extending over much of Utah and western Colorado. Mullens and Freeman (1957) separate the rocks into two types: stream deposits and floodplain deposits. Stream deposits are sediments that were deposited under the influence of water currents, whereas the floodplain deposits are sediments deposited from water not noticeably influenced by current action. Ninety percent of the total thickness is composed of stream deposits near the apex of the fan, but this proportion decreases in an orderly way toward the toe.

Changes in the texture and composition of the Salt Wash sediments permit identification of four major facies (Figure 7-25). The conglomeratic sandstone facies is confined to southcentral Utah. It consists mainly of sandstones containing pebbles as much as 4 inches in diameter. The sandstone and mudstone facies consists of interstratified sandstones and impure claystones, which surround the conglomeratic sandstone facies on the northwest, north, and east. A claystone and lenticular sandstone facies consisting of lenses of sandstone and a dominant matrix of claystone is present in northeastern Utah and part of

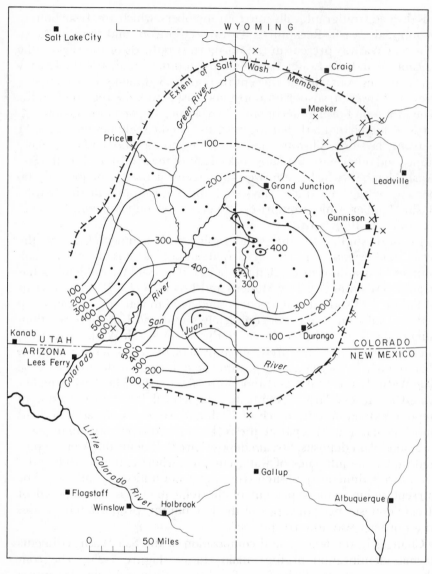

Figure 7-24 Isopach map of Salt Wash member of Morrison Formation showing thickness in feet. (From Mullens and Freeman, 1957.)

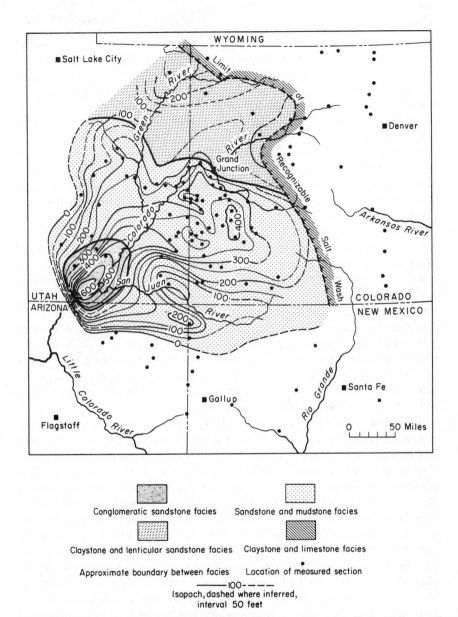

Figure 7-25 Facies map of Salt Wash member of Morrison Formation (From Mullens and Freeman, 1957.)

northwestern Colorado. The fourth facies, of claystone and limestone, lies east of the limit of recognition of the Salt Wash. However, the gradual decrease in sandstone content and increase in claystone and limestone content indicate that beds are continuous and essentially contemporaneous with the typical Salt Wash.

While the Salt Wash Member was being deposited, another major sediment source was providing materials that were being deposited as the Recapture Member. Thus the Salt Wash and Recapture Members are two broad, fan-shaped alluvial plains, or fans, that were constructed by deposition from two separate aggrading stream systems. The two fans coalesce along a common margin, which passes as a wide belt through the Four Corners area.

The climate during deposition of the lower part of the Morrison was dry, as suggested by preservation of sand dunes (Craig et al., 1955). However, sufficient moisture was present to support both reeds and large trees along stream courses and to permit the existence of small bodies of standing water in which thin beds of limestone were deposited. There are more fossil tree remains near the apex of the fan, and this distribution may reflect a greater abundance of vegetation at the apex as a result of the slightly higher elevation and proximity to a greater water supply near the source area. Again, the Salt Wash Member is not typical of the alluvial deposits of arid regions. The transport of sediment for hundreds of miles from northeastern Airzona into northern Colorado indicates a relatively abundant water supply.

The main interest in the Salt Wash Member of the Morrison Formation is the uranium and vanadium that are mined from it in many places in Colorado, Utah, and Arizona. The ore occurs as tabular masses in the thicker parts of stream-deposited sandstone lens and, in general, it is restricted to a single zone within the Salt Wash Member. If the uranium and vanadium were transported in solution through the Salt Wash Member after its deposition, movement of the metal-bearing solutions was affected by the transmissibility of the Salt Wash. The stream deposits are obviously more permeable than the floodplain deposits. The distal part of the fan is characterized by a low proportion of stream to floodplain deposits and a lack of continuity of the stream deposits. Movement of solutions through these stream deposits is impeded because of this lack of continuity, and the opportunity for concentration of dissolved metals is unlikely. The ideal situation for the concentration of ore minerals in the stream deposits is therefore where stream sediments constitute about half the thickness of the deposit. They are continuous, and the movement of the metal-bearing solutions is impeded only locally. Since movement of the metal-bearing solutions is not restricted at the fan apex or in the upper part of the fan, the solutions pass freely through this area and there is little chance for concentration of ore minerals.

The ideal conditions for accumulation of ore deposits exist in the central part of the Salt Wash wedge. In fact, the area containing the major ore deposits in the Salt Wash is, in general, within the central part of the fan. It must be remembered, however, that ore deposits in the Salt Wash are generally confined to one stratigraphic zone of stream deposits. Therefore, only a small part of the total deposit is ore bearing. Nonetheless, it does seem clear that significant ore deposits are not found in either the distal portion or the apex of this fan.

Riverine Plain.   The Riverine Plain (Butler, 1950; Schumm, 1968) lies in the states of New South Wales and Victoria in southeast Australia. It is the alluvial plain across which the Murray and Murrumbidgee Rivers flow westward from the eastern highlands of Australia. The Riverine Plain is, as its name suggests, a flat, alluvial plain, with a gradient of about 1.5 feet per mile. In the Murrumbidgee irrigation area, there has been considerable drilling for purposes of evaluating groundwater resources. The deepest bores, as described by Pels (1960, 1964) penetrated 465 feet of alluvium before encountering bedrock. Only the upper 150 feet is due to fluvial deposition, and the remainder of the sediments were deposited in lakes and swamps. However, of the upper 150 feet, only approximately 45 feet is composed of sandy sediments, and the rest is clay. Thus the situation is very different from that of the piedmont deposits described previously, because the greater part of the deposit is composed of very fine sediments, and the sands represent, for the most part, channel-fill deposits in the clay. The Riverine Plain deposits are analogous to the most distal deposits of a fluvial fan.

Butler (1958) has identified five depositional units in the upper surface of the plain (Figure 7-26). Three of these are fluvial, one is aeolian, and one is mixed fluvial–aeolian. A mixed fluvial–aeolian deposit, the Katandra sediments, is the oldest of the five. In most exposures the Katandra is a tight gray clay, but it is actually composed of a complex of channel, floodplain, and aeolian sediments. Cut into this clay bedrock are channels, and these have been filled with sandy sediments that were transported by the ancestral Murrumbidgee River. The oldest paleochannel sediments were deposited in deep channels eroded into the Katandra. After these Quiamong channels aggraded, a blanket of aeolian clay (parna) was deposited over the Katandra–Quiamong landscape (Butler, 1958; Butler and Hutton, 1956). Then the youngest of the paleochannels incised through the aeolian sediments and into the older Katandra riverine sediments. These channels were filled with

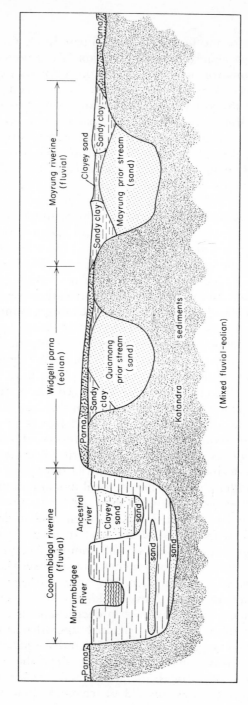

Figure 7-26 Stratigraphic relations on Riverine Plain, New South Wales, Australia. (From Schumm, 1968.)

fluvial sands, the Mayrung sediments. The most recent fluvial sediments, which form the floodplain of the Murrumbidgee River, are the Coonambidgal riverine deposits.

The older paleochannels, or the prior streams of Butler, can be found over large areas of the Riverine Plain forming a distributary pattern (Schumm, 1968, pl. 2). The most recent channel changes on the surface of the Riverine Plain have been discussed in Chapter Five.

Prior to the development of the several river control and flood irrigation schemes along the Murrumbidgee River, extensive flooding occurred over the Riverine Plain surface. During periods of major flooding, the greatest velocities of flow occurred where flow was concentrated, and, of course, on locally steeper parts of the Riverine Plain. At these locations there was erosion, which probably formed discontinuous gullies of the type found on steeper parts of alluvial valley floors (Schumm and Hadley, 1957). In addition, channel incision would have occurred, as unconfined flood waters plunged into another channel, for example, into the Murray River to the south. The 40-foot deep scours into the cohesive Katandra sediments must have initially resembled the arroyos of the southwestern United States, and a similar origin could account for these deep linear scours into the Katandra sediments of the Riverine Plain. No matter how the original incision began, once formed such a channel would enlarge, and it would concentrate floodwaters, eroding upslope until it intersected the source of the floodwaters, the paleo-Murrumbidgee channel. Until the eroding channel intersected the main river, it probably was transporting only sediment eroded from its bed and banks and sediment held in suspension by the floodwaters. However, when the paleo-Murrumbidgee channel was tapped, both water and sediment from the main river were diverted into the new, deep, stream channel. Therefore, the greater part of the water and sediment carried by the paleo-Murrumbidgee River would eventually have been diverted into this channel. As large quantities of bed load were introduced into it, the channel aggraded. Aggradation and widening of the prior-stream channel probably continued until a stable channel formed that was capable of transporting the runoff and sand load delivered to it.

The efficiency of the channel system on a plain of this inclination (1.5 feet per mile) can vary greatly as the character of the channels change. For example, the present rivers on the surface of the plain are highly sinuous, and their gradients are approximately one-half of that of the slope of the plain itself. However, during the time that the prior streams were active, the gradient of the stream was essentially the gradient of the plain, because the sinuosity of these channels was very low (Figure 5-4).

In the straight steep channels it was possible to move coarse sediments far down the surface of the plain.

It is in the prior-stream channels that the coarsest sediments of the Riverine Plain are found. For this reason they are sources of groundwater. However, where the prior-stream deposits are isolated from the modern rivers, the sands are dry. Only where the modern rivers cross and cut into the older linear sand bodies is water introduced into these paleochannels. These observations have some bearing on the economic potential of a paleochannel. There are many channels in ancient fluvial deposits that are barren of uranium or gold, even when neighboring channels are productive. Obviously a channel must be connected with the ore source before it can contain economically valuable minerals that are formed either as placers or as secondary chemical deposits.

In contrast to the fans described previously, the Riverine Plain, because of its fine sediments, sinuous stream, and gentle slope, is considered to be analogous to the distal part of a wet fan.

PIEDMONT EROSION

Pediments

When sediment production from Zone 1 is sufficiently low that alluvial fans do not form, erosional features dominate the piedmont. Cut rock surfaces with relatively thin gravel caps sweep away from mountain fronts and escarpments. Pediments have been a source of geomorphic controversy for decades (Hadley, 1967). No attempt is made here to discuss pediments in depth; instead, only one type is described, because it provides clear evidence of episodic erosion. This pediment is developed on relatively weak rock at the base of a mountain or scarp that is composed of, or at least capped by, relatively resistant rocks. Generally in this geologic situation multiple pediment surfaces are common and these seem to have developed, at least in some instances, without climatic, baselevel, or tectonic controls. Therefore, they are an excellent example of episodic erosion that is perhaps a function of geomorphic thresholds. In short, traditional explanations may not be required.

John Rich (1935) describes these pediments (Figure 7-27), which are typical of those formed at the base of the Book Cliffs in Colorado and Utah, an escarpment typical of many in the Colorado Plateau. The Mancos shale forms the bulk of the scarp, and all the piedmont, but the scarp is capped by the Mesa Verde sandstone. This situation differs

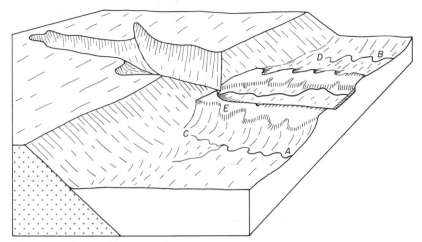

Figure 7-27 Development of multiple pediments by stream capture. (From Rich, 1935.)

somewhat from Rich's illustration, as he shows erosion along a fault scarp, but the principle is the same.

Rich begins his discussion with uplift of the resistant rocks and stream incision into the fault block, a typical Davisian model. The stream removes a coarse and large sediment load from the mountains and therefore requires a steep gradient to transport this load across the piedmont zone. However, streams draining only the piedmont area of soft rocks (Figures 7-27A, B) have a much gentler gradient, and they have incised into and eroded the weaker rocks. The streams draining from the highlands maintain a steeper gradient and are at a significantly higher level near the scarp. The result is that streams C or D will capture the high-level stream, thereby leaving surface E as an abandoned pediment. Following capture, gravels are moved from the canyon and spread over the Mancos shale surface to form the pediment's gravel cap. Obviously this process of piedmont denudation is not dependent on anything but stream capture.

Hunt et al. (1953) have demonstrated that capture and drainage pattern shift are very active processes on the north flank of the Henry Mountains, Utah. As the process continues the complete record is lost because the uppermost pediment surfaces are destroyed by lateral widening of the valleys, a circumstance suggested for the Douglas Creek terraces (Chapter Six).

Episodic erosion of a piedmont zone of the sort described above will cause rejuvenation of Zone 1 and periodic flushing of stored sediments from Zone 1 onto the piedmont. When this occurs, erosion of a pediment by lateral planation and backwearing of valley side slopes is replaced by gravel deposition and lateral stream shifting. In this situation the erosion of the pediment and gravel deposition are two separate processes (Hunt et al., 1953). The clean contact between the pediment gravels and the relatively impermeable shale bedrock produces a surface along which groundwater migration and the migration of ore-bearing solutions is possible.

DISCUSSION

Although the piedmont is usually viewed as a depositional zone, it is obvious that a great deal of erosion also can be expected there. Even when the dominant landforms are depositional, such as alluvial fans, the great variability in fan morphology reveals that the deposition may be episodic, being interrupted by periods of fan trenching and sediment reworking.

At present, semiarid and arid region fans are of concern to those planning pipelines, power lines, and roads, and even urban development. Perhaps when the fan is trenched, development should be restricted to the upper fan, because the lower fan is a zone of active deposition (Figure 7-14); when the fan is not trenched, roads and so forth should be placed as far as possible from the fan apex to avoid the area of maximum deposition. However, the instability of fan channels and their tendency to scour and widen during large floods require a degree of caution in any endeavor on these landforms (Scott, 1973; Schick, 1973).

There is a need to recognize within one area the critical threshold slope at which trenching of the fan will occur. Obviously the very simple experimental situation (Figure 7-13) will be complicated in the field by geologic and drainage-basin size differences and by differential uplift, but a complete geomorphic analysis of the area may nevertheless provide a quantitative basis for the recognition of incipiently unstable fans.

The experimental studies of fan growth, although designed initially to test the concept of geomorphic thresholds, have provided data on a new type of pediment deposit, the wet or fluvial fan, that was undoubtedly much more common during the geologic past. The Witwatersrand, Tarkwa, Van Horn, and Morrison deposits may all be of this general type. Therefore, the behavior of the experimental fluvial fan may provide a means of interpreting some of the depositional features and mineral concentrations in these ancient deposits.

There are differences, of course, and the sedimentology of piedmont deposits depends on the nature and amount of sediment delivered from Zone 1. For example, the Van Horn conglomerate was deposited by braided bedload channels, whereas the Morrison Formation and the Riverine Plain were probably formed for the most part by mixed-load and even suspended-load channels.

Periodic reworking of piedmont deposits as geomorphic thresholds are exceeded provides a mechanism for the concentration of heavy minerals at several levels within the deposit. In addition, the permeable units of such a deposit provide a route for mineralizing solutions.

There should be abundant evidence in the geologic record of fluvial sediments, which were deposited under humid conditions prior to the advent of erosion-retarding vegetation. These deposits should resemble those of the wet experimental fan, and they should contain zones of heavy mineral concentrations, if such materials were produced within Zone 1.

The heavy mineral placers therefore need not be related to erosion of local heavy mineral concentrations in the rocks of the source area. Rather they could be due to concentration by reworking of minerals that were widely dispersed through Zone 1 rocks. Recall that the magnetite was uniformly distributed through the source area sediment during the experiment, but upon erosion it was concentrated in valley placers (Figure 6-32) and in proximal fan placers (Figure 7-15). Some channel deposits in the Witwatersrand and Tarkwa sediments probably have an origin in fan trenching and channel backfilling of the type observed on the experimental fan.

Both the experimental studies and the discussion of stream capture in the piedmont provide an explanation for paleochannels that contain ore minerals and barren paleochannels that may be stratigraphically and sedimentologically very similar. For example, during the experiments it was noted that on the surface of the fan, midfan trenches developed that were not directly connected to the source area. These were formed as a result of concentration of runoff on the fan surface, and they were never conduits of sediment derived directly from the source area. Thus concentrations of heavy minerals in these midfan trenches were negligible. Therefore, on a piedmont plain or alluvial fan the channels that are going to contain economic mineral deposits must be connected with the sediment source area proper.

On the Riverine Plain the contact between the Katandra sediments and the younger paleochannels is irregular and even discontinuous. If there were a significant increase in sediment production from the Murrumbidgee headwaters, and if the sediments were coarse sand and gravel, a sheet deposit would be formed as the modern channel migrated laterally and laid down its coarse sediment load near the contact between the highlands and the plain. Such a deposit would resemble the Shinarump conglomerate of the southwestern United States (Malan, 1968). The Shinarump is of interest because uranium is found in the inner channels scoured into the underlying finer Moenkopi Formation.

The Shinarump is essentially an extensive blanket of coarse-grained sediments that varies greatly in thickness because of the incision and subsequent filling of channels in the underlying fine-grained sediments. These channels, although containing coarser sediments, resemble the anastomosing ancestral-stream patterns of the Riverine Plain. The Shinarump channels have deep scours on the outside of some of the bends and in relatively straight portions of the channels (Young, 1964). They are not continuous and probably reflect the undulatory or up-and-down longitudinal profile of a channel that is eroded into bedrock (Chapter Six).

Uranium-bearing solutions migrated through the Shinarump channels, but some of these paleochannels are barren, and it may simply be that this particular channel was isolated from the groundwater system. This is analogous to the situation on the Riverine Plain where some prior-stream channels do not contain groundwater.

Channels can be isolated by means of stream capture or beheading along a mountain front. In such cases all the sediment and water are diverted into another channel by the capture, and parts of the old channel are left relatively high and dry above the new level of channel activity (Figure 7-27). An example of this may be the channel changes that have occurred along the eastern front of the Rocky Mountains. The channels that formerly drained east from the Rocky Mountains were beheaded by the South Platte River, which now lies at an elevation below these paleochannels. If this piedmont area were buried, it is probable that the modern lower-level channels would contain groundwater, whereas the older channels at a higher level would remain dry. If during this situation ore solutions entered the deposit, ore bodies would only develop in the stratigraphically lower channels.

Finally, the channels of an extensive fluvial deposit can be classified in a way that conforms to the facies changes of the Morrison Formation. Bed-load channels dominate the proximal and midfan area. Farther down the piedmont, mixed-load channels are characteristic, and finally, on a fluvial fan the most distal part shows evidence of suspended-load

channels. The very different geomorphic and sedimentologic characteristics of each channel type should allow them to be identified in deposits
such as the Salt Wash and Westwater members of the Morrison Formation.

At least under certain conditions both piedmont deposition and erosion are episodic, as a result of the natural erosional and depositional
processes at work. The behavior of the experimental fan and the stratigraphic character of the Witwatersrand and Van Horn conglomerates
suggest that where sediment loads are high, geomorphic thresholds will
exert an important influence on the geomorphology and stratigraphy of
piedmont erosional and depositional features.

Multiple pediment surfaces described by Rich and Hunt confirm
episodic erosion by stream capture (a geomorphic threshold), and Ritter
(1972) provides an example of episodic terrace formation in a piedmont
situation. He describes three adjacent valleys on the eastern side of the
Beartooth Mountains, Montana. Only one stream rises in the mountains,
yet each valley contains several terraces that are capped with gravel
derived from the mountains. The age of the gravel and the terraces
varies from valley to valley, as the position of the mountain-fed channel
was shifted from one valley to the other by a capture process similar to
that outlined for pediments above. Ritter concludes that "It is impossible
to understand the geomorphic history of any one valley without considering the events in neighboring valleys or without employment of the
stream capture model." If these terraces cannot be correlated from one
valley to the next, regional correlation is impossible, and this conclusion
applies also to the pediment surfaces formed by stream capture.

REFERENCES

Anstey, R. L., 1965, Physical characteristics of alluvial fans: U. S. Army Natick Lab. Tech.
    Rep. ES-20, 109 pp.

Bull, W. B., 1964, Geomorphology of segmented alluvial fans in western Fresno County,
    California: U. S. Geol. Surv. Prof. Paper 352-E, pp. 89–128.

Bull, W. B., 1968, Alluvial fans: J. Geol. Educ., v. 16, pp. 101–106.

Butler, B. E., 1950, A theory of prior streams as a causal factor of soil occurrence in the
    Riverine Plain of southeastern Australia: Aust. J. Agric. Res., v. 1, pp. 231–252.

Butler, B. E., 1958, Depositional syststems of the Riverine Plain in relation to soils:
    Commonwealth Scientific and Industrial Research Organization, Soil Publ. 10, 35 pp.

Butler, B. E. and Hutton, J. T., 1956, Parna in the Riverine Plain of southeastern Australia
    and the soils thereon: Aust. J. Agric. Res., v. 7, pp. 536–553.

Craig, L. C. and others, 1955, Stratigraphy of the Morrison and related formations,

Colorado Plateau region, a preliminary report: U. S. Geol. Surv. Bull. 1009-E, pp. 125–166.

Denny, C. S., 1965, Alluvial fans in the Death Valley region, California and Nevada: U. S. Geol. Surv. Prof. Paper 466, 62 pp.

Eckis, Rollin, 1928, Alluvial fans of the Cucamonga district, southern California: J. Geol., v. 36, pp. 225–247.

Gole, C. V. and Chitale, S. V., 1966, Inland delta building activity of Kosi River: Am. Soc. Civil Eng. J. Hydraul. Div. HY-2, pp. 111–126.

Hadley, R. F., 1967, Pediments and pediment-forming processes: J. Geol. Educ., v. 15, pp. 83–89.

Hunt, C. B., Averitt, Paul and Miller, R. L., 1953, Geology and geography of the Henry Mountains Region, Utah: U. S. Geol. Surv. Prof. Paper 228, 239 pp.

Hunt, C. B. and Mabey, D. R., 1966, Stratigraphy and structure, Death Valley, California: U. S. Geol. Surv. Prof. Paper 494-A, 162 pp.

Hooke, R. L., 1967, Processes on arid-region alluvial fans: J. Geol., v. 75, pp. 438–460.

Hooke, R. L., 1968, Steady state relationships on arid-region alluvial fans in closed basins: Am. J. Sci., v. 266, pp. 609–629.

Lindsey, D. A., 1972, Sedimentary petrology and paleocurrents of the Harebell Formation, Pinyon conglomerate and associated coarse clastic deposits, northwestern Wyoming; U. S. Geol. Surv. Prof. Paper 734-B, 68 pp.

Lustig, L. K., 1965, Clastic sedimentation in Deep Springs Valley, Calif.: U. S. Geol. Surv. Prof. Paper 352-F, pp. 131–192.

McGowen, J. H. and Groat, C. G., 1971, Van Horn Sandstone, West Texas: an alluvial fan model for mineral exploration: Univ. Texas, Bur. Econ. Geol., Rep. Invest. 72, 57 pp.

McPherson, H. J. and Hirst, F., 1972, Sediment changes on two alluvial fans in the Canadian Rocky Mountains, in Olav Slaymaker and H. J. McPherson (editors), Mountain Geomorphology: Tantulus Research, Vancouver, pp. 161–175.

Macke, David, 1976, Stratigraphy and sedimentology of exerimental alluvial fans; unpublished M.S. Thesis, Colorado State University, 105 pp.

Malan, R. C., 1968, The uranium mining industry and geology of the Monument Valley and White Canyon Districts, Arizona and Utah, in Ore deposits of the United States: AIME, v. 1, pp. 790–804.

Miall, A. D., 1970, Devonian alluvial fans, Prince of Wales Island, Arctic Canada: J. Sediment. Petrol., v. 40, pp. 556–571.

Mullens, T. E. and Freeman, V. L., 1957, Lithofacies of the Salt Wash Member of the Morrison Formation, Colorado Plateau: Geol. Soc. Am. Bull., v. 68, pp. 505–526.

Pels, Simon, 1960, The geology of the Murrumbidgee irrigation areas and surrounding districts: Water Conservation and Irrigation Commission, New South Wales, Groundwater and Drainage Series, Bull. 5, 43 pp.

Pels, Simon, 1964, The present and ancestral Murray River system: Aust. Geogr. Stud., v. 2, pp. 111–119.

Pretorius, D. A., 1974a, The nature of the Witwatersrand gold-uranium deposits: Univ. Witwatersrand, Econ. Geol. Res. Unit, Inf. Circ. 86, 50 pp.

Pretorius, D. A., 1974b, Gold in the Proterozoic sediments of South Africa: systems, paradigns and models: Univ. Witwatersrand, Econ. Geol. Res. Unit, Inf. Circ. 87, 22 pp.

Rich, J. L., 1935, Origin and evolution of rock fans and pediments: Geol. Soc. Am. Bull., v. 46, pp. 999–1024.

Ritter, D. F., 1972, The significance of stream capture in the evolution of a piedmont region, southern Montana: Z. Geomorphol., v. 16, pp. 83–92.

Ryder, J. M., 1971, Some aspects of the morphometry of paraglacial alluvial fans in south-central British Columbia: Can. J. Earth Sci., v. 8, pp. 1252–1264.

Schick, A. P., 1973, Alluvial fans and desert roads: a problem in applied geomorphology: Z. Geomorphol., Suppl. 20, pp. 418–425.

Schumm, S. A., 1968, River adjustment to altered hydrologic regimen—Murrumbidgee Rivers and paleochannels, Australia: U. S. Geol. Surv. Prof. Paper 598, 65 pp.

Schumm, S. A. and Hadley, R. F., 1957, Arroyos and the semiarid cycle of erosion: Am. J. Sci., v. 255, pp. 161–174.

Scott, K. M., 1973, Scout and fill in Tujunga Waih—a fan head valley in urban southern California—1969: U. S. Geol. Surv. Prof. Paper 732-B, 29 pp.

Sestini, G., 1973, Sedimentology of a paleoplacer: the gold-bearing Tarkwaian of Ghana, in G. C. Amstutz and A. J. Bernard (editors), Ores in Sediments: Springer-Verlag, Berlin, pp. 275–306.

Sigov, A. P., Lomayev, A. V., Sigov, V. A., Storozhenko, L. Y., Hkrypov, V. N., and Shub, I. Z., 1972, Placers of the Urals, their formation, distribution and elements of geomorphic prediction: Sov. Geogr., v. 13, pp. 375–387.

Williams, G. E., 1973, Late Quaternary piedmont sedimentation, soil formation and paleoclimates in South Australia: Z. Geomorphol., v. 17, pp. 102–125.

Wilson, M. D., 1970, Upper Cretaceous-Paleocene synorogenic conglomerates of South-western Montana: Am. Assoc. Pet. Geol. Bull., v. 54, pp. 1843–1867.

Weaver, W. E., 1976, Experimental study of alluvial fans: unpublished Ph.D. Dissertation Colorado State University, in preparation.

Young, K. G., 1964, Distribution of uranium deposits in the White Canyon–Monument Valley district, Utah–Arizona: Econ. Geol., v. 59, pp. 850–873.

CHAPTER EIGHT

Coastal Plain (Zone 3)

T he downstream boundary of the fluvial system would appear to be at the shore, but fluvial influences are felt seaward of the interface between marine and fluvial processes. The climate and lithologic characteristics of Zone 1 exert a significant influence on the sediment load transported by the channels of Zone 2 and then moved by marine processes to deeper depositional sites on the continental shelf and to the ocean floor via submarine canyons and deep-sea fans (Hayes, 1967). Therefore, even where coastal processes may dominate, the fluvial system cannot be ignored.

The final component of the fluvial system, coastal plains and deltaic landforms, is of particular interest because it is in the flat areas of fluvial deposition that excellent examples of episodic change, such as channel avulsion and delta-lobe shift, can be examined. Stratigraphic studies of delta deposition offer confirmation of episodic adjustment of river channels as a result of threshold conditions. For example, avulsion in many cases is due simply to a channel that raised its floor by deposition as delta growth progressively lengthened its channel.

The vast literature on coastal morphology and processes, and especially on the stratigraphy and sedimentology of deltas, is not given a comprehensive treatment here. Rather the theme of change without external influence is emphasized, and the coastal landforms and deposits are discussed primarily with respect to their influence by upstream controls, although the groups of variables upon which the competition between fluvial and marine processes are based also receive attention.

ALLUVIAL PLAIN CHANNELS

On an alluvial or coastal plain the relations presented in Chapter Five indicate the nature of channel morphology that can be expected. Gradients are gentler and sediments are finer, but a major factor of importance is that the channels are not confined between closely spaced valley walls. This means that where there is deposition the potential for lateral channel migration is great. Therefore, dramatic changes of position and pattern are likely as a result of both upstream controls and deposition that is manifested in delta growth and channel deposition. Needless to say, a sea level change would significantly influence the coastal streams (Figure 5-33).

In spite of being usually either a mixed- or suspended-load type of channel, delta channels in particular are much less sinuous than expected (Table 5-9); in fact, they may be almost straight as exemplified by the Mississippi River below New Orleans. These exceptions may be the proof of the assertion in Chapter Five that meandering is a result of river adjustment to a valley slope that is too steep. In Zone 3, as the alluvial surface of deposition is formed, it is constructed at the angle required for the transport of water and sediment to the sea. Hence, meandering on this surface will reduce stream gradient and produce aggradation. The channels therefore remain straight in order to move their loads across a depositional surface that has just the inclination required for the task.

Avulsion

A characteristic of the coastal plain situation is that rivers can shift position by avulsion. One of the most dramatic examples of this is the 1851 avulsion, which shifted the mouth of the Yellow River over 200 miles to the north of its former position (Freeman, 1922). Avulsion generally is in response to two factors: (1) channel aggradation due to progressive extension of a delta into the sea (the increased length of the stream requires aggradation to maintain the gradient upstream), and (2) a shorter, steeper route to the sea that the river can adopt.

This type of event has occurred many times in the Mississippi Valley and on its delta. On the delta the development of new distributary channels by avulsion produces new delta lobes and the complex cyclic stratigraphy of deltas. When the avulsion occurs far upstream, it may produce a new delta at a new location. Figure 8-1 shows the Mississippi River deltas and lobes that have formed during the past 5000 years, and Figure 8-2 shows the age and duration of each. A more detailed study indicates that there have been 14 lobes formed during the past 7500 years. For example, the Le Fourche Delta complex is composed of five lobes (Frazier, 1967).

The propensity for change is inherent in the coastal fluvial area, as it is on an alluvial fan. In fact, without control structures built by the Corps of Engineers, the Mississippi River would now follow a shorter course to the Gulf of Mexico through the Old River–Atchafalaya River channel (Figure 8-3), a route 180 miles shorter (Hardin, 1956). At the present time the water moving through the Atchafalaya River, which is 30 percent Mississippi River water, is building a new delta in Atachafalaya Bay (Shlemon, 1975).

Perhaps the most detailed study of periodic avulsion on a grand scale has been performed by Fisk and his colleagues (1944, 1952). They used vast quantities of information provided by the U. S. Army Corp of Engineers and data obtained themselves from aerial photographs and

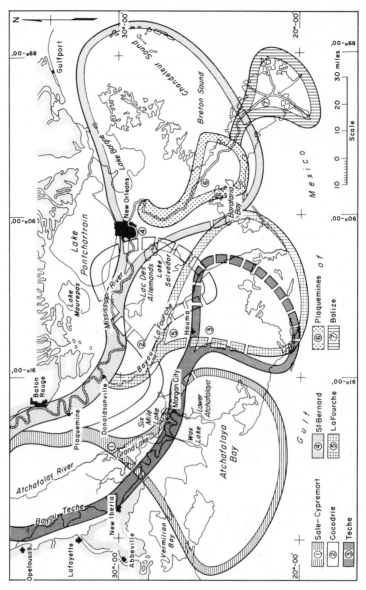

Figure 8-1 Mississippi River deltas. (From Kolb and Van Lopik, 1966.)

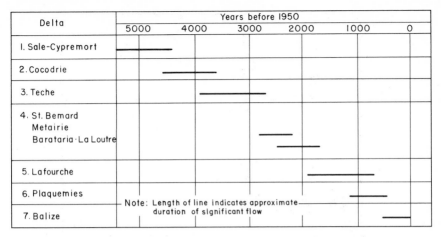

Delta	Years before 1950					
	5000	4000	3000	2000	1000	0
1. Sale-Cypremort						
2. Cocodrie						
3. Teche						
4. St. Bemard Metairie Barataria·La Loutre						
5. Lafourche						
6. Plaquemies	Note: Length of line indicates approximate duration of significant flow					
7. Balize						

Figure 8-2   Age of Mississippi River deltas. (From Kolb and Van Lopik, 1966.)

field studies to develop a history of channel and delta growth and change in the lower Mississippi River valley. Their very detailed study and recognition of 20 stages of river courses during the past 2000 years has been questioned by Saucier (1974), who recognizes only five meander belts. He also concludes that in many cases courses recognized in the southern part of the valley cannot be correlated with those in the north without radiocarbon dates, and that the Pleistocene history of the river as outlined in Figure 5-33 pertains only to the valley south of Vicksburg. Nevertheless, during Mississippi River Holocene history, two types of avulsion have taken place repeatedly. The first is a major river diversion that occurs hundreds of miles from the sea. The result is a new delta. The second occurs on the delta itself, and it produces a new delta lobe.

The first case can be demonstrated by the change in position of the Mississippi River where it shifted from the position of the Teche Delta to that of the LaFouche Delta. This change was caused by a shift of the river from the west to the east side of its valley at a position approximately 150 miles from the sea (Figure 8-3). The avulsion significantly shortened the course of the river. The river remained in this general position during growth of the LaFouche Delta (Figure 8-4), which increased the length of the channel and caused aggradation upstream (Figure 5-22). When the LaFouche delta had grown to essentially its maximum extent, the river was approximately 1334 miles long. Then the LaFouche delta was abandoned with a shift of the river to its present position along the east bluff below Vicksburg (Figure 8-4). Both of these events dramatically shortened the course of the river (Figure 5-22).

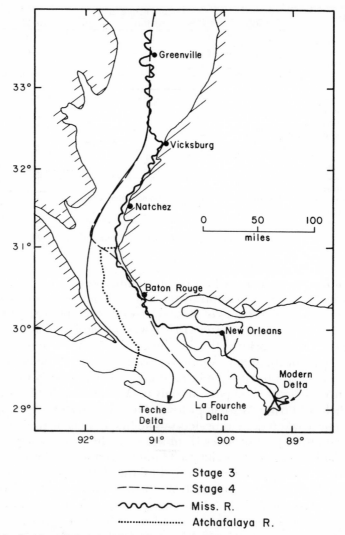

Figure 8-3 Position of Mississippi River during Teche Delta (Fisk stage 3; Saucier meander belt 3) and La Fourche Delta (Fisk stages 4, 5, 6, 7; Saucier meander belt 4) formation. Note position of modern Atchafalaya River and outline of modern delta. (After Fisk et al., 1944.)

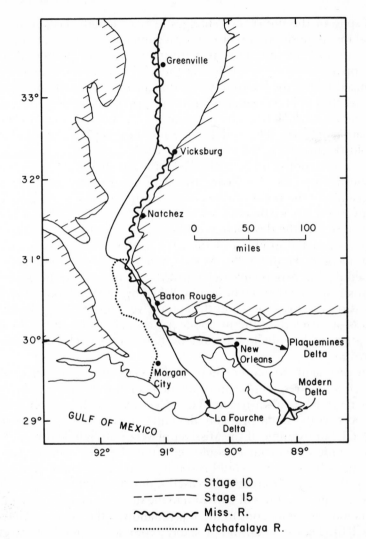

Figure 8-4   Position of Mississippi River during late La Fourche Delta construction (Fisk stage
10; Saucier meander belt 4) and Plaquemines St. Bernard Delta (Fisk stage 15; Saucier meander
belt 5) formation. Note position of Atchafalaya River and outline of modern delta (after Fisk et
al., 1944).

In spite of the impressive changes in river length, Fisk et al. (1952) found that deposition or scour in the channel upstream was not obvious. They concluded that river activity upstream from the point of diversion was apparently unaffected during the avulsion. The explanation they advanced is that the avulsion was a slow process rather than an abrupt channel shift. This conclusion has been supported by the recent dating of deltas and delta lobes, which indicates a considerable overlap between formation of a new delta or delta lobe and the complete abandonment of the old (Figure 8-2).

One factor not considered by Fisk et al. in their analysis is that the change in slope can be accomplished by destruction of the meander pattern above the point of diversion. In other words, if the gradient of the diversion is twice that of the Mississippi River and the sinuosity of the Mississippi is 2, the destruction of the meander pattern would permit a steepening of the gradient of the river in the upstream reach without major incision (Figure 5-23). As the gradient of the distributary was decreased during progressive delta growth, a reduction in the gradient of the Mississippi could then be accomplished by the development of meanders as on the Riverine Plain (Chapter Five, Figure 5-34). By the very process of developing the meander pattern, all evidence for the older, straighter, wider, shallower, and perhaps braided channel would be destroyed.

The diversion, no matter where it takes place and no matter what type of river is involved, results in dramatic response of that channel to the steeper gradient downstream. The effect of this change on sediment transport to the delta probably depends on the nature of the stream involved. For example, if the Mississippi were a straight bed-load stream, a shortening of its course would have the effect of a major baselevel lowering, which in turn would result in scour of the channel, rejuvenation of tributaries, a greatly increased sediment production, and movement of large quantities of alluvium to the new delta lobe. This would be a situation very analogous to the rejuvenation of the experimental basin in the REF (Figure 4-12), and probably a complex response would result. For example, when the Yellow River diverted to the north, a knickpoint formed in the channel at the point of diversion and its upstream migration lowered the riverbed for a considerable distance. The river was still adjusting its grade in 1938 (Todd and Eliassen, 1940). In other words, after 87 years the Yellow River was still responding for a distance of about 80 miles to a change in baselevel.

A river similar to the Mississippi could be steepened by destruction of the meander pattern, as noted above and although incision would be minimized, the channel enlargement and meander-pattern destruction would produce quantities of sediment that would be shifted to the delta. In the process of moving this increased sediment load through the new channel, periods of aggradation and scour would occur repeatedly as the channels adjusted to this dramatic change in gradient. Artificial meander cutoffs simulate this adjustment, but on a reduced scale; for example, the river reaches affected by cutoffs on the Mississippi River have required 40 years before attaining relative stability, which in most cases is due to channel stabilization procedures (Winkley, 1976).

The extensive investigations of the potential for diversion of the Mississippi River into the Old River–Atchafalaya River course can be used to examine the process of avulsion in more detail (Fisk et al., 1952). The Atchafalaya is actually the farthest upstream distributary of the Mississippi River (Figure 8-4). In fact, in 1956 it was the third largest river flowing to the sea in the United States. Near Angola, Louisiana, a meander bend of the Mississippi River, due to its lateral shift to the west, intersected an old channel, and since that intersection, Mississippi River water has been diverted south to the Gulf near Morgan City, Louisiana. The distance from this point of diversion is 320 miles to the Gulf by way of New Orleans, but only about 140 miles by way of the Atchafalaya River. In 1951 the diversion channel was carrying 23 percent of the flow of the Mississippi River, and Hardin (1956) stated that, when this proportion became 40 percent, the new channel would develop rapidly and would capture the discharge of the Mississippi River (Figure 8-5). It was anticipated that this event would take place between 1968 and 1985, and most probably around 1975. The flow is now controlled by a structure that prevents the completion of the avulsion process.

It is surprising that once diversion of water began down the Atchafalaya River the entire flow did not adopt this short course. It did not do so because the Atchafalaya channel could not accommodate such a large discharge and the resistance to flow in that channel prevented the complete diversion; however, the upper reaches of the Atchafalaya were widened by bank erosion and as this process continued an increasing quantity of Mississippi River water was diverted (Fisk et al., 1952).

Fisk and his colleagues (1952) studied the nature of earlier diversions of the Mississippi River as a basis for predicting events related to the Atchafalaya Diversion. These historical studies indicate that the conditions favorable for the Atchafalaya Diversion were established about the year 1500. Hence, unlike the Yellow River, where a major avulsion occurred, and unlike the diversion of the Colorado River into the Salton Sea area in 1905 and 1907, the evidence shows that Mississippi courses have not been abandoned abruptly.

There is no evidence that permanent diversion of the Mississippi

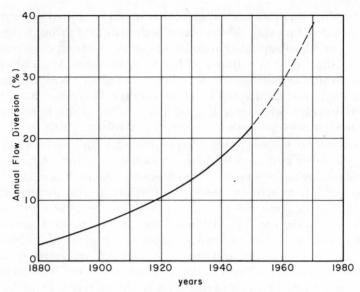

Figure 8-5   Discharge through Old River-Atchafalaya channel as a percentage of total annual discharge of Mississippi River. (From Fisk et al., 1952.)

River has been brought about by crevassing or overtopping of banks during floods such as occurred on the Yellow River. Instead, abandonment of Mississippi River courses is accomplished through gradual and progressive enlargement of the diversion channel over long periods, as there is a considerable time overlap among the deltas and delta lobes (Figure 8-2), and this supports Fisk's conclusion that the diversion of the Mississippi River from one course to another requires periods of at least 100 years. Fisk concludes that the course changes of the Mississippi are fundamentally different from the rapid diversions of rivers like the Yellow because the Mississippi channel is relatively deep and is able to transport its sediment load without difficulty.

The usual process of avulsion begins when the Mississippi River fortuitously intersects a channel such as the Atchafalaya, which follows a course essentially parallel to the Mississippi River. The most important factor is that a previously established channel exists into which the water can flow. Fisk points out that bank failures only provide a temporary diversion of water into the adjacent lowland and that most Mississippi crevasses are healed when river stage again falls. The sudden decrease in velocity as the floodwaters escape results in sediment deposition and plugging of the gap. This was demonstrated at the Bonnet Caire Spillway, 3 miles upstream from New Orleans. When floodwaters were diverted from the river to Lake Pontchartain through the spillway, quantities of sand and silt were deposited in the broad floodway, and there was little tendency to scour the channel to form a permanent diversion channel. Only when a distributary can maintain a channel throughout the year, including low-water stages, does flow during higher stages enlarge the channel to eventually form a diversion.

Initially the diversion channel is too small to transport all the Mississippi discharge, but it enlarges with time until it is capable of transplanting up to 50 percent of the flow of the river. This stage is critical and bankfull flow in both the old and the new courses is sufficient to sweep sediment load downstream without plugging either channel. Because of its gradient advantage, however, the distributary channel is able to continue to enlarge, whereas a slight decrease in flow through the main channel is sufficient to cause part of a load to be dropped, which plugs the old main channel.

It is possible that during this slow process of diversion the channel above the diversion is slowly adjusting to the new, steeper gradient that is being established as flow increases down the more direct and steeper course. As noted above the adjustment can be made by means of a pattern change.

PALEOCHANNELS

Coastal and deltaic deposits contain an abundance of paleochannels, but this topic is considered in Chapter Four and so only one aspect of the subject as related to coal deposits is considered here.

In the coastal and deltaic environment, organic materials accumulate to produce peat and coal beds. The shifting of streams and distributary channels over this area, in many cases produces disruptions in the continuity of the coal beds. These washouts of the coal miners (Williamson, 1967) may have a serious economic impact on the mining operations. There are many minor erosional features, but washouts are large and represent the channel deposits of rivers flowing across peat swamps. Occasionally coal beds are eroded over relatively large areas in a seemingly haphazard fashion, apparently because of the lateral shift of river courses.

The washouts or sand-filled paleochannels can be a significant problem for the mining engineer if they are encountered in large numbers. In many cases only closely spaced drilling will reveal the magnitude of the problem, but this is not economical. The basic problem is to identify, if possible, the channel patterns within a coal basin. A single channel is rarely a problem, but if it bifurcates into multiple distributary channels, the problem is much more serious.

Streams draining from adjacent higher areas will cross coal swamps in a variety of patterns, depending on the configuration of the basin itself. For example, if a dendritic drainage pattern develops, the mining problems will be considerable, and exploitation of the coal may not be economically feasible.

In Figure 8-6 several examples of rivers draining from higher areas to the sea are shown. Obviously the parallel single-channel rivers pose only a minor problem, but as the basin morphology changes, the complexity of the pattern increases.

Variations in the washout pattern of coal basins of the northern Transvaal, South Africa, have been recognized and they seem to show variations of the type seen in Figure 8-6. The significant factor is the overall shape of the landscape and its effect on drainage pattern development (Chapter Four).

DELTAS

Deltas are not readily classified except by pattern. The two extremes of delta types are the arcuate delta of the Nile and the birdsfoot delta of the Mississippi (LeBlanc, 1972). The differences have been attributed almost wholly to the eroding effects of waves and currents. Wright and Colemen (1973) suggest that the ratio between stream discharge and wave power is an index of the relative effectiveness of river versus coastal processes and that, as the coastal processes become progressively dominant, the delta becomes progressively less irregular at the

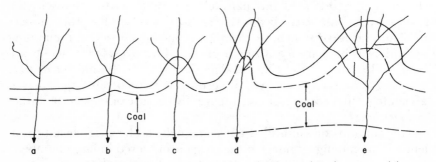

Figure 8-6 Possible channel patterns (washouts) in coal. When a plain slopes toward the sea, single channels traverse the coal swamp (a, b), but as valleys concentrate runoff a more complex dendritic pattern results (c, d, e).

shoreline. However, other factors are type, quantity, and size of the sediment load transported by the stream. For example, with other conditions the same, an arcuate delta could be deposited by a bed-load or a mixed-load stream, which bring relatively large quantities of coarse sediment to the coastline. Under these conditions the channel cannot be maintained in one position; it shifts, building up the surface of the delta in a manner similar to alluvial fan growth, and a fan-delta results (McGowen, 1970). On the other hand, when the river is transporting large quantities of fine sediment, essentially a combination suspended-load, mixed-load stream, the fine sediments develop relatively stable banks and levees, which are extended outward to form the characteristic bird-foot delta (Axelsson, 1967, p. 28) or an elongate delta. However, if wave action is important, the bird-foot will not form, even though the channels are transporting large quantities of fine material.

There are four major categories of influences (Morgan, 1970) that determine deltas and coastal stream morphology: river regime, coastal processes, structural stability, and climate. The quantity of sediment load and the particle size transported by the stream are the major upstream influences (Galloway, 1975, p. 90), but flow variations are also important. Rivers with seasonal flow go through extremes of discharge, and this causes variations in the nature and quantity of sediment transported to the delta. The result could be cyclic sedimentation due to normal seasonal fluvial processes.

Wave energy, tidal range, and current strength are important factors involving the modification of the delta. In addition, a coast may or may not be structurally stable, and, of course, the nature of the delta and the rate at which sediment is delivered to it are influenced by this geologic control. Climate, in addition to controlling sediment load and discharge to a large extent, also affects vegetation growth on the delta itself. Dense vegetation is more effective in trapping sediment, and, under these conditions, delta growth is accelerated. Part of the diversity among deltas may exist because they are in different stages of development, but this appears not to have been investigated.

Delta Morphology

Silvester and de la Cruz (1970) attempted a quantitative investigation of delta morphology after collecting information on 53 deltas throughout the world, for which information on morphology, climate, and hydrology was available. Their results can be considered to be a preliminary quantitative attempt to develop relations between delta morphology and other environmental factors. They studied several delta characteristics, such as delta length, area, maximum width, ratios between maximum width and the number of distributary mouths, and ratios between maximum width of the delta and the total number of distributaries. The results showed that both delta length and delta area are directly correlated with water discharge. However, there is an inverse relationship between delta length and area, and river slope and the continental shelf slope. The greater the water discharge, the larger the drainage basin, and, therefore, the greater the sediment production; a large delta results, but the larger the discharge, the flatter the slope of the stream. The flatter the gradient of the continental shelf, the shallower the water and, for a given sediment delivery to the coast, the larger the delta.

A positive correlation between delta slope and river slope exists. River slope reflects discharge and sediment load, and the delta responds to these controls in the same way as the river channel. Concerning shape, the greater the river slope, the higher the river velocity, and hence, a more elongate delta forms.

Swell duration and swell direction are important factors determining delta width. The greater the incidence of swell, the more energy is available for spreading the deltaic material along the coast, and the spreading is enhanced by the angle at which the waves intersect the coast.

Although Silvester and de la Cruz (1970) found that distributary size and number were not related to the other variables, they did determine that as discharge increased there were fewer but larger distributary channels. The results of this investigation indicate that the most important upstream controls on delta morphology are, of course, water discharge, flow velocity, and sediment load (Coleman and Wright, 1975). In all the analyses water discharge was more significant than sediment load, but sediment load was directly related to discharge.

The results, which are not surprising, resemble those obtained for alluvial fans. The larger the drainage basin, the larger the alluvial fan, and the larger the delta. The variables that influence sediment production from a watershed, and all the factors discussed as controlling drainage basin morphology in Table 2-1, also are important in influencing delta growth. However, deltas are usually a very long distance from Zone 1, and there may be factors influencing the production and transport of water and sediment through the channel that would interfere with the establishment of a well-defined relationship between the morphologic and geomorphic characteristics of Zone 1 and the morphology of the deltas in Zone 3. Nevertheless, the effects of climate change on runoff and sediment yield (Chapter Three) should markedly affect delta morphology and growth rates.

Experimental Study of Delta Morphology. An experimental study of delta growth by Chang (1967) provides some valuable information on delta response to fluctuations of sediment yield and discharge. Chang used a large 100-foot-long flume (Figure 5-8), but only the lower one-third was the site of delta growth. Sand was fed at a constant rate into a channel that led to the water-filled basin, where a fan-delta formed. During most of the experiments, water level, sediment load, and water discharge were maintained constant. Figure 8-7 shows delta growth during a 47-hour and 50 minute period. A symmetrical deposit formed, but at times (12:20, 23:30, 35:00, 35:30 hours) due to channel shifting and delta-head scour, fingerlike projections extended beyond the normal delta margin. Unfortunately, only plan views of the deltas are presented by Chang; variations in relief were not measured.

It is clear that because of the sediment used (0.37 and 0.47 mm median-grain-size sand, with minor amounts of silt and clay) the delta is actually a submerged alluvial fan or fan delta. Therefore, the results are restricted to this type of deposit. In addition, channel avulsion could not occur except on the fan delta itself, as the feeder channel was confined between fixed walls.

Figure 8-8 shows the increase of delta area with time during Chang's runs 15 through 17a. Water discharge was constant (6.3 l per second). The rate of fan growth was least during run 15, which has the smallest amount of sediment fed into and transported through the channel (5.6 g per second). The sediment transported through the channel was identical for runs 16 and 17 (8.8 g per second), but the depth of water in the basin was shallower for run 17; therefore, delta 17 had a much more rapid increase in area through time. The thickness of deltas 15 and 16 was about 23 cm, whereas 17 was only 7 cm thick. During run 17a the sand load was reduced to zero. The channel degraded, the delta head was incised, and a rapid increase in delta area resulted. At the same time a dramatic change in the shape of the delta occurred. Figure 8-9 shows the marked elongation of the fan-delta during run 17a as the upper part of the delta was eroded and new lobes were built at the toe of the delta.

Note that the rapid increase in area was short-lived, and after about 10 hours (Figure 8-8) the rate of delta growth significantly decreased. The delta morphology that developed following sediment-load reduction resembles that of the trenched alluvial fan (Figure 7-1).

Figure 8-10 shows delta area changes during Chang's run 20a

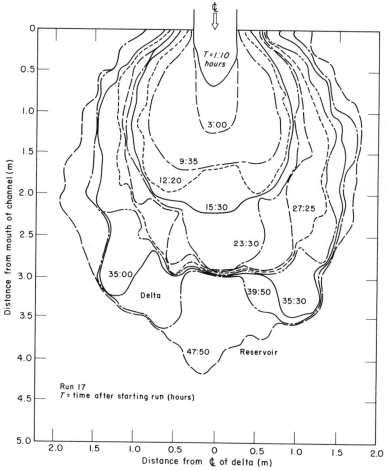

Figure 8-7   Plan view of experimental fan-delta growth during 47 hours and 50 minutes. (From Chang, 1967.)

when sediment load was doubled (2.5 to 5.0 g per second), and an increase in the rate of delta growth is apparent. However, the rate of growth is not rapid and most of the sediment apparently was deposited near the head of the delta during the first 40 hours of the run. During run 20b the sediment load was decreased (from 5.0 to 2.5 g per second), and a rapid increase in delta area resulted as the stored sediment was eroded and flushed to the distal part of the delta. Both an increase and a decrease of sediment load produced an increase in the rate of delta

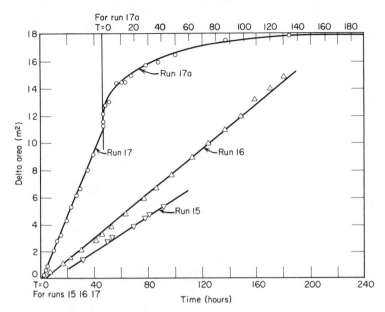

Figure 8-8 Relation between delta area and run time for experiments 15–17. See discussion in text. (From Chang, 1967.)

growth. However, the decreased rate produced only a short period of rapid growth as the delta head was eroded. Also, a major difference in the delta shape resulted from the changes in sediment load. There was a marked elongation of the delta during delta-head erosion (low width/length ratio). A much higher width/length ratio developed with an increase of sediment loads and delta-head deposition (Figure 8-11). Aggradation stores sediment near the delta head, but, as in the alluvial fan situation, when delta-head erosion occurs, sediment is moved to the distal part of the delta, causing major elongation.

As Chang's experimental deltas grew, the lengthening of the delta produced the expected aggradation in the upstream portions of the feeder channel. However, the feeder channel was fixed in position by wooden walls and avulsion due to aggradation as in a natural channel was prevented.

It is possible that not only will the rate of increase of delta area and length decrease with higher sediment loads, but that erosion of the delta with construction of a new lobe at its toe, following a decrease of sediment load will be a likely event in nature. The lengthening of a delta because of this factor could mistakenly be related to lower wave power.

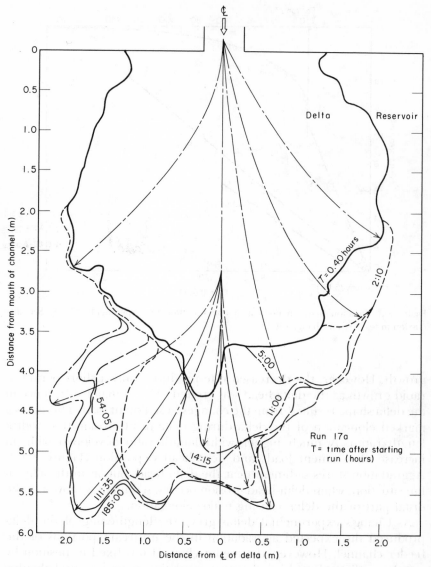

Figure 8-9 Plan view of delta showing effect of reduction of sediment delivery to delta during experiment 17a. Figure 8-7 shows delta prior to sediment-load reduction. (From Chang, 1967.)

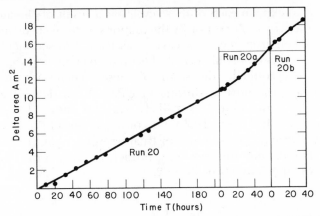

Figure 8-10   Relation between delta area and run time. Curve shows rate of delta growth with uniform sediment delivery to delta (experiment 20), with increase of sediment load (run 20a) and with reduction of sediment load (run 20B). (From Chang, 1967.)

Nevertheless, a decrease of sediment load permits wave action to begin the process of delta destruction (Stephens et al., 1976), but the decrease in the quantity of sediment delivered to the margins of the delta may be a function of upstream storage and release of sediment rather than climate or tectonic changes.

Most delta deposits are composed of many cycles of deposition. The

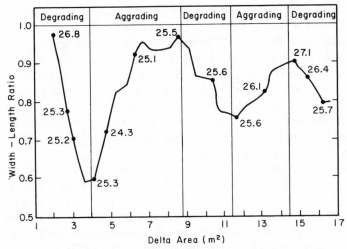

Figure 8-11   Change of delta shape during periods of deposition and erosion on experimental delta. In this example (experiment 20) the changes are due, in part, to baselevel change. Numbers indicate water-surface elevation in centimeters. (From Chang, 1967.)

tendency is to explain each of these cycles as a result of climate change or tectonic activity in Zone 1 or by fluctuations of sea level or subsidence in the coastal environment. The earlier discussions of sediment production variability, geomorphic thresholds, and river metamorphosis suggest that some could be the result of these changes within Zones 1 and 2. In fact, the normal shifting of channels on deltas and coastal plains has been mentioned as a likely cause of some of these cycles (Beerbower, 1964; Brown, 1969). Of course, sea-level fluctuations and faulting also trigger a complex upstream response, as is discussed in Chapter Three, and this certainly influences delta growth and the dynamics of the channels of Zone 2.

DELTA DEPOSITS

Just as on the Riverine Plain, where the Murrumbidgee River was not confined (Chapter Five), it is possible to locate paleochannel remnants on the surface and at depth on deltaic and coastal plains where channel shift permits burial and preservation of channels. The record of fluvial deposition therefore will be very complete.

The range of channel types from suspended load to bed load and their associated sediments have been recognized in ancient rocks of the coastal environment (Friend and Moody-Stuart, 1972). Depending on the proximity and sediment production of Zone 1, the coastal plain sediments could resemble those of Death Valley or of the gentle Riverine Plain of New South Wales.

Galloway and Brown (1973) describe the Cisco high constructional deltas of Pennsylvania age of north central Texas and relate these to mixed-load or bed-load channels. Thus it appears that the distinctions made earlier between the types of stream systems and nature of the sediment load, that is, the factors influencing the characteristics of the channels of Zone 2, apply equally to the channels of the coastal areas and to the types of delta construction that are observed and that have been described from the ancient rocks.

Among the numerous studies of ancient delta deposits, only one (Ferm, 1970), which is characterized by the development of multiple lobes and the shifting of the sites of deposition through time, is reviewed here. Deltas grow as sediment-laden streams pass over the emerged surface, and sands, silts, and clay are deposited at the delta front. The finer sediments are, of course, deposited in the offshore marine environment at the toe of the delta. Progradation, which is a major aspect of modern delta sedimentation, alternates with lateral shift or offset of the prograded lobes. This involves the gradual, or even abrupt, abandonment of one delta lobe and diversion of sediment-laden flow into an adjoining open-water area. The new active delta lobe progrades into the sea. At the same time the abandoned lobe is completely overlapped by deposits formerly restricted to the margins of the delta wedge. In other words, the sandy units will be buried beneath fine-grained floodplain-type sediments. According to Ferm (1970) this combined process of progradation and lateral shift produces, in time, a deposit that can be referred to as a delta system or complex. This complex consists of a series of overlapping and offset prograded detrital wedges, which are to some degree separated from one another by various kinds of deposits usually formed in the marginal portions of the delta. Ferm's (1970) conclusion is that cyclic deltaic deposits can be best attributed to deltaic progradation and lateral delta migration. Neither tectonic nor baselevel control is required. This explanation is in accord with that of Moore (1966) for cyclic deltaic sediments, and it certainly is compatible with everything known about modern delta growth.

Basically the depositional cycle in the deltas reflect sediment storage and removal from upstream. As the delta grows, aggradation upstream stores sediment in the upstream valleys. When avulsion takes place some or much of the stored sediment is remobilized and incorporated into the new delta. This sequence of events, although at a very different scale, is not unlike the storage and erosion of sediment at the head of the experimental fan. The concepts of geomorphic thresholds and complex response should be very important in understanding delta morphology and sedimentology.

DISCUSSION

An indication of the economic importance of coastal plains, deltas, and the continental shelf is the immense literature describing the morphology and, particularly, the sedimentary characteristics and stratigraphy of these areas. Some contribution to the explanation of the morphology and internal character of these deposits can be made by considering them within the framework of the geomorphic concepts discussed previously, and it is only this aspect of the coastal zone that is discussed here.

The characteristic channel migration on deltas and coastal areas can be explained by normal processes of delta growth and channel shift. However, each shift will cause an adjustment upstream and may induce a complex response that will appear in the stratigraphic record as a series of cyclic sedimentary units. Therefore, the threshold concept applies to coastal plain and delta growth, and it should be important in the development of delta sediment character and stratigraphy. In sedimentologic and stratigraphic terms, deltaic deposition does not occur everywhere contemporaneously, and it is not continuous anywhere. Each period of deposition is separated by a period of little or no deposition, and a hiatal surface separates discrete stratigraphic units (Frazier, 1974).

The avulsion of rivers on alluvial plains and deltas is a normal process, and the threatened abandonment of the New Orleans course of the Mississippi River, with the resulting economic deterioration of that city, has its precedents in ancient times. In particular, the riverine civilizations of the Indus, Tigris, and Euphrates valleys were influenced by avulsion and neotectonics. This contrasts with the Nile Valley where, although the Nile can migrate laterally, it is confined to its valley and a major avulsion is not possible. Thus Luxor and Cairo have been river cities for thousands of years, but the ruins of the ancient cities of Ur, Lagash, and Nippur (Figure 8-12) are all now located far from rivers. These great cities of antiquity declined in importance when, by avulsion, the river took a course that left them on a backwater channel (Mackay, 1945).

In contrast to vertical adjustment by channels confined in valleys, the most likely way that a channel can adjust on an alluvial plain is by episodic shift by avulsion; however, the fluvial morphology of coastal area channels should not be significantly different from the types of channels described elsewhere.

The literature indicates that upstream factors, water discharge, and sediment load are important controls of delta morphology and dynamics. Therefore, the works of flow regulation, river control structures, precipitation augmentation, and so forth, all must be considered to be likely to exert an influence on the fragile delta environment. If the delta exists as the result of a balance between stream power and coastal energy, then change in Zones 1 and 2 should eventually influence delta morphology. For example, the dams on the Missouri and Colorado rivers retain large quantities of sediment. This will be replaced to some extent by bank erosion and channel scour, but when this source is depleted or protected by bank stabilization structures, the sediment delivery to the delta will decrease and coastal erosion then could become the dominant process. This sequence may require decades or even centuries, as the controls far upstream gradually exert a downvalley influence, but the coast will inevitably be affected. The magnitude·of the effect will depend on the balance between stream and coastal processes.

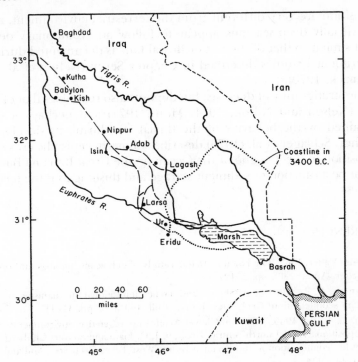

Figure 8-12 Map showing modern and ancient courses (dashed lines) of Tigris and Euphrates rivers with location of ancient cities and the modern cities of Baghdad and Basrah. (From Mackay, 1945.)

Finally, the morphology and stratigraphy of deltas shows the depositional breaks that concern Ager (Chapter One) and the type of channel shift that can be related to geomorphic thresholds. Delta extension and concurrent upstream deposition set up a situation whereby avulsion is inevitable. The avulsion in turn produces a long period of channel instability. For example, the Yellow River after 80 years was still adjusting to avulsion, and after 40 years the Mississippi River is still being affected by cutoffs and the channel shortening of 1930s. Channel shortening and gradient steepening not only cause incision, but also channel widening and midbar deposition, and they increase the likelihood of cutoffs upstream and downstream, a complex response.

A final suggestion is that the effects of the fluvial system can be extended into the deep marine environment where sediments from rivers move down canyons in the continental shelf and accumulate as deep-sea fans. Although the mechanisms of sediment transport and deposition are very different from the terrestrial environment, at least superficially deep-sea fans appear to follow an evolutionary development similar to that of the wet or fluvial fan, as documented during the experimental studies described in Chapter Seven (Nelson et al., 1970; Normack, 1970).

The stratigraphy of deep-sea fan deposits also resembles that of fluvial fans (Nelson and Nilson, 1974; Mutti, 1974) and perhaps it can be explained by the behavior of the fluvial fan during its development. Further, Schlager et al. (1976) describe submarine episodic erosion and deposition in the Tongue of the Ocean on the Great Bahama Bank that might be a function of sediment storage and flushing as is the terrestrial process.

REFERENCES

Axelsson, Valter, 1967, The Laitaure Delta: a study of deltaic morphology and processes: Geogr. Ann., v. 49, pp. 2–127.

Beerbower, J. R., 1964, Cyclothems and cyclic depositional mechanisms in alluvial plain sedimentation: Geol. Surv. Kansas Bull. 169, v. 1, pp. 31–41.

Brown, L. F. Jr., 1969, Virgil and lower Wolfcamp vegetative environments and the depositional model north-central Texas, in J. G. Elam and Stewart Chuber (editors), Cyclic sedimentation in the Permian Basin: West Texas Geol. Soc., Midland, Texas, pp. 115–134.

Brown, L. F. Jr., 1971, Geometry and distribution of fluvial and deltaic sandstones, north, central Texas: Gulf Coast Assoc. Geol. Soc., Trans. v. 19, pp. 34–47.

Chang, Hai-Yang, 1967, Hydraulics of rivers and deltas: unpublished Ph.D. Dissertation, Colorado State University, 176 pp.

Coleman, J. M. and Gagliano, S. M., 1964, Cyclic sedimentation in the Mississippi River deltaic plain: Gulf Coast Association of Geological Societies, v. 14, pp. 67–80.

Coleman, J. M. and Wright, L. D., 1975, Modern river deltas: variability of processes and sand bodies, in M. L. Broussard (editor), Deltas: Houston Geological Society, pp. 99–150.

Ferm, J. C., 1970, Allegheny deltaic deposits: Soc. Econ. Paleontol. Mineral. Spec. Publ. 15, pp. 246–255.

Fisk, H. N. et al., 1944, Geological investigation of the alluvial valley of the lower Mississippi River: U. S. Army Corps of Engineers, Mississippi River Commission, Vicksburg, Mississippi, 78 pp.

Fisk, H. N. et al., 1952, Geological investigation of the Atchafalaya Basin and the problem of Mississippi River diversion: U. S. Army Corps of Engineers, Waterways Experimental Station, 2 vols., 145 pp.

Frazier, D. E., 1967, Recent deltaic deposits of the Mississippi River: their development and chronology: Gulf Coast Association of Geological Societies, v. 17, pp. 287–315.

Frazier, D. E., 1974, Depositional episodes: their relationship to the Quaternary stratigraphic framework in the northwestern portion of the Gulf Basin: Bureau of Economic Geology, University of Texas, Geological Circular 74-1. 28 pp.

Freeman, J. R., 1922, Flood problems in China: Am. Soc. Civil Eng. Trans., v. 85, pp. 1405–1460.

Friend, P. F. and Moody-Stuart, M., 1972, Sedimentation of the Wood Bay Formation (Devonian) of Spitsberger: Regional Analysis of a Late Orogenic Facies, Nor. Polarinst., Skr. 157, 77 pp.

Galloway, W. E., 1975, Process framework for describing the morphologic and stratigraphic evolution of deltaic depositional systems, in M. L. Broussard (editpor), Deltas: Houston Geological Society, pp. 87–98.

Galloway, W. E. and Brown, L. F. Jr., 1973, Depositional systems and shelf-slope relations on cratonic basin margin, uppermost Pennsylvanian of northcentral Texas: Am. Assoc. Pet. Geol. Bull., v. 57, pp. 1185–1218.

Hardin, J. R., 1956, Old River diversion control: the general problem: Proc. Am. Soc. Civil Eng., J. Waterways Div., v. 82, WW 1, 13 pp.

Hayes, M. O., 1967, Relationship between coastal climate and bottom sediment type on the inner continental shelf: Marine Geol., v. 5, pp. 111–132.

Kolb, C. R. and Van Lopik, R. R., 1966, Depositional environments of the Mississippi River deltaic plain southeastern Louisiana, in M. L. Shirley and J. A. Ragsdale (editors), Deltas and their Geologic Framework: Houston Geological Society, Houston, Texas, pp. 17–61.

LeBlanc, R. J., 1972, Geometry of sandstone reservoir bodies: Am. Assoc. Pet. Geol. Mem. 18, pp. 133–189.

McGowen, J. H., 1970, Gum Hollow fan delta, Nueces Bay, Texas: Bur. Econ. Geol., Univ. Texas, Austin, Rep. Invest. 69, 91 pp.

MacKay, Dorothy, 1945, Ancient river beds and dead cities: Antiquity, v. 19, pp. 135–144.

Moore, Derek, 1966, Deltaic sedimentation: Earth Sci. Rev., v. 1, pp. 87–104.

Morgan, J. P., 1970, Depositional processes and products in the deltaic environment: Soc. Econ. Palentol. Mineral. Spec. Publ. 15, pp. 31–47.

Mutti, Emiliano, 1974, Examples of ancient deep-sea fan deposits from circum-Mediterranean geosynclines: Soc. Econ. Paleontol. Mineral. Spec. Publ. 19, pp. 92–105.

Nelson, C. H., Carlson, P. R., Byrne, J. V., and Alpha, T. R., 1970, Development of the Astoria Canyon-Fan physiography and comparison with similar systems: Marine Geol., v. 8, pp. 259–291.

Nelson, C. H. and Nilsen, T. H., 1974, Depositional trends of modern and ancient deep-sea fans: Soc. Econ. Paleontol. Mineral. Spec. Publ. 19, pp. 69–91.

Normark, W. R., 1970, Growth patterns of deep-sea fans: Am. Assoc. Pet. Geol. Bull., v. 54, pp. 2170–2195.

Saucier, R. T., 1974, Quaternary geology of the lower Mississippi Valley: Arkansas Archaeol. Surv. Res. Ser. No. 6, 26 pp.

Schlager, W., Hooke, R. L. and James, N. P., 1976, Episodic erosion and deposition in the Tongue of the Ocean (Bahamas): Geol. Soc. Am. Bull. v. 87, pp. 1115–1118.

Shlemon, R. J., 1975, Subaqueous delta formation—Atchafalaya Bay, Louisiana, in M. L. Broussard (editor), Deltas: Houston Geological Society, Houston, Texas, pp. 209–222.

Silvester, Richard and de la Cruz, D. de R., 1970, Pattern forming processes in deltas: J. Waterways Harbors Div., Am. Soc. Civil Eng., v. 96, pp. 201–217.

Stephens, D. G., Van Nieuwenhuise, D. S., Mullin, P., Lee, C., and Kanes, W. H., 1976, Destructive phase of deltaic development: North Santee River delta: J. Sediment. Petrol., v. 46, pp. 132–144.

Todd, O. J. and Eliassen, S., 1940, The Yellow River problem: Am. Soc. Civil Eng. Trans., v. 105, pp. 346–416.

Williamson, I. H., 1967, Coal Mining Geology: Oxford University Press, London, 266 pp.

Winkley, B. R., 1976, Response of the Mississippi River to the cutoffs, in Rivers 76: Am. Soc. Civil Eng. Symp. Inland Waterways Navigation, Flood Control, Water Diversions, pp. 1267–1284.

Wright, L. D. and Coleman, J. M., 1973, Variations in morphology of major river deltas as functions of ocean wave and river discharge regimes: Am. Assoc. Pet. Geol., Bull., v. 57, pp. 370–398.

CHAPTER NINE

The
Fluvial
System

A large part of the surface of the earth is composed of fluvial systems of all sizes. The systems are open, and the character of the system and its components exerts an influence beyond its boundaries, as demonstrated when fluvial sediments reach a marine environment. Although the fluvial system can be fragmented into subsystems (Zones 1, 2, and 3) for purposes of study or management, nevertheless each component of the system is influenced by upstream and downstream controls. Therefore, an understanding of variations in the stratigraphic column, sediment delivery ratios, and stream, delta, and alluvial fan behavior and morphology requires an understanding of the total fluvial system. It is with this foundation that the complexity of the morphologic system and the variability of the cascading system is explicable.

A major contribution of the geomorphologist to environmental studies and to other cooperative efforts with engineers, conservationists, and land managers is his awareness of the significance of time and landscape history. The earth scientist must anticipate the long-term behavior of changing landscape so that man-induced changes "will be in harmony with natural forces 50, 100 or 500 years from now, as well as with conditions of the moment" (Frye, 1971, p. 9). Therefore, a model of landscape evolution is needed for both practical and scientific purposes. However, the Davis model of landform evolution , or any other for that matter, does not provide sufficient understanding for accurate predictions of future change. The major obstacle to the acceptance of any idealized model of progressive erosional evolution of a fluvial system during a short span of time (Figure 1-1) is the great morphologic variability that occurs within the fluvial system. For example, relatively wide valleys and flat slopes exist at the mouth of a drainage basin, but, normally near the divides drainage density is higher and the slopes are steeper. Thus, when there is a change in any part of the system, it is difficult for the other components of the system to adjust in such a way that dynamic equilibrium is restored over a short period of time; the relaxation time is long. This was demonstrated by the complex response of the small experimental drainage basin (Figure 4-12). The channel near the mouth of the basin was unable to cope with the changing sediment production of the upstream areas.

In the preceding chapters three new concepts are presented that provide a means of understanding seemingly anomalous landforms or the erratic behavior of a landform through time. These are (1) geomorphic thresholds, (2) complex response, and (3) episodic erosion. The geomorphic threshold is an intrinsic threshold that depends on the erosional or depositional changes within the system, for example, the steepening of a fan-head or valley-fill deposit until failure occurs, the increase of channel sinuosity until a series of cutoffs straighten the channel, and the channel shift or avulsion on plains or deltas. Complex response is the process of hunting for a new equilibrium because of change induced by the exceeding of either an intrinsic or an extrinsic threshold. It is best exemplified by the response of the REF drainage basin (Figure 4-12) and the Iowa (Figure 6-24) and southwestern United States gullies and arroyos to rejuvenation. Finally, when the change is a major one relative to the size of the drainage basin or the system component involved, episodic erosion or deposition can occur (Figure 6-25). With high sediment loads and rapid system adjustment, progressive erosion or deposition cannot immediately or even quickly restore a new equilibrium condition. Rather incision is impeded by deposition, and deposition is impeded by erosion. The growth of the wet alluvial fan (Figures 7-10 and 7-11) and the Douglas Creek incision history (Figure 6-26) are examples; the concept may well apply to the erosional evolution of the landscape during early stages of development (Figure 4-18).

An attempt to show how each of these concepts applies to geomorphology is presented in Figure 9-1. Episodic erosion or deposition in-

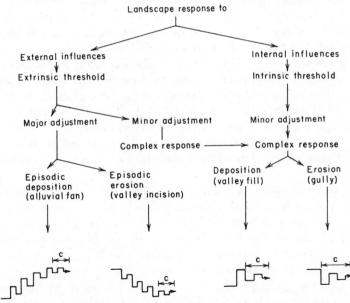

Figure 9-1 Types of landform response to change. Note that final adjustment to the external influence is in each case a typical complex response (C). Sketches show variations of surface elevation with time.

volves geomorphic thresholds and complex response, but episodic erosion and deposition are triggered by a major change of the system. On
the other hand, complex response alone is a response to a less significant
change, and it involves hunting for a new equilibrium. As episodic
deposition or erosion approaches a new equilibrium, the final phase will
be a complex response (Figure 9-1). These concepts produce a new and
very different conception of the erosional evolution of the landscape
during, at least, Holocene time.

It may be that this model, as stated before, applies only in areas where
sediment transport is high. Certainly it is difficult to envision pauses in
the downcutting, of the type at Douglas Creek, when a river is cutting
through very resistant rocks and erosion is slow. It seems necessary that
a stream be transporting appreciable amounts of sediment before the
events that have been detected on the wet alluvial fan or in the Douglas
Creek valley will take place. However, in most cases rejuvenation of a
drainage system will produce relatively large amounts of sediment, and
the complex response should be typical of many rejuvenated drainage
basins.

These three geomorphic concepts at the very least provide the basis
for new interpretations of some minor landscape features, such as the
most recent valley fill or the low terrace that appears not to be related to
climate or baselevel change. Obviously these features can be related to a
climatic fluctuation, land-use, or other extrinsic control as indicated on
Figure 9-1, but frequently such an explanation is not convincing, especially as these episodic adjustments can be expected as a natural part of
the evolution of the fluvial system. In Zone 1 some valley-fill deposits,
terrace formation, and placer formation can be related to these natural
processes (Figures 4-12, 6-24, and 6-32). In Zone 2 river-pattern change
and avulsion can be a part of the expected behavior of rivers (Figure
5-23). In Zone 3 fan-head trenching and delta-channel avulsion can be a
natural part of the depositional evolution of these landforms (Figure
7-11).

The concepts provide a basis for prediction, which is the essential
criterion of a science. The ability to predict with assurance the response
of a landscape to weather modification and changing land use or to
natural climate or baselevel changes would be of great practical value
and reinforces the need for a long-term view of landform change. For
example, at a given location, how secure are buried radioactive wastes
from meander shift or channel incision? The need in this case, and
obviously in many others, is to anticipate beyond the tenure of an elected
official's term of office—which, of course, requires a geomorphic view of
the landscape and man's place within it.

The ability to identify potentially unstable components of a landscape and to predict the future behavior of currently unstable landforms should be one major goal of geomorphology. The very morphologic and geologic complexity of a landscape will impede attempts to achieve this goal, but such an approach to the landscape is a significant alternative to simple description and postdiction.

Some applications of this approach fall within four general groupings: (1) soil conservation and land management, (2) civil engineering, (3) geomorphology, and (4) geology (Schumm, 1977). A few examples are presented for each category to illustrate the potential of this geomorphic approach.

SOIL CONSERVATION AND LAND MANAGEMENT

The ability to identify incipiently unstable parts of the landscape would be of inestimable aid to the land manager and would permit the conservation engineer to practice preventive conservation. For example, if relations similar to those of Figure 4-14 could be developed elsewhere it would be possible to select within a drainage basin those reaches of the main valley or those tributary channels that are on the threshold of failure. The expenditure of funds in preventive conservation is a more efficient use of limited resources than the "after the fact" attempts to retard erosion or to heal previously developed erosional features. However, if erosion has begun, then selection of the most appropriate time and place for the application of control techniques could be based on the complex response of the system to rejuvenation. As Figures 4-11, 4-12, 6-24, and 7-13 show, incision is usually followed by deposition. If the conservation engineer can recognize when the reversal from erosion to deposition will begin, he will be able to work with the system instead of against it.

A remarkable example of what may be a threshold event is the dramatic decrease in the suspended sediment load passing through the Grand Canyon between the years 1940 and 1942. The decrease in sediment was from 50 to 100 million tons per year at a given discharge (Figure 9-2). Thomas et al. (1963) attribute this decrease to drought in the major sediment-producing areas, but others have claimed that it is the result of over 20 years of conservation and flood-control efforts in the Colorado River drainage basins. The latter explanation seems ludicrous, except that trenching of the wet experimental fan did not take place until 40 percent of the source area was covered with plastic (Figure 7-7) in an attempt to reduce sediment production from hillslopes. Although a

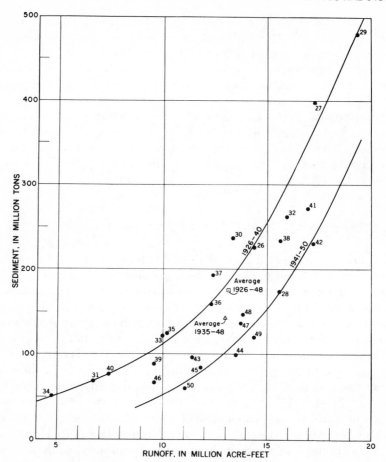

Figure 9-2   Relation between annual runoff and suspended sediment load of Colorado River at Grand Canyon, 1926 to 1957. (From Thomas et al., 1963.)

decrease in upland erosion was induced by the plastic sheets, this was compensated for by additional channel and valley erosion. The experimental result suggests that the effects of upstream controls may be long delayed, but eventually they may appear abruptly.

Hadley (1974) considered the decrease of sediment load in the Colorado River basin, and he determined that, although water discharge did not decrease significantly except on the San Juan River, sediment load decreased in the Colorado, Green, and San Juan rivers (Table 9-1). He concluded that major reductions in livestock numbers and the erosion control efforts of the previous decades are responsible for the

TABLE 9-1 RATIOS OF SUSPENDED SEDIMENT LOADS AND DIS-
CHARGE FOR TWO PERIODS OF RECORD, COLORADO RIVER BASIN
(FROM HADLEY, 1974)

Gaging station	Period 1	Period 2	Ratio Period 2/Period 1	
			Discharge	Sediment
Colorado River, Grand Canyon, Arizona	1926–1941	1942–1969	0.94	0.49
Colorado River near Cisco, Utah	1930–1942	1943–1962	0.97	0.50
Green River at Green River, Utah	1930–1942	1943–1962	1.16	0.68
San Juan River near Bluff, Utah	1930–1942	1943–1962	0.78	0.38

dramatic sediment load decreases in the period from 1940 to 1942.
Further work is needed, but Hadley's conclusions are not inconsistent
with the geomorphic threshold concept presented above.

RIVER ENGINEERING

As in a drainage basin, so along a river variations of valley slope,
sediment load, and discharge cause local reaches to be unstable. If, for a
river, a relation between stream power and sinuosity or between valley
slope and sinuosity can be established (Figures 5-14 and 5-16), then a
plan for stabilization may include an increase of sinuosity as a means of
decreasing stream power. Such an approach may be a valid substitute for
the bank stabilization and realignment techniques currently in use, but it
would require the construction of dikes to begin development of a
sinuous pattern.

For river reaches where sinuosity is very high, a period of instability
and meander cutoff can be expected (Figure 9-3). If these reaches are
identified, selective cutoffs may partly reduce the impact of the inevitable river pattern change or avulsion. This is in no way a recommenda-
tion for channelization. The brutal forcing of a channel into an unnatural straight alignment almost always produces serious consequences.
Unless the new course is cut in resistant materials the channel will
attempt to resume its meandering course. In addition, the greatly in-

Figure 9-3   Channel of Rio Puerco, New Mexico, which has straightened by a series of cutoffs. Upstream and downstream the channel is meandering; the cutoffs were apparently a response to increasing sinuosity and decreasing gradient in this reach (Figure 5-23).

creased gradient of the straightened channel will normally cause incision and rejuvenation upstream, thereby producing a high sediment load that will probably enlarge and aggrade the aligned channel and cause floodplain destruction. Again, the channels that will benefit most from partial or full channelization probably can be identified by a careful study of channel morphology.

GEOMORPHOLOGY

The concept of dynamic metastable equilibrium explains many of the details of the denudational history of a landscape. If some terraces and alluvial deposits are the result of thresholds and complex response, then a less-complicated climatic and tectonic history can be advocated. The manner in which a landscape evolves through time can be that of the Davis erosion cycle, but the modifications of that scheme (Figure 4-17) improve it as a basis for realistic landscape interpretation. As noted above, the concepts of geomorphic thresholds and complex response provide a basis for predictive geomorphology. For example, where within an arid valley should a large expensive facility be placed? The valley is flanked with alluvial fans in different stages of dissection. A careful geomorphic study of the fans and the geologic, hydrologic, and geomorphic characteristics of the source areas above them will indicate the safest spot in this valley for construction.

The predictions of the geomorphologist should aid developers and planners in achieving sound decisions that take the historic view of landforms into consideration.

GEOLOGY

The threshold and complex response concepts are especially applicable to geologic problems. The behavior of a river or the entire fluvial system through time provides an explanation for certain stratigraphic conditions, for some placer deposits, for environments favorable to the formation of epigenetic deposits of uranium and for some petroleum and natural gas reservoirs. The interruption of progressive denudation or progressive deposition produces a complex stratigraphy that, upon reflection, is essential to the formation of mineral deposits in fluvial sediments. The interruptions of deposition and the changing rates of deposition with time probably are a response to events that take place in Zones 1 and 2 of a fluvial system. Ager (1973) was not necessarily concerned with fluvial deposition, but, based on what we know about the response and the behavior of drainage basins and streams, there is no reason to expect a continuous deposition of sediment during the downwearing of a landscape. In fact, the storage of sediment within the system and its periodic flushing should produce a seemingly very incomplete stratigraphic and sedimentologic sequence. If the erosional history of a landscape is more complex than previously considered, then the depositional record of these events will also be complex.

EVIDENCE

Unfortunately it is very difficult to prove ideas presented here. Support can be obtained through the use of experimental studies, but the transference of the results from the experimental studies to the field poses some problem, because during recent geologic time, Pleistocene and Holocene climatic changes have been so great that they have essentially overwhelmed the other landscape influences. Hence, most Pleistocene stratigraphers and geomorphologists will attribute terraces and alluvial fills at all scales to climatic change. This need not be the case, but it is very difficult to demonstrate that a particular terrace is not, in fact, due to climatic change. It would seem, then, that geomorphologists will have to turn to the stratigraphic record to determine what happens during the long spans of time involved in the erosional reduction of the landscape. In the depositional basins of the world, there should be sequences of sedimentary units that provide data to evaluate the ideas discussed here and to determine whether or not the ideas put forth have merit.

For example, cyclic sedimentation has concerned stratigraphers for some time. A great deal has been written on this subject, not all, of course, related to fluvial processes, and the symposium volume edited by Merriam (1964) and the book by Duff et al. (1967) adequately review the problem. The concern, of course, is whether or not such cycles actually exist, and if they do, the reason for them. It appears from the research reviewed here on the behavior of fluvial systems that the development of cyclic sedimentation is inevitable in fluvial sedimentary deposits.

Cycles of several dimensions should be found within a fluvial depositional unit. On Figure 4-17, which shows the progress of the erosion cycle through time, sediment yield can be substituted for elevation or relief on the abscissa of that figure. The curves then show sediment produced by the fluvial system during denudation of the landscape. There should be approximately four orders of cycles in the deposits associated with this erosional evolution. The primary cycle is related to denudation following uplift, with maximum sediment production at the beginning of the erosional event and a progressive decrease in quantity and size of material through time to yield a massive fining upward sequence (Figure 4-17a). However, interruptions of this sequence due to isostatic adjustment also produce high sediment yields from the source area (Figure 9-4). Therefore, within the primary cycle associated with tectonics, there are second-order cycles associated with isostatic adjustment and, perhaps, major climatic change. Between these events, third-order cycles are related to the exceeding of geomorphic thresholds, the metastable equilibrium. These third-order cycles are of much smaller dimensions, and yet they are important for the concentration of heavy minerals and the development of channeling in fluvial deposits. Fourth-order cycles are related to episodic erosion and to the complex response of the fluvial system to any of the above changes, either tectonic, isostatic, climatic, or threshold. These cycles of smaller dimension result from the attempt of the system to adjust to changes related to the primary, secondary, and tertiary cycles. Finally, fifth-order cycles occur that are related to the seasonality of hydrologic events or to major flooding, and in the stratigraphic record these will appear as thin fining-upward depositional units.

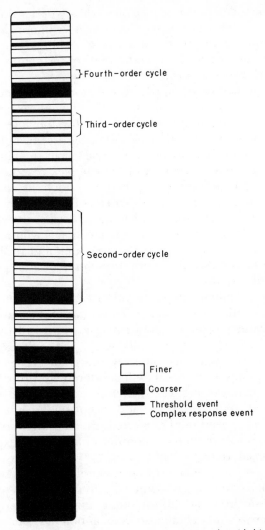

Figure 9-4 Diagrammatic model of primary sedimentation cycle with higher order components.

DISCUSSION

The concepts presented may be controversial and perhaps partly in error; nevertheless, the author believes that the approach utilized here and a model of the erosional evolution of the fluvial landscape, which includes the concepts of geomorphic thresholds, complex response, episodic erosion and deposition, provides a means of developing a better understanding of the dynamics of landform evolution and, perhaps more importantly, a means of identifying within a landscape those components of the system that are inherently or incipiently unstable but are amenable to man's control.

Further research should support the concepts presented here and demonstrate their worth not only in terms of modern environmental and land and river management, but also for the interpretation of ancient fluvial deposits and other deposits that are strongly influenced by the fluvial system. It must be emphasized that, in spite of the emphasis on the threshold concept and the complex response of the fluvial system, these hypotheses are presented simply as another means of explaining and, more importantly, predicting the occurrence of certain geomorphic and geologic phenomena. Using the approach of Mosley and Zimpfer (1976) no single explanation is wholly adequate to explain landforms, and the historic, equilibrium, and probabilistic approaches all have validity and each presents partial explanations of complex natural systems.

For example, the alluvial deposits within a valley may show the influence of tectonics and climate change. Thus most of the alluvial chronology can be explained as the result of extrinsic controls. However, other alluvial features can probably be explained by the complex response of the fluvial systems. Other sedimentary units may reflect hydrologic events, and perhaps they are best considered as probabilistic. The sedimentary sequence of Figure 9-4 therefore can only be explained by the use of several hypotheses. In fact, all but one of several multiple working hypotheses need not be rejected; rather many can be incorporated into a more comprehensive and more satisfactory explanation of the features considered.

Landform evolution has always been closely linked conceptually to organic evolution, and the concept of episodic erosion especially as related to intrinsic thresholds appears to be a significant departure from tradition. However, a model of episodic evolution has been advanced by Eldridge and Gould (1972), as an explanation for abrupt changes in the fossil record. They believe that many breaks in the fossil record are not the result of an imperfect record, but rather they reflect the manner in which evolution occurs. They advance the concept of punctuated equilibria as a replacement for progressive evolution or phyletic gradualism, stating that "a lineage's history includes long periods of morphologic stability, punctuated here and there by rapid events of speciation in isolated subpopulations." The result is a paleontologic record of episodic evolution (Eldridge and Gould, 1972, pp. 109–110).

Kuhn (1970) of course, has concluded that the advance of a science itself is episodic. A new paradigm revolutionizes the basis of a science, and rapid progress is made, for a time. For example, the concept of geomorphic thresholds permits and even demands a reassessment of some past work and provides a basis for future efforts.

REFERENCES

Ager, D. U., 1973, The nature of the stratigraphic record: Macmillan, London, 114 pp.

Duff, P. McL. D., Hallam, A. and Walton, Eik, 1967, Cyclic sedimentation: Elsevier, Amsterdam, 280 pp.

Eldridge, Niles and Gould, S. J., 1972, Punctuated equilibria: an alternative to phyletic gradualism, in T. J. M. Schopf (editor), Models in Paleobiology: Freeman, Cooper and Co., San Francisco, pp. 82–115.

Frye, John C., 1971, A geologist views the environment: Illinois State Geol. Surv., Environ. Geol. Notes No. 42, p. 9.

Hadley, R. F., 1974, Sediment yield and land use in southwest United States: Int. Assoc. Sci. Hydrol. Publ. 113, pp. 96–98.

Kuhn, T. S., 1970, The structure of scientific revolutions, 2nd ed.: University of Chicago Press, Chicago, 210 pp.

Mosley, M. P. and Zimpfer, G. L., 1976, Explanations in geomorphology: Z. Geomorphol. v. 20, pp. 381–390.

Merriam, D. F., 1964, Symposium on cyclic sedimentation: State Geol. Surv. of Kansas Bull. 169, 2 vols., 636 pp.

Schumm, S. A., 1977, Applied Fluvial Geomorphology, in J. R. Hails (editor), Applied Geomorphology: Elsevier, Amsterdam, in press.

Thomas, H. E. et al., 1963, Effects of drought in the Colorado River basin: U. S. Geol. Surv. Prof. Paper 372-F, 50 pp.

Index